The Rules of Riot
*Internal Conflict and
the Law of War*

The Rules of Riot

Internal Conflict and the Law of War

By James E. Bond

Princeton University Press, Princeton, New Jersey

LCC: 73-5390
ISBN: 0-691-05651-X

Library of Congress Cataloging in Publication
data will be found on the last printed
page of this book

This book has been composed in Linotype Times Roman

Printed in the United States of America
by Princeton University Press,
Princeton, New Jersey

To Garth

In the hope that he will survive into
a more humane and civilized age

ACKNOWLEDGMENTS

First, I want to acknowledge my indebtedness to the four men whose example lured me into teaching. Mr. Dane Harris and Drs. F. A. Harper, Joseph O'Rourke, and Philip Wilder infused their instruction with such a sense of excitement and promise that I never doubted but that I must teach. I am not so presumptuous as to think I can recreate in my classroom the magic they performed in theirs, but I shall always encourage among my students as they did among theirs the faculty of critical appraisal. They taught me how to think rather than what to think; and if I concluded that human intelligence is all too fallible, I also concluded that we must nevertheless act on our learning and understanding. This book bears, I hope, the stamp of their intellectual integrity.

I owe an intellectual debt to three lawyers with whom I taught at the Judge Advocate General's School. Mr. Lawrence Gaughan, with whom I am once again happily associated on the law faculty at Washington and Lee, Mr. John McMahon, who is now practicing admiralty law in New York City, and Mr. Jordon Paust, who is presently working on a doctoral degree at Yale University, are all confident and forceful advocates. Each of us held strong and often sharply divergent views on the law of war, and I profited greatly from our lively exchanges. I also appreciate the gentle encouragement and kind consideration my two superior officers Colonel Albert Rakas and Major James B. Coker gave me. They enabled me to finish the manuscript "on Army time" and therefore much earlier than would have otherwise been the case.

Finally, I thank my wife. Georgana has been correcting, revising, and editing me (with mixed results) since we entered high school together fifteen years ago. She would, of course, disclaim any responsibility for the final product, as she did recently when a student upbraided her with my shortcomings. "I don't claim any of the credit," she said, "but I don't accept any of the blame either." The remark was characteristically accurate and modest. She knows my failures are not hers, and she would never appropriate my successes. Her modesty does not, however, alter the fact that whatever the merit in my work, much of it is hers.

J.E.B.

TABLE OF CONTENTS

The Rules of Riot

*Internal Conflict and
the Law of War*

INTRODUCTION

International lawyers, reacting to the unhappy events in Southeast Asia as well as to the whole post-World War II pattern of guerrilla movements and wars of national liberation, have begun discussing the law of intervention. When and where and how may states intervene in the internal conflicts of another state? These scholars justify their inquiries on many grounds, one of which is worth emphasizing here: they all believe that these kinds of conflicts will bedevil the international community for the foreseeable future.

The point is worth emphasizing because I propose to examine still another facet of these conflicts, specifically, the applicability thereto of the law of war. What kinds of force may participants in these conflicts use? Against whom may they use force? Under what conditions may they use force?

Traditionally, international law did not tell sovereign states how they could treat their own nationals; and nations dealt with bandits, rebels, and other malcontents largely as they wished. In 1949, however, nations adopted common Article 3 of the Geneva Conventions, often called a "miniature convention."[1] Article 3 proscribes inhumane treatment of non-combatants in armed conflicts not of an international nature.

Very little has been written about Article 3, however, and it poses many problems. What is an "armed conflict not of an international nature"? Would Article 3 apply

---

[1] The text of Article 3 is set out in footnote 106 of Chapter 1. The article is included in all four of the 1949 Geneva Conventions, which constitute the heart of the international law of war. See footnotes 78-82 for a more detailed reference to the Conventions.

to a Watts-like riot? to the guerrilla movement in the Portuguese provinces in Africa? to Biafra? Would it apply, at least as between the government and its rebel citizens, in a war "internationalized" by foreign troops, as in Vietnam?

Inevitably, one also faces the problem of pouring substantive content into the language of Article 3. What is a "regularly constituted court"? Which "judicial guarantees" are "recognized as indispensable by civilized peoples"? What does Article 3 mean when it says that the sick and wounded shall be cared for? Does one look, for example, to the more detailed provisions of the two Geneva Conventions for the Protection and Amelioration of the Sick and Wounded for guidance? Or does one accept as determinative the gloss of state practice, that is, how signatory states have treated rebel sick and wounded? Or is there some third alternative, such as a standard of reasonableness or a shock-the-conscience test? Perhaps one who feels unable to define "inhumane treatment" may nevertheless confidently assert that he will recognize it when he sees it. In short, one must not only determine when Article 3 applies, one must decide what it prohibits.

Though Article 3 purports to protect all those "taking no active part in the hostilities," its protective ambit, even under the most liberal interpretation, may not be broad enough. The Article, for instance, does not advert at all to the problem of post-trial detention and punishment, much less to the problem of detention without trial. The widely publicized, deplorable conditions at the South Vietnamese prison on Con Son Island suggest that post-trial detention and punishment of those who oppose the government are major problems that should be regulated by international law.

Whatever Article 3 prohibits and whenever it applies,

it does not, moreover, regulate the use of weapons, selection of targets, or, in a phrase, the conduct of hostilities. Does this body of the law of war or some part of it, much codified in international agreement and much established and continually modified through customary practice, apply to internal conflicts? Under traditional international law the answer would be no. Today, however, the international community is greatly concerned about the human rights of people everywhere, and it may be ready to extend additional protections not granted in Article 3 to those caught up in a violent dispute with their government.

The question is *what* protections. Should, for example, the government be prohibited from using against rebels weapons that it could not legally employ in an international conflict? Dum-dum bullets illustrate the problem. Though illegal under international law, they are used by many armies in suppressing insurrections and even by some police forces against common criminals. Similarly, there are no international legal restraints on government destruction of rebel-held property. In international conflicts customary and conventional law prohibit any destruction of specific types of property and all unnecessary destruction. These examples show how little of the traditional law of war applies to internal conflicts.

The answer to the question "What, if any, protections of the law of war should apply to internal conflicts?" depends ultimately on an analysis of competing policies. There are, after all, sound reasons for the traditional reluctance of the international community to regulate governmental conduct toward its own nationals. Particularly in the context of guerrilla warfare, peace and stability may be promoted by preserving the government's wide discretion to deal with rebels as it sees fit. Many observers agree that a harsh and severe policy is one of the few effective ways to prevent or defeat a guerrilla movement. The world community also has an interest in insuring both self-determination and human rights, however. The latter, if not the former, may be sacrificed by a government determined to repress any armed threat to its authority. Perhaps, then, international law ought to draw a line beyond which the government cannot go in its fight to survive. Legal scholars have not yet addressed themselves to this problem of line-drawing, which will be the focus of this study.

CHAPTER I

The Historical Development of the Law of War and Its Present Crisis

A. A Brief History of the Law of War

War has plagued mankind since Cain slew Abel. In the 3,500 years since man began writing his history, he has recorded only 270 years of peace;[1] and even many of those eras and countries popularly regarded as peaceful have been suffused with violence. During the Pax Romana, for example, Roman legions battled barbarians scattered around the perimeter of the empire.[2] The United States was born in revolution and has enjoyed only two decades of peace in the last two centuries.[3] Though the nature of war has changed as civilization has changed, it has never disappeared as the poets dreamed; and the 2,400 years since Plato's death have proved his prediction that only the dead have seen the end of war.

If man has not yet beaten his swords into plowshares, he has appeased his conscience by regulating the conduct of war. Even the ancients, though condemned for their savagery, observed some minimal restraints. Christian knights obeyed throughout the Middle Ages a chivalrous code that dictated humane treatment toward at least their Christian enemies; and the Church occasionally construed Christ's teaching to forbid particular conduct, as in 1132 when the Lateran Council branded the cross-

[1] L. Montross, WAR THROUGH THE AGES 313 (3rd ed. 1960).
[2] *Id.* at 83-86.
[3] Q. Wright, A STUDY OF WAR 56 (Abridged ed. 1964).

bow and arbalist "unchristian" weapons.[4] But not until
1625 did Grotius synthesize a coherent body of general
principles from the practice of past generations and the
work of theologians, philosophers, and literati. During
the last century nations have elaborated these general
principles in detailed conventions that, while widely criti-
cized for their inadequacies, represent a high-water mark
in man's effort to ameliorate the suffering caused by war.

1. *Ancient Antecedents*

Such has been the evolution in the laws of war that
some of today's fundamental rules originated among the
ancients. It is true that the ancients were often brutal and
cruel: they slew men, women, and children; they leveled
cities, laid waste the fields, and salted the earth.[5] One
scholar has suggested that the "description of the Assyr-
ian coming down 'like a wolf on the fold' " would apply
"equally to Babylonians, Medes, Persians, Phoenicians,
and Carthaginians."[6] The Jews, however, though often
similarly cruel, were also occasionally humane. The Old
Testament records both their savagery and their generosi-
ty: Abraham declined the defeated Sodomite King's offer
of his goods, saying: "I will not take a thread nor a shoe-
latchet nor aught that is thine";[7] but Samuel heard Jeho-

[4] C. Fenwick, INTERNATIONAL LAW 556 (3rd ed. 1948).

[5] C. Phillipson, II INTERNATIONAL LAW AND CUSTOMS OF AN-
CIENT GREECE AND ROME 203 (1911).

[6] C. Fenwick, *supra* n. 4 at 5. Of like character were Jengliz
Khan's Golden Horde who were described thus: "Swarming like
locusts over the face of the earth, they have brought terrible
devastation . . . laying it waste with fire and carnage. . . . For
they are inhuman and beastly, rather monsters than men, thirst-
ing for and drinking blood, tearing and devouring the flesh of
dogs and men." L. Montross, *supra* n. 1 at 144.

[7] GENESIS 14:23.

vah command: "Now go and smite Amalek, and utterly destroy all that they have, and spare them not; but slay both man and woman, infant and suckling, ox and sheep, camel and ass."[8] Amid all the carnage of war among the ancient tribes and peoples, one nevertheless finds evidence of the Judeo-Christian doctrines of forgiveness and mercy that have greatly influenced the development of the laws of war.

While the humanitarian pulse first beats in the practices of the Jews, detailed rules of warfare first emerge among the Greeks and Romans. The Greeks and Romans, for example, spared particular peoples and buildings from destruction.[9] When Alexander destroyed the city of Thebes in 335 B.C. and put its citizens to the sword, he left standing the poet Pindar's home and spared his descendants.[10] The modern law that protects churches, schools, libraries, museums, and similar buildings from bombing and that accords a special status to doctors and ministers stems from the Greek and Roman tradition of respect for poets, philosophers, artists, and men of intellectual distinction and from their rules, which recognized temples and embassies as inviolable.[11] The Greeks and Romans customarily observed the modern prohibition

[8] I SAMUEL 15:3. Judged by contemporary standards, Samuel should either have asked the Lord to clarify His order, or he should have refused to obey it. To his credit he did fail to carry it out completely.

[9] H. Wheaton, LAW OF NATIONS 14 (1845).

[10] "There are some things of such a nature, as to contribute, no way, to the support and prolongation of war: things which reason itself requires to be spared even during the heat and continuance of war . . . : such are Porticos, Temples, statues, and all other elegant works and monuments of art." H. Grotius, RIGHTS OF WAR AND PEACE 366-7 (A. Campbell trans. 1901).

[11] C. Phillipson, *supra* n. 5 at 221.

outlawing poison or poisonous weapons, whose use was regarded as cowardly.[12] Plato states another rule that has been codified in the present law: the dead must not be despoiled, or their burial denied.[13] Truces were arranged for a variety of reasons, among which one was to allow burial of the dead.[14]

Enemies also exchanged prisoners during truces. More often, however, the captor ransomed his prisoners.[15] Even more frequently, he executed or enslaved them (and their families). Though these practices persisted throughout the ancient era, the Romans dealt less harshly with their enemies.[16] Caesar often spared lives and refrained from destroying stormed cities.[17] This practice of sparing non-combatants and their property was not without precedent, for Grotius quotes Xenophon as saying that a convention was made between Cyrus and the Assyrians that there should be "peace with the cultivators, war with the soldiers."[18]

No law of war dictated these apparently humanitarian

[12] *Id.* at 208-09. Parallel prohibitions on poison are found in other cultures. For example, the Code of Manu, which dates from pre-Christian times, forbade Hindus from using poisoned arrows.

[13] Plato, THE REPUBLIC 171-72 (MacDonald, ed. 1945). As outlined in the chapter entitled "Usage of War," Plato's suggestions for mitigating the severity of warfare anticipated many of the modern codes.

[14] C. Phillipson, *supra* n. 5 at 280. But see H. Wheaton, *supra* n. 9 at 2. That the rule was important, as well as occasionally disregarded, is illustrated in Sophocles' ANTIGONE, where the heroine defies her uncle Creon, the king, and buries her dead brother Polynices.

[15] Students of the ILIAD will recall that though Achilles sold some of his prisoners, he ransomed others.

[16] C. Phillipson, *supra* n. 5 at 251.

[17] *Id.* at 240.   [18] H. Grotius, *supra* n. 10 at 362.

practices, nor did the Greeks and Romans invariably observe them. They, too, committed atrocities.[19] Grotius, surveying the history of warfare among the ancients, conceded that human law did not prohibit slaughter and devastation.[20] He nevertheless singled out for praise many examples of humanitarian conduct; and they were frequent enough to justify Phillipson's conclusion: "Still, if hostilities proved inevitable in Hellas, much was done to humanize warfare, and to remove it from the terrible atrocities and the unquenchable bloodthirstiness which prevailed among most of the nations of antiquity."[21] The Greeks and Romans went beyond the occasional Jewish practice of extending mercy and forgiveness to their vanquished foes by regularly observing the customs outlined above.

Though these customs have been characterized as humanitarian, the Greeks and Romans often articulated pragmatic rationali for their observance, thus introducing the motive of self-interest that has long been the curious handmaiden of humanitarianism in the development of the laws of war.[22] Alexander, for example, reminded his

[19] Baldwin, *New Look at the Law of War: Limited War and FM* 27-10, 4 MIL. L. REV. 1, 14 (1959). One of the most frequently cited is the Greek execution of the heralds whom Darius sent to demand earth and water as evidence of submission to him. The incident is the more shocking because it violated one of the few "rules" that the ancients observed. The Persian king's reaction is interesting. When urged to execute Athenian representatives in court, Xerxes replied that the Greeks had "violated the law of all mankind," and he "would not do that very thing he blamed in them." C. Fenwick, INTERNATIONAL LAW 8 (4th ed. 1965).

[20] H. Grotius, *supra* n. 10 at 332.

[21] C. Phillipson, *supra* n. 5 at 219.

[22] Military commanders have greatly influenced the development of the law of war. The author of the second treatise on

troops in Asia Minor that they should not destroy that
which would soon be theirs.[23] There is also evidence that
he moderated the ferocity of his campaigns because the
peoples of Asia Minor thought his conduct barbarian.
Alexander, after all, like the Romans after him wished
to assimilate conquered peoples into an imperial empire,
and he concluded that territorial expansion and consoli-
dation were best served by a firm but generous policy.[24]
Similarly pragmatic motives explain the evolution in
treatment of prisoners. It made little sense to behead a
man when one could trade him for another or, better yet,
ransom him for silver. In all these practices there was
doubtless, too, the expectation of reciprocal treatment.
The Greek emphasis on reprisal, which, according to
Phillipson, "came to be established . . . as a regularized
juridical act,"[25] implies that reciprocal observance of rules
or practices was expected.

2. The Medieval Period

The Catholic Church arose out of the ruins of the
Roman Empire, and its theologians contributed to the development of the law of war the concept of the just war.
Before Augustine no one had questioned the right of
earthly princes to order their soldiers onto the battlefield
for whatever reason. Now the Church admonished its
sons that unjust war was no more than robbery on a ma-

---

international law was, for example, a Spanish judge advocate
general; and the Swedish commander Gustavus Adolphus is said
to have placed Grotius' classic alongside the BIBLE beneath his
pillow when he slept.

[23] Grotius discusses the desirability of "moderation in acquir-
ing dominion" extensively in Chapter xv of Book III. H. Grotius,
supra n. 10 at 372-374.

[24] C. Phillipson, *supra* n. 5 at 251.   [25] *Id.* at 357.

jestic scale.[26] A just war was one whose aim was "to avenge injury, that is when that people or city against whom war is to be declared has neglected either to redress injuries done by its subjects, or to restore what they have wrongfully seized."[27] The just war doctrine, which, of course, justified the Crusades, did not prevent warfare between Christian princes and fell into disrepute. With the rise of the sovereign state, men came to accept once again the legitimacy of war as an instrument of foreign policy. Clausewitz's is the classic statement of the belief: "War is nothing but a continuation of political intercourse by other means."[28] The work of the Catholic theologians has nevertheless borne fruit in the efforts in this century to proscribe use of force in international relations.

Of greater interest for our particular purpose was the concomitant development during the Middle Ages of a "law of arms." The law of arms was broader than the present law of war, for it governed discipline within armies and other internal administrative matters, as well as regulated the battlefield conduct of soldiers toward their enemies.[29] It applied, moreover, whenever Christians fought one another, whether in international wars or in conflicts that would today appear more analogous to internal wars.[30] The detailed rules of the law of arms

[26] St. Augustine, THE CITY OF GOD 169 (J. Healy trans. 1931).

[27] *Id.* at 231. The canonists elaborated the just war doctrine in considerable detail. *E.g.*, Gozybowski, *The Polish Doctrine of the Law of War in the Fifteenth Century: A Note on the Genealogy of International Law*, 8 JURIST 386 (1958).

[28] Von Clausewitz, ON WAR 16 (Jolles trans. 1943).

[29] M. Keen, THE LAWS OF WAR IN THE LATE MIDDLE AGES 239 (1965).

[30] "The rules of chivalry applied 'wherever there was war,'" according to Keen, *id.* at 240.

were based on a code of chivalry, and their influence was such that one scholar has commented: "The notion of a law of nations was preceded and prepared for by the chivalric ideal of a good life of honor and loyalty."[31]

What had been discretionary among the ancients—the granting of quarter—became an obligatory duty as between knights, for example; and a refusal to grant quarter remains to this day a war crime. Keen begins his study of the law of arms with what he labels "a curious incident": "[During the siege of Limoges in 1370] three French knights, who had defended themselves gallantly, seeing at length no alternative to surrender, threw themselves on the mercy of John of Gaunt and the Earl of Cambridge. 'My Lords,' they cried, 'we are yours: you have vanquished us. Act therefore to the law of arms.' John of Gaunt acceded to their request, and they were taken prisoner on the understanding that their lives would be protected."[32] The incident is curious only because the English did not have to grant quarter under the peculiar circumstances of the siege. Generally, knights could and did demand quarter.[33]

It is not surprising that an age dominated by the Church should respect its buildings and staff. Churches and churchmen could not be attacked under any circumstances.[34] Though the general immunity has been preserved in modern codes, it is no longer absolute.[35]

---

[31] Huizinga, *The Political and Military Significance of Chivalric Ideas in the Late Middle Ages*, MEN AND IDEAS 203 (1960).

[32] *Supra* n. 29 at 1.

[33] Denial of quarter remains a war crime today. Hague Regulation 23(d) states: "It is especially forbidden to declare that no quarter will be given."

[34] M. Keen, *supra* n. 29 at 189.

[35] Today forces could legitimately attack a church, for instance, if the enemy were using its steeple as an observation post. This

Since the knight was a Christian sword for hire and was generally paid out of the pockets of his defeated foes, he needed to know how deeply he could dig. The law of spoils division permitted the taking of more property than present law would justify, but the victor's rights were not unlimited. First, he had to establish that he had taken the booty in a just war; otherwise, his opponent could demand restitution.[36] Second, the foe could surrender on condition that he be allowed to keep certain property.[37] There was finally a set of rules which apportioned spoils among the victors.[38]

3. The Rise of the Nation-State and the Development of the "Classical" Law of War

The Treaty of Westphalia in 1648 is usually celebrated as the birthdate of the modern state system. It is no coincidence that during the Thirty Years War which the treaty ended Grotius published the work that established his paternity as the father of international law, for, as Quincy Wright has pointed out, *Rights of War and Peace* was inspired by Grotius' "humanitarian desire to ameliorate the practices which he had witnessed during the Thirty Years War."[39] At that juncture in history when groups of people first began to think of themselves as independent, equal, sovereign states, Grotius set out a legal framework within which they could conduct their relations. Since warfare had been the midwife to this new international order, it is not surprising that the law

---

example illustrates the general rule that a building loses its immunity if used for a military purpose. See Chapter II, pp. 25-26 *infra*.

[36] M. Keen, *supra* n. 29 at 139.

[37] *Id.* at 128-29.   [38] *Id.* at 145-54.

[39] Q. Wright, *supra* n. 3 at 334.

of war was the first branch of international law to develop.

One fact evidences the brilliance of the framework Grotius outlined: the detailed codal provisions in the present laws of war are still based on the fundamental principles he articulated. First, he advocated a policy of minimum destruction. Grotius' statement that one should not destroy that whose loss does not strengthen him or weaken the enemy[40] is echoed in the Preamble to the 1868 St. Petersburg Declaration: "the only legitimate object which States should endeavor to accomplish during War is to weaken the military forces of the enemy."[41] Grotius, furthermore, detailed application of the principle: soldiers could not attack churches and temples, burn fields, or raze houses.[42] Second, he advocated the protection of non-combatants, whose welfare remains today the chief concern of the law of war, as seen in the common Geneva Convention provision that "persons taking no active part in the hostilities . . . shall in all circumstances be treated humanely."[43] Advising against undertakings that might "involve innocent persons in destruction," Grotius enumerated the categories of those entitled to protection: (1) children; (2) women; (3) men whose kind of life is repugnant to arms—those who perform sacred offices, scholars, husbandmen, and merchants (which included artisans and workmen).[44] Finally, Grotius recommended sparing the lives of enemy soldiers who surrender: ". . .

[40] H. Grotius, *supra* n. 10 at 367. Grotius is quoting Polybius.
[41] R. Phillimore, III INTERNATIONAL LAW 160 (3rd ed. 1885).
[42] H. Grotius, *supra* n. 10 at 365-67.
[43] Article 3, which is common to all four Geneva Conventions of 1949, is often called a "miniature convention" because it embodies the fundamental principles of the law of war.
[44] H. Grotius, *supra* n. 10 at 361-62.

equity commands us to spare those who surrender unconditionally, or ask for their lives".[45]

During the years following publication of *Rights of War and Peace*, Grotius' ideas were accepted as accurate statements of customary international law,[46] and treatise writers cited it as authority for their statements of law.[47] Military commanders began to practice Grotian principles. Napoleon, for example, permitted the defeated defenders of the garrison of El Airsh to go free on the condition that they go to Bagdad and not serve against the French for a year.[48] By the mid-nineteenth century these principles had begun appearing in military manuals.[49]

[45] H. Grotius, *supra* n. 10 at 363.

[46] Not all 17th century scholars agreed with Grotius, however. Van Bynkershoek wrote: "War is a contest by force. I have not said by lawful force, for in my opinion, every force is lawful in war. Everything is lawful against an enemy." A TREATISE ON THE LAW OF WAR 2 (Du Sonceau, ed. 1810). Fortunately, the Grotian view prevailed.

[47] G. Baker, I. HALLECK'S INTERNATIONAL LAW 13-14 (1908).

[48] G. Baker, II. HALLECK'S INTERNATIONAL HUMANITARIAN LAW, 24 (1908).

[49] Pictet, *International Humanitarian Law*, 6 INT'L. REV. OF THE RED CROSS 456, 466 (1966). The first detailed military regulation was "Instructions for the Government of Armies of the United States in the Feld," which Professor Francis Lieber of Columbia University drew up at the request of President Lincoln. General Orders No. 100 provided guidance to Union Forces during the Civil War. The following passages suggest the tone of the regulation:

"Military necessity admits of all direct destruction of life or limb of *armed* enemies, and of other persons whose destruction is incidentally *unavoidable* in the armed contests of the war; it allows of the capturing of every armed enemy, and every enemy of importance to the hostile government, or of peculiar danger to the captor; it allows of all destruction of property, and obstruction of the ways and channels of traffic, travel, or communication, and of

Even before 1850 states had embodied them in treaties,[50] which Grotius had recognized as a method of regulating conduct in war.[51] The United States–Prussia Treaty of Amity and Commerce of 10 September 1785[52] is an example of such an agreement. Articles 23 and 24 are but elaborations of Grotian principles. For example, Article 23 stated in part: "Upon the entrance of the armies of either nation into the territories of the other, women and children, ecclesiastics, scholars of every faculty, cultivators of the earth, merchants, artisans, manufacturers, and fishermen, unarmed and inhabiting unfortified towns, villages, or places, and in general all persons whose oc-

---

all withholding of sustenance or means of life from the enemy; of the appropriation of whatever an enemy's country affords necessary for the subsistence and safety of the army, and of such deception as does not involve the breaking of good faith either positively pledged, regarding agreements entered into during the war, or supposed by the modern law of war to exist. Men who take up arms against one another in public war do not cease on this account to be moral beings, responsible to one another and to God.

"Military necessity does not admit of cruelty—that is, the infliction of suffering for the sake of suffering or for revenge, nor of maiming or wounding except in fight, nor of torture to extort confessions. It does not admit of the use of poison in any way, nor the wanton devastation of a district. It admits of deception, but disclaims acts of perfidy; and, in general, military necessity does not include any act of hostility which makes the return to peace unnecessarily difficult."

That a civil war rather than an international conflict should produce such a regulation evidences, as did Grotius' comment cited in footnote 23 *supra*, the general desirability of applying the law of war to internal conflicts.

[50] *Note*, INTERNATIONAL LAW DOCUMENTS 1950-51 1 (1952).

[51] H. Grotius, *supra* n. 10 at 170.

[52] 8 STAT. 84; T.S. 292; 8 BEVANS 78; 2 Treaties (MALLOY) 1477.

cupations are for the common subsistence and benefit of mankind, shall be allowed to continue their respective employment, unmolested in their persons. Nor shall their houses or goods be burnt or otherwise destroyed, nor their cattle taken, nor their fields wasted. . . ."

The contracting parties also showed concern for the welfare of prisoners of war: "In order that the fate of prisoners of war may be alleviated, all such practices as those of sending them into distant, inclement, or unwholesome districts, or crowding them into close and noxious places, shall be studiously avoided." Desirable as such agreements were, they had one common defect: they lacked universal application. They governed only particular wars or campaigns, as, for instance, the cartel of March 12, 1780, between France and England establishing the ransom in pounds sterling for captured field-marshals.[53]

a. THE CODIFICATION OF THE LAW OF WAR

The movement for general codification began in 1861 with the publication of a pamphlet entitled "A Memory of Solferino." Its author Henri Dunant[54] recounted seeing 38,000 men fall dead or wounded in the space of only fifteen hours at the Battle of Solferino. Dunant expressed two wishes: (1) that nations should establish national relief societies to aid war victims and (2) that nations should agree by treaty to respect the work of these societies during war.[55]

Following an international conference at Geneva in the fall of 1863, diplomatic representations from twelve

[53] G. Baker, *supra* n. 48 at 26.

[54] Mr. Dunant received the Nobel Peace Prize in 1901 for his half century of labor in the cause of codification.

[55] G. Draper, THE RED CROSS CONVENTIONS 1-2 (1958).

nations agreed in 1864 to the first Geneva Convention for the Amelioration of the Condition of the Wounded in Time of War,[56] which came into force in 1865. As its title suggests, the Convention dealt solely with care for the sick and wounded. Its ten brief articles did guarantee these basic rights: (1) protection of hospitals, their staff, and medical equipment and supplies; (2) protection for members of the civilian population who had taken sick and wounded into their homes; (3) the right of repatriation.

The almost immediate demands for revision that followed adoption of the Convention set a frequently repeated pattern in the codification process. Although the 1868 draft Geneva Convention never came into force, Germany and France and the United States and Spain nevertheless observed its provisions in two major 19th-century wars.[57] In the same year the great European powers issued the St. Petersburg Declaration, the first international agreement outlawing the use of particular weapons. It specifically forbade "the employment . . . of any projectile of a weight below 400 grammes, which is either explosive or charged with fulminating or inflammable substances."[58]

The first attempt to regulate treatment of prisoners of war through an international convention was made at Brussels in 1874. Articles 23 through 34 established a regime for capture, internment, and treatment of prisoners of war.[59] The Brussels Declaration, though never

---

[56] 22 STAT. 940; T.S. 377; 1 BEVANS 7; 2 Treaties (MALLOY) 1903. The Treaty was ratified or adhered to by 54 states. It was replaced by the 1906 Geneva Convention and the 1929 Geneva Convention as between parties to those instruments.

[57] *Note, supra* n. 50 at 2.   [58] R. Phillimore, *supra* n. 41.

[59] A. Higgins, THE HAGUE PEACE CONFERENCES 273 (1909).

transformed into a convention, did establish principles that found expression in later agreements. For example, the Article 29 requirement that "every prisoner is bound to declare, if questioned on this point, his true name and rank" can be traced from Article 9 of the 1907 Hague Regulations through Article 5 of the 1929 Geneva Prisoner of War Convention to Article 17 of the 1949 Geneva Prisoner of War Convention, which obliges a captive soldier to state "only his surname, first names and rank, date of birth, and army, regimental, personal or serial number. . . ."

Another of those later agreements was the 1899 Hague Convention with Respect to the Laws and Customs of War on Land.[60] The 1899 Hague Peace Conference,[61] which was convened among other things to adapt the 1864 Geneva Convention to naval warfare and to revise and implement the Brussels Declaration of 1874, achieved both these goals. Of the three conventions promulgated, the second dealt with the law and customs of war on land and the third with maritime warfare.[62] Hardly had the ink dried on these agreements than Russia, who had promoted the Peace Conference, and Japan, also a Convention signatory, were at each other's throats. A commentator remarked: "The terms of the two Conventions were well observed. Naturally deficiencies were

[60] 32 STAT. 1803; T.S. 403; 1 BEVANS 247; 2 Treaties (MALLOY) 2042.

[61] A sound historical sketch of the 1899 and 1907 Hague Conferences is found in A. Higgins, *supra* n. 59. The legislative history of the two Conferences is contained in J. Scott, REPORTS TO THE HAGUE CONFERENCES OF 1899 AND 1907 (1916).

[62] The first of the three conventions was a "Convention for the Pacific Settlement of Disputes." 32 STAT. 1779; T.S. 392; 1 BEVANS 230; 2 Treaties (MALLOY) 2220. The texts of all three are in A. Higgins, *id.* at 97, 206, and 358 respectively.

discovered in the practical application of both conventions, but in the main they were found to be workable."[63]

In 1906 thirty-six states agreed to replace the ten-article Geneva Convention of 1864 with a thirty-three-article instrument. The new Geneva Convention for the Amelioration of the Conditions of the Wounded of the Armies in the Field expanded upon the principles enunciated in the 1864 Convention. Not only were the sick and wounded to be cared for; belligerents had a responsibility to search for the sick and wounded. Not only were citizens who treated the sick and wounded entitled to protection; military authorities were encouraged to "appeal to the charitable zeal of the inhabitants to receive, and, under [their] supervision, to care for the sick and wounded. . . ."[64] The 1906 agreement also specifically prohibited such disgusting battlefield practices as robbing dead bodies.[65] Additionally, the Convention spelled out the rights of medical personnel. Finally, it obligated signatories to seek enforcement legislation "to repress, in time of war, individual acts of robbery and ill treatment of the sick and wounded. . . ."[66]

A year later essentially the same nations met again at The Hague. They signed thirteen conventions covering a broad range of subjects. The most important is the Hague Convention (IV) and the Regulations Annexed Thereto Respecting the Laws and Customs of War on Land.[67] The Regulations proscribed weapons that caused unnecessary suffering and barred indiscriminate bom-

[63] A. Higgins, *id.* at 43.

[64] Article 5, 1906 Geneva Convention 35 STAT. 1885; T.S. 464; 1 BEVANS 516; 2 Treaties (MALLOY) 2183.

[65] *Id.*, Art. 3.   [66] *Id.*, Art. 28.

[67] 36 STAT. 2277; T.S. 539; 1 BEVANS 631; 2 Treaties (MALLOY) 2269.

bardment. These regulations, which have since become customary international law,[68] still constitute the bulk of international law regulating the conduct of hostilities. Although the Hague and Geneva Conventions did not legally bind the countries fighting World War I (because some among the belligerents had not signed them), the participants generally complied with their provisions and even concluded more detailed agreements covering treatment of civilians and prisoners of war.[69] Experience in World War I nevertheless revealed several gaps in Convention protection.

Following the armistice, nations set about plugging these holes. First, they tried to extend prohibitions on land bombardment to aerial bombardment, much as their 19th century predecessors had extended the Geneva principles protecting soldiers to sailors. They failed. The 1923 Rules on Aerial Bombardment,[70] drafted by the International Commission of Jurists, were never adopted. Those seeking a ban on gas warfare enjoyed greater

[68] The International Military Tribunal for the Far East concluded: ". . . Although the obligation to observe the provision of the [Hague] Convention as a binding treaty may be swept away by operations of the 'general participation clause,' or otherwise, the Convention remains as good evidence of the customary law of nations, to be considered by the Tribunal along with all other available evidence in determining the customary law to be applied in any given situation." OFFICIAL TRANSCRIPT OF THE JUDGEMENT OF THE INTERNATIONAL MILITARY TRIBUNAL FOR THE FAR EAST 65.

[69] *Note, supra* n. 50 at 3-4.

[70] See J. Spaight, AIR POWER AND WAR RIGHTS 498-508 (3rd ed. 1947). The effort to restrict aerial bombardment began before the turn of the century. Several parties to the 1899 Hague Conference agreed to a declaration prohibiting the discharge of projectiles and explosives from balloons or by other similar new methods. *Cf.* 2 AM. J. INT'L. SUPP. 216 (1908).

success. Signatories of the Geneva Gas Protocol of 1925[71] renounced the use of "asphyxiating, poisonous or other gases, and all analogous liquids, materials, or devices. . . ." In 1929 the nations replaced the 1906 Geneva Convention with two new Conventions: the Geneva Convention for the Amelioration of the Condition of the Wounded and Sick of Armies in the Field[72] and the Geneva Convention Relative to the Treatment of Prisoners of War.[73] Since their predecessor had elaborated the original 1864 Geneva Convention, the new agreements fleshed out the 1906 Convention with more detailed rules. The POW agreement, in particular, set out specific rules governing prisoner of war camps. The animating spirit behind many of the rules was the simple principle that the POW should receive the same treatment—in housing, food, clothing, and medical care—accorded the country's own soldiers. The Convention also dealt with the subject of labor, wages, and discipline and permitted the sending and receipt of mail.

As the world struggled to arrest its drift toward a second world war, interest in further reform waned. The International Committee of the Red Cross proposed and the 15th International Conference approved a draft convention to protect civilians in occupied territory. In 1938 the 16th International Conference endorsed a series of

[71] M. Hudson, III. INTERNATIONAL LEGISLATION 1670-1672 (1931). Although President Nixon has resubmitted the Protocol to the Senate for its advice and consent, the United States is not presently a party to the agreement. One of the three declarations issued at the 1899 Hague Conference anticipated the ban on gas warfare. It prohibited the use of projectiles, "the only object of which is diffusion of asphyxiating or deleterious gases."

[72] 47 STAT. 2074; T.S. 847; 2 BEVANS 965; 118 L.N.T.S. 303.

[73] 47 STAT. 2021; T.S. 846; 2 BEVANS 932; 118 L.N.T.S. 343.

modifications to the 1929 Geneva Conventions. None was adopted.[74]

Almost all the World War II belligerents had, however, ratified the 1929 Geneva Conventions and the 1907 Hague Conventions, all of which had in any case become customary international law. Japan, though not a signatory to the POW Convention, assured the United States it would treat American prisoners as the Convention provided.[75] France, Germany, Italy, Britain, and the United States executed a series of agreements to protect interned civilians.[76]

Even before the guns fell silent, the ICRC initiated studies aimed at revising existing conventional law. Following a series of conferences beginning in 1946, Switzerland invited its brethren nations to a Diplomatic Conference for the Establishment of International Conventions for the Protection of War Victims.[77] And establish such conventions they did. In August 1949, four conventions were promulgated:

(1) the Geneva Convention for the Amelioration of the Wounded and the Sick in the Armed Forces in the Field.[78]

(2) the Geneva Convention for the Amelioration of the Condition of Wounded, Sick, and Shipwrecked Members of Armed Forces at Sea.[79]

(3) the Geneva Convention relative to the Treatment of Prisoners of War.[80]

[74] Veuthey, *The Red Cross and Non-International Conflicts*, 10 INT'L. REV. OF THE RED CROSS 411, 412 (1970).

[75] *Note, supra* n. 50 at 5.   [76] *Id.*

[77] See FINAL RECORD OF THE DIPLOMATIC CONFERENCE OF GENEVA, 1949.

[78] 6 U.S.T. 3114; T.I.A.S. 3362; 75 U.N.T.S. 31.

[79] 6 U.S.T. 3217; T.I.A.S. 3363; 75 U.N.T.S. 85.

[80] 6 U.S.T. 3316; T.I.A.S. 3364; 75 U.N.T.S. 135.

(4) the Geneva Convention relative to the protection of Civilian Persons in Time of War.[81]

These conventions, which enjoy almost universal adherence, largely govern treatment of non-combatants today.[82]

b. RESTRAINTS ON USE OF FORCE

Over the last fifty years efforts to outlaw the use of force altogether have paralleled the codification process. In 1928 the major powers signed the Kellogg-Briand Pact, which condemned "recourse to war for the solution of international controversies." They renounced war "as an instrument of national policy. . . ."[83] Although one of the 1907 Hague Conventions prohibited bondholding states from calling out their gunboats to collect debts[84] and the League of Nations Covenant imposed "cooling off" periods before war could be declared,[85] the Kellogg-Briand

[81] 6 U.S.T. 3516; T.I.A.S. 3365; 75 U.N.T.S. 287.

[82] The principal provisions of these conventions are discussed and their historical background is sketched in G. Draper, *supra* n. 55. The standard reference work is Jean Pictet's four-volume COMMENTARIES, which analyze each article individually. FIELD MANUAL 27-10, THE LAW OF LAND WARFARE, contains the United States interpretation of the main articles.

[83] 46 STAT. 2343; T.S. 796; 2 BEVANS 732; 94 L.N.T.S. 57. Whether the Kellog-Briand Pact made the waging of aggressive war a crime, as the International Military Tribunal held, has been hotly debated. *Cf.* G. Schwarzenberger, II. INTERNATIONAL LAW 487-94 (1968).

[84] Convention Respecting the Limitation of Force for the Recovery of Contract Debts, 36 STAT. 2241; T.S. 537; 1 BEVANS 607; 2 Treaties (MALLOY) 2248.

[85] 10. *E.g.*, LEAGUE OF NATIONS COVENANT, art. 12, para. 1 provided: "The Members of the League agree that if there should arise between them any dispute likely to lead to a rupture, they will submit the matter either to arbitration or judicial settlement or to inquiry by the Council, and they agree in no case to resort to war until three months after the award by the arbitrators or the

Pact is regarded as the first authoritative effort to prohibit war since Augustine articulated the just war doctrine. Both the Nuremberg and Tokyo war crimes tribunals concluded that the initiation of a war of aggression was not only an international crime, but the supreme international crime, "differing only from other war crimes in that it contains within itself the accumulated evil of the whole."[86] Though some have questioned the soundness of the tribunals' judgments, they bolstered their conclusion by citing, in addition to the Kellogg-Briand Pact, the Draft Treaty of Mutual Assistance sponsored by the League of Nations in 1923, providing in Article 1 that "aggression is an international crime"; the Preamble to the 1924 League Protocol for the Pacific Settlement of International Disputes, stating that a war of aggression violates the solidarity of nations and is therefore an international crime; the declaration adopted by the League Assembly on September 24, 1927, decrying war as an international crime; and the resolution unanimously adopted on February 18, 1928, by the twenty-one American republics at Havana, providing that a "war of aggression constitutes an international crime against the human species."[87]

Whether aggressive war was a war crime in 1939, it is today—though scholars despair of ever agreeing upon an authoritative definition.[88] The cornerstone of the international system established under the United Nations Charter is the broad prohibition in Article 2(4) on "the threat or use of force" in international relations. The Charter

---

judicial decision or the report by the Council." Although provisions like these may now seem quaint, they reflected the contemporary judgment that World War I began "accidentally."

[86] 1 TRIAL OF THE MAJOR WAR CRIMINALS 186 (1947).

[87] *Id.* at 218-44.

[88] *E.g.*, J. Stone, LEGAL CONTROLS OF INTERNATIONAL CONFLICT 330-34 (1959).

does permit the use of force in two exceptional circumstances: (1) when employed in self-defense; and (2) when authorized by the Security Council. These general norms, however, neither proscribe revolution nor prevent a government from using armed force to maintain its authority. Generalized as they are, they have not provided a detailed rationale for distinguishing legitimate from illegitimate third-party intervention in internal conflicts. The quest for an integrated legal theory that would explain *when* states might use force in internal conflicts has preoccupied a growing number of scholars[89] with the unfortunate consequence, as we shall presently see, that they have neglected the equally important question about *how* participants may employ that force.

The chart below shows how the legal scheme by which man now seeks to regulate the use of force and the conduct of war evolved.

B. RECENT CHANGES IN THE NATURE OF WARFARE

While, as we have seen, man has recorded war as a constant phenomenon so long as he has written history, he has depicted it as continually changing.[90] The laws of

---

[89] *Cf.* Bond, *Survey of the Normative Rules of Intervention*, 52 MIL. L. REV. 51 (1971). Present-day scholars have concentrated almost exclusively on restraint of force problems. Increasingly, they have focused their attention on either (1) delineating a sub-charter set of norms that regulate use of force (*e.g.*, Lillich, *Forcible Self-help under International Law*, 22 NAVAL WAR COLLEGE REV. 56 [1970]) or (2) integrating norms restricting intervention into the Charter rubrics (*e.g.*, Moore, *The Control of Foreign Intervention in Internal Conflict*, 9 VA. J. INT'L. L. 205 [1969]).

[90] See Kelly, *A Legal Analysis of the Changes in War* 13 MIL. L. REV. 89 (1961).

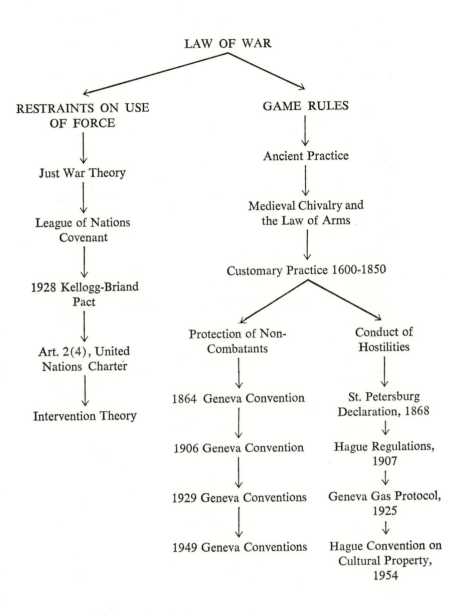

LAW OF WAR

RESTRAINTS ON USE
OF FORCE

Just War Theory

League of Nations
Covenant

1928 Kellogg-Briand
Pact

Art. 2(4), United
Nations Charter

Intervention Theory

GAME RULES

Ancient Practice

Medieval Chivalry and
the Law of Arms

Customary Practice 1600-1850

Protection of Non-
Combatants

1864 Geneva Convention

1906 Geneva Convention

1929 Geneva Conventions

1949 Geneva Conventions

Conduct of
Hostilities

St. Petersburg
Declaration, 1868

Hague Regulations,
1907

Geneva Gas Protocol,
1925

Hague Convention on
Cultural Property,
1954

war have had perforce to change as well; the evolution in
their development sketched above has been a response to
the changing nature of warfare. Prior to the Napoleonic
wars, for example, small professional armies fought one
another for rather limited objectives.[91] The dawn of the
industrial age and the introduction of the citizen army
drastically altered the pattern. The non-professional soldier, spurred by ideology, marched off to war. Those who
stayed behind to run the factories contributed as much to
the military effort, for they fueled the war machine. The
American Civil War has been called the first modern war;
it was the first war in which a majority of the citizens participated in the fight.[92] General Sherman, who proved to
be a man of his word, declared: ". . . this war [the Civil
War] differs from European wars in this particular; we are
not only fighting hostile armies, but a hostile people, and
must make old and young, rich and poor, feel the hard
hand of war, as well as their organized armies."[93] Widespread revulsion at the consequent devastation and suffering from tactics such as General Sherman employed ig-
nited the codification movement. Indeed, the Civil War
saw the first adoption by a belligerent of a detailed code
governing his conduct of hostilities and his treatment of
non-combatants.[94]

Though one of the few beneficial consequences of war
has thus been law reform, the revised rules have usually
proved inadequate in subsequent conflicts. No Januses,

[91] Vattel could conclude that "at the present day, war is carried
on by regular armies; the people, the peasantry, the towns-folk,
take no part in it, and as a rule, have nothing to fear from the
sword of the enemy." Clausewitz dismissed such war as "play
war." II. INTERNATIONAL LAW 7 (Dept. of Army Pam. 27-161-2
1962).

[92] *Id.*   [93] Quoted in C. Fenwick, *supra* n. 4 at 568.
[94] See n. 49 *supra*.

these reformers, and with both eyes cocked toward correcting the abuses of the last war, they have not perceived the challenges of the next. Professor Kelly has pointed out: "By tracing fundamental changes in the character of war in the last four hundred years, four distinct periods can be discerned. . . . The laws, fashioned in one period, lose much of their force when applied to the next."[95] One example will illustrate the point. The men who met at The Hague in 1907 did not anticipate the aerial age. They devised rules of bombardment that provided no answers to the questions of target selection, the duty to warn, the validity of strategic or tactical bombing that have befuddled war planners since World War I.[96]

The present insistent demands for reform of the laws of war stem from just such inadequacies: the failure of the present law to regulate the problems peculiar to the altered nature of war in our time. First, fighting has become localized. War is internal rather than international in scope. Traditionally, the laws of war have not applied to internal conflicts. Second, guerrilla tactics are widely employed. Such tactics and those who use them have generally been considered beyond the pale of international law. The result is that the laws of war neither regulate conduct nor protect participants in the kind of warfare characteristic of our time.

C. INADEQUACIES IN THE PRESENT LAW OF WAR

1. *The Increasing Incidence of Internal Warfare*

Evidence of the increasing incidence of internal war is probably as recent as the latest newscast. Though by no

[95] Kelly, *supra* n. 90 at 95.
[96] See DeSaussure, *The Laws of Air Warfare: Are There Any?* 23 NAVAL WAR COLLEGE REV. 35 (1971).

means a new phenomenon—revolution has been endemic
in the modern nation-state system—the frequency and
violence of internal conflict distinguish present warfare
from the paradigm pattern of conflict epitomized by
World War II. One scholar has observed that internal war
"is practically the essence of contemporary political life."[97]
From the pages of the *New York Times* the same authority gleaned "well over 1,200 unequivocal examples [of
internal war] between 1946 and 1959."[98] Although one
may dispute the precise number of internal wars (whose
number will reflect one's definition of "internal war"),
riots, insurrections, insurgencies, coup d'états, and revo-
lutions bedevil established authorities throughout the
world. The Free French movement in Quebec and the bitter fighting between Protestants and Catholics in Northern
Ireland remind us that stable governments in the Northern Hemisphere are not immune from what was once
thought a disease of the "have not" nations below the
equator. Even Vietnam and the Middle East, the two major contemporary conflicts that fit most closely the traditional model of international war, are rooted in internal
conflicts and continue to demonstrate aspects of internal
warfare.

2. *The Pervasive Use of Guerrilla Tactics*

In all of these internal conflicts, the participants use
guerrilla tactics. Although Ho Chi Minh and Che Guevara
did not invent guerrilla warfare—General Washington
was a successful practitioner of the art in the 18th century—they and their disciples have proselytized the Third
World so successfully that people commonly and some-

[97] Eckstein, *Introduction*, INTERNAL WAR 3 (H. Eckstein ed.
1963).
[98] *Id.*

what misleadingly speak of guerrilla wars.[99] Since guerrilla tactics may be and have been used in both international and internal conflicts, guerrilla wars are presumably ones in which participants resort exclusively to guerrilla strategy. This is often the case in internal conflicts where government forces have abandoned as ineffective conventional methods of warfare and have themselves adopted those methods usually identified with rebel or insurgent groups. Britain in Malaysia and France in Algeria[100] both imitated their tormentors, and the American army now trains its troops in "counterinsurgency warfare."[101] Whatever it is called and however it may differ from city to countryside, guerrilla warfare is the pervasive mode of contemporary conflict. All parties fight in dispersed and mobile groups; conduct surprise attacks, ambushes, and sabotage; and use terror.[102]

3. *Existing Inadequacies in the Law*

Since internal war is not an entirely new phenomenon, international legal scholars have long before the present decade asked themselves whether the laws of war applied to such conflicts. Until 1949 and the adoption of common Article 3 of the Geneva Conventions, the consensus answer was that only customary international law

[99] *E.g.*, Ney, *Guerrilla War and Modern Strategy*, 2 ORBIS 66 (1958).

[100] Wales, *Algerian Terrorism*, 22 NAVAL WAR COLLEGE REV. 26 (1969).

[101] See *e.g.* FIELD MANUAL 31-16, COUNTERGUERRILLA OPERATIONS (1967).

[102] D. Bindschedler-Robert, THE LAW OF ARMED CONFLICT 38 (1970). For an analysis of terror as a weapon, see Thornton, *Terror as a Weapon of Political Agitation*, INTERNAL WAR 71 (H. Eckstein, ed. 1963).

(as opposed to the international laws of war found in
treaties) applied and then only in cases of civil wars or,
to use the correct term of art, "belligerencies." To qualify
as belligerents, rebel groups had to pass five litmus paper
tests: (1) are there general hostilities? (2) do the rebels
act like an army? (3) do they have an effective government? (4) do they control substantial territory? and (5)
do third states recognize the rebels as belligerents?[103] The
classic example of a belligerency is the South during the
American Civil War. Others have demonstrated the sense-
lessness of the tests,[104] which are in any case no longer
respected in a variety of other contexts. But if they remain
determinative of when groups must respect the laws of
war, few will be the contemporary conflicts to which even
the customary laws apply. Among recent internal conflicts
probably only the Biafran secessionist movement could be
analogized to the classic model of a belligerency (although no state formally recognized the existence of a
belligerency.)[105]

In 1949, nations did adopt common Article 3 of the
Geneva Conventions, which binds the signatories to observe certain fundamental humanitarian principles in
"armed conflict not of an international character."[106]

---

[103] H. Lauterpacht, II OPPENHEIM'S INTERNATIONAL LAW 250
(7th ed. 1952).

[104] *E.g.*, Farer, *Intervention in Civil Wars: A Modest Proposal*,
I THE VIETNAM WAR AND INTERNATIONAL LAW 509, 514 (R. Falk,
ed. 1968).

[105] Two states did, however, recognize Biafra, Ijalaye, *Was
Biafra Ever a State in International Law*, 65 AM. J. INT'L L. 551,
555 (1971).

[106] See footnote 43 *supra*. Article 3 provides:

"In the case of armed conflict not of an international character
occurring in the territory of one of the High Contracting Parties,

While the phrase could be construed broadly enough to embrace almost any kind of internal disturbance, some legislative history suggests that the delegates believed they were describing nothing other than the classic kind of belligerency.[107] It is at least clear from past practice that the parties to internal conflicts have seldom interpreted

---

each party to the conflict shall be bound to apply, as a minimum, the following provisions;

"(1) Persons taking no active part in the hostilities, including members of armed forces who have laid down their arms and those placed hors de combat by sickness, wounds, detention, or any other cause, shall in all circumstances be treated humanely, without any adverse distinction founded on race, colour, religion or faith, sex, birth or wealth, or any other similar criteria.

"To this end, the following acts are and shall remain prohibited at any time and in any place whatsoever with respect to the above-mentioned persons;

"(a) violence to life and person, in particular murder of all kinds, mutilation, cruel treatment and torture;

"(b) taking of hostages;

"(c) outrages upon personal dignity, in particular, humiliating and degrading treatment;

"(d) the passing of sentences and the carrying out of executions without previous judgment pronounced by a regularly constituted court affording all the judicial guarantees which are recognized as indispensable by civilized peoples.

"(2) The wounded and sick shall be collected and cared for.

"An impartial humanitarian body, such as the International Committee of the Red Cross, may offer its services to the Parties to the conflict.

"The Parties to the conflict should further endeavor to bring into force, by means of special agreements, all or part of the other provisions of the present Convention.

"The application of the preceding provisions shall not affect the legal status of the Parties to the conflict."

[107] II-B FINAL RECORD OF THE DIPLOMATIC CONFERENCE OF GENEVA 121 (1949).

the conditions for its applicability as broadly as com-
mentators have thought desirable.[108]

Even if Article 3 were applicable to a wider range of
internal conflicts than either state practice suggests or
reasonable interpretation permits, its provisions do not
constitute a complete codification of the law of war for
internal conflicts. They do not purport, for example, to
regulate the conduct of hostilities.[109] Article 3 is silent on
the permissible scope of destruction. It does not, for example, grant immunity to hospitals, churches, or museums. Whole villages may be and often are burned to the
ground. Nor does Article 3 prohibit the use of any weapon
or weapons system. A convention such as the Geneva Gas
Protocol of 1925 applies only to international conflicts,
and parties have used gas warfare in some internal conflicts.[110] All Article 3 does is extend some minimum humanitarian protections to non-combatants. These provi-

---

[108] *Cf.* Ford, *Resistance Movements and International Law*,
7-8 INT'L. REV. OF THE RED CROSS 515, 579, 627, 7 (1967-1968).

[109] But see Farer, *Humanitarian Law and Armed Conflicts:
Toward The Definition of "International Armed Conflict"* 71
COLUM. L. REV. 37 (1971). At 40 Farer says: ". . . the international legal rules governing combat operations—largely codified
in the Hague Conventions—have traditionally been held to apply
only to international armed conflicts. Hence such practices as
the destruction of towns and villages to achieve insignificant military objectives or indiscriminate zonal bombardment allegedly
designed to harass unseen enemy forces may not be covered by
the international law of internal war, although one could possibly
argue that these tactics violate Article 3's injunction to treat
'humanely . . . [p]ersons taking no active part in the hostilities'
and its prohibition of 'violence to life and persons.' "

[110] The most egregious case has been the civil war in Yemen.
Cf. Meselson & Viney, *The Yemen*, CHEMICAL AND BIOLOGICAL
WARFARE 99-102 (S. Rose ed. 1968).

sions—as, for example, the requirement that "the sick and wounded be cared for"—are so general that parties have evaded their responsibility.[111] Governments have repeatedly rebuffed efforts by the International Committee of the Red Cross to treat sick and wounded rebels.[112]

Moreover, the minimum provisions of Article 3 do not prevent many kinds of maltreatment common in internal conflicts. Article 3 does not specifically advert at all to the problems of detention and punishment although it does forbid "the passing of sentences and carrying out of executions without previous judgment pronounced by a regularly constituted court, affording all the judicial guarantees which are recognized as indispensable by civilized peoples." Quite aside from what constitutes "all the judicial guarantees . . . recognized as indispensable by civilized peoples," the chief problems in internal conflicts have been pre- and post-trial detention and summary and excessive punishment. Governments usually pursue extraordinary criminal processes against rebels.[113] They detain for interrogation purposes without charge, for example, or hold persons incognito. At the conclusion of a court-imposed sentence, authorities may extend terms of confinement if the prisoner does not seem "rehabilitated."[114] Capital punishment is frequently imposed. Rebel units, which usually lack any judicial infrastructure, may dispense even more summary justice.

[111] Farer, *supra* n. 108 at 39.

[112] *Cf. Help to War Victims in Nigeria,* 9 INT'L. REV. OF THE RED CROSS 353 (1969).

[113] J. Kelley and G. Pellatier, LEGAL CONTROL OF THE POPULACE IN SUBVERSIVE WARFARE 31-287 (1966).

[114] T. Mien, VIETNAM: NATIONAL SECURITY NEEDS IN A CONSTITUTIONAL GOVERNMENT (unpublished thesis, The Judge Advocate General's School 1971).

The situation would scarcely be better if the Geneva
Conventions in their entirety and all the other conventional treaty law were applicable; for although the delegates to the 1949 Geneva Diplomatic Conference understood guerrilla tactics, they did not tailor the Convention
solutions to the problems of guerrilla warfare. Rather,
they ignored them. Captured guerrillas, for example, are
generally not entitled to prisoner of war status. Although
many countries that had been occupied during World
War II fought for recognition of guerrilla forces,[115] the
United States and other major countries resisted inclusion
of guerrillas within the POW category. The upshot was
"a comparatively innocuous provision," of which Professor Baxter says: "Despite some extravagant claims made
for Article 4, it does little to increase the categories of
persons who are, as 'lawful belligerents,' to come under
the protection of the Prisoners of War Convention."[116]
Basically, Article 4 says that one is a prisoner of war if
(1) he is a member of a national armed force or (2) if
he is a member of a group that fulfills the following four
conditions:

(a) that of being commanded by a person responsible
for his subordinates;

(b) that of having a fixed distinctive sign recognizable at a distance;

(c) that of carrying arms openly;

(d) that of conducting their operations in accordance
with the laws and customs of war.

No guerrilla is likely to qualify for POW status under

[115] *Cf.* Trainin, *Questions of Guerrilla Warfare in the Law of
War*, 40 AM. J. INT'L. L. 534 (1946).

[116] Baxter, *The Geneva Conventions of 1949*, 9 NAVAL WAR
COLLEGE REV. 59 (1956).

such conditions. While the guerrilla force will probably have a hierarchical command (happily for generals if not for privates, even the Russians and the Chinese, after flirting with a "classless" army, have found a rank structure necessary), its members are not likely to wear a "fixed distinctive sign recognizable at a distance," nor will they always bear arms openly. The whole classification scheme is irrelevant to conflicts in which guerrilla tactics are used. Participants in these wars simply do not fall into the neat categories set out in the Geneva Conventions. In short, the guerrilla under the Geneva Conventions remains what he has always been: an outlaw.

D. Demands for the Revision and Extension of the Law of War to Internal Conflict

The preceding discussion of inadequacies in the present law of war is neither detailed nor exhaustive, as the problems to be examined in subsequent chapters will show. It does, however, spotlight the nature of the present crisis: the law of war is not tailored to guerrilla warfare in internal conflicts. Scholars, private groups, governments, and international organizations, recognizing this fact, have all joined voices in an insistent demand for reform.

1. The Work of the International Committee of the Red Cross and Other Private Groups

Among private organizations, the International Committee of the Red Cross has labored longest and hardest to extend the law of war to internal conflicts. As early as 1912 it submitted to the International Red Cross Conference a Draft Convention on the role of the Red Cross in civil wars or insurrections.[117] In 1921 the Tenth Conference resolved that all victims of civil wars or social or revolutionary disturbances had a right to relief in conformity with the general principles of the Red Cross,[118] and the 1938 Conference reiterated its demand that humanitarian principles be applied in internal conflicts.[119] Every International Conference in the last decade, including the last one held at Istanbul in 1969, has called upon all the parties to armed conflict of any kind to respect human rights. From the civil war in Upper Silesia in 1921 to the recent unhappy events in Biafra and Jordan, the ICRC has acted on that demand and sought to alleviate suffering in internal wars.[120]

In addition to its humanitarian activities on the battlefield, the ICRC has studied the problem of applying the law of war to internal conflict and has recommended several substantive changes. It submitted to the Nineteenth International Conference of the Red Cross a series of "Draft Rules for the Limitation of the Dangers Incurred by the Civilian Population in Time of War."[121] It has convened three private meetings of experts to study the plight of non-combatants in internal conflicts: Aid to Political Detainees (1953);[122] Applicability of Humanitarian Principles in Cases of Internal Disturbances

[117] Veuthey, *supra* n. 74 at 411.

[118] *Id.* at 412.   [119] *Id.*

[120] *E.g.*, International Committee of the Red Cross, *The ICRC and the Yemen Conflict* (1964).

[121] *Protection of Civilian Populations Against the Dangers of Indiscriminate Warfare*, 7 INT'L. REV. OF THE RED CROSS 300 (1967).

[122] International Committee of the Red Cross, *Report Aid to Political Retainees* (1953).

(1955);[123] and Aid to Victims of Internal Disturbances
(1962).[124] Presently, the ICRC is consulting experts on
the general topic, Reaffirmation and Development of International Humanitarian Law Applicable in Armed Conflict, and has already published a Preliminary Report on
the Consultation of Experts concerning Non-International Conflict and Guerrilla Warfare.[125] Governmental experts have now met to consider draft proposals on the
subject and a diplomatic conference is scheduled for
February, 1974.

2. The Work of the United Nations

Although the United Nations initially evinced little
interest in revising or codifying the law of war,[126] it has
recently thrown its weight behind proposals for reform.
Pursuant to the recommendation of the 1968 International Conference on Human Rights at Tehran,[127] the

[123] International Committee of the Red Cross, *Report Applicability of Humanitarian Principles in Cases of Internal Disturbances* (1955).

[124] International Committee of the Red Cross, *Report Aid to Victims of Internal Disturbances* (1962).

[125] International Committee of the Red Cross, PRELIMINARY REPORT ON THE CONSULTATION OF EXPERTS CONCERNING CONFLICT AND GUERRILLA WARFARE (1970).

[126] YEARBOOK OF THE INT'L. LAW COMM. 20.4.1949, p. 475.
Amid the euphoria of establishing the United Nations, some
scholars assumed that since the Charter forbade war, revising
laws regulating its conduct would therefore be unnecessary.

[127] Resolution 23 requested that the General Assembly ask the
Secretary-General to study:
"(a) steps which could be taken to secure better application
of existing humanitarian international conventions and rules in
all armed conflicts;
"(b) the need for additional humanitarian international conventions or of possible revision of existing conventions to ensure

Secretary-General has prepared and issued a report entitled *Respect for Human Rights in Armed Conflict.*[128] The General Assembly has endorsed and encouraged these efforts and through a series of resolutions has itself sought to change existing law.[129] It has, for example, declared illegal the use of nuclear, chemical, or biological weapons in any armed conflict. Furthermore, it has demanded that the guerrillas fighting in the Portuguese provinces in Africa be treated as prisoners of war. The United Nations Commission on Human Rights has also considered the problem and recommended revision and extension of the law of war to non-international conflicts. The Secretariat has begun to work closely with the ICRC in what has now become a joint effort to update the law of war.

The recent revival of interest in war law reform, both within the United Nations and elsewhere, is a logical outgrowth of the post-war preoccupation with human rights. One of the most astute students of the law of war has concluded that "the revision of the law of armed conflict . . . had come perilously near to stagnation before the impact of the movement for a regime of human rights was brought to bear."[130] Scholars no longer view the law of war and human rights as separate legal regimes. Instead, they see them as complementary halves of a single

---

the better protection of civilians, prisoners, and combatants in all armed conflicts, and of the prohibition and elimination of the use of certain methods and means of warfare."

[128] U.N. DOC. A/8052 (18 Sept. 1970).

[129] *Documentary note*, REAFFIRMATION AND DEVELOPMENT OF HUMANITARIAN LAW AND CUSTOMS APPLICABLE IN ARMED CONFLICTS 3-5 (1969).

[130] Draper, *The Ethical and Juridicial Status of Constraints in War*, 55 MIL. L. REV. 169, 177 (1972).

regime of international humanitarian law. Colonel Draper has succinctly explained the nature of this regime: "The regime of human rights will come in time to be the normal ordering in civil society; if war breaks out, inter- or intra-state, that regime does not dissipate. First, it is there waiting in the background the whole time to take over once the conflict abates. Second, a lower level of that regime then comes into play by way of derogation made strictly necessary by the emergency situation. That lower regime is the Law of Armed Conflicts."[131]

E. CONCLUSIONS

Five conclusions emerge from this historical survey and analysis of the law of war.

1. The law of war is no more static than any other body of legal rules. As the conditions demanding regulation have changed, the law of war has changed.

2. Revisions and reform in the law have, however, usually lagged behind altered means of conducting warfare. Draftsmen have seldom anticipated technological innovations, for example; and rules intended for an earlier era have been stretched to govern another.

3. As the law of war has become increasingly detailed and codified, it has been applied to an ever-widening range of armed conflicts.

4. The agitation for extending the law of war to internal conflict may indicate that it is an idea whose time has come. Many of the present rules, initially articulated by scholars, were included in draft agreements that never came into force before finally finding limited expression in a formal international instrument. The limited expression was then expanded in successive conventions.

[131] *Id.*

The idea that parties to internal conflicts should respect the law of war has a similar lineage: long advocated by scholars and included in draft instruments, it finally emerged in Article 3 of the 1949 Geneva Conventions.

5. The task now is to articulate an integrated legal regime for the conduct of hostilities and the treatment of non-combatants in internal conflicts. This new regime must draw upon both the traditional law of war and newer developments in the human rights field.

CHAPTER II

The Rationale for Applying Humanitarian Law to Internal Conflict

Though the phrase "law of war" has struck some observers as a contradiction in terms—Cicero remarked that law was silent in war[1]—its evolution and codification traced in the preceding chapter attest man's continuing effort to ameliorate insofar as possible the suffering caused by war. No one questions that the reduction of human suffering is the chief goal of the law of war, but only recently have observers recognized that internal conflicts breed the same kind of human suffering against which the law of war has set its face in international conflicts.

A. THE CHARACTER OF INTERNAL CONFLICT

Internal conflicts have become chambers of horror. Destruction, brutality, and death do not, after all, recognize international boundaries; they stalk their prey wherever men fight one another. While accurate figures do not exist, estimates on destruction of property and loss of life in internal conflicts run high. In Algeria, for example, French soldiers killed over 100,000 rebels or suspected rebel sympathizers between 1954 and 1960. The French themselves lost over 13,000 soldiers.[2] During the more recent Nigerian civil war, as many as 2,000,000 Biafrans may have died.[3] The 1972 revolt in East Pakistan cost

[1] Quoted in Q. Wright, II. A STUDY OF WAR 863 (1942).
[2] J. Kraft, THE STRUGGLE FOR ALGERIA 99 (1961).
[3] *New York Times*, Sept. 27, 1970, at 22, col. 3.

50,000 to 200,000 Bengalis their lives.[4] The strategy of attrition practiced in other internal wars provides local undertakers with a steady business. In five years of episodic fighting in Chad, for example, several thousand native and government soldiers have slain each other.[5] The Portuguese lose approximately one hundred soldiers every year fighting guerrilla movements in their African provinces.[6]

One cannot smell the stench nor see the horror of these deaths in the statistics alone. The dead rot unburied. Vultures in East Pakistan could not fly because they were so fat with human blood. The Mau Mau in Kenya hacked their fellow tribesmen and European settlers to death with machetes and then incinerated them with wives and children in their homes.[7] A Portuguese lieutenant rounded up a group of Angolese natives, told them he wanted to snap their picture with his telephoto lens, then blew them to bits with what was in fact a bazooka.[8] A reporter in Ceylon, covering the 1971 revolt there, filed this report with the Associated Press: "Bodies of young men presumably killed by policemen and soldiers have been floating down rivers in groups toward the sea near Colombo. . . . Some of them were decapitated and others riddled with bullets, their wrists bound behind their backs."[9] These vignettes illustrate not only the horror of death but apparent violations of the basic human rights guaranteed in international conflicts by the laws of war.

The pattern of such violations repeats itself in each internal conflict and parallels those excesses all too com-

[4] Id., May 20, 1971, at 41, col. 1.
[5] Id., June 26, 1969, at 40, col. 3.
[6] Id., July 8, 1970, at 10, col. 1.
[7] C. Wills, WHO KILLED KENYA? 78 (1943).
[8] New York Times, Aug. 6, 1969, at 43, col. 1.
[9] Id., April 25, 1971, at 1, col. 6.

mon in international conflicts. Compare, for example, the following two descriptions of prisoner interrogation:

"In military posts and police stations . . . frequent use was made of the 'magneto,' or hand-telephone generator, for applying electric shocks to prisoners. The ducking of bound prisoners to the point of drowning, as well as the application of burning cigarettes to tender skin, and the internal use of pressurized gases and liquids—all became standard operating procedures."[10]

"[H]eads of prisoners [are] held under water and bayonet blades pressed against their throats. . . . In more extreme cases, victims have had bamboo slivers run under their fingernails or wires from a field telephone connected to arms, nipples or testicles."[11]

These similar accounts reflect, in the first case, alleged French practices in Algeria and, in the second case, alleged American practice in Vietnam. Again, in Algeria a French colonel executed five prisoners in retaliation for a rebel attack on a supply convoy and hung their bodies in the village market as a warning.[12] In Guinea convicted conspirators against the Touré government were executed and their bodies dangled from bridges leading into the capital.[13] In Ceylon the lifeless bodies of two insurgents were nailed through the wrists to road signs.[14]

Destruction is similarly widespread. Guerrillas in Chad raid villages, steal everything of value, and burn them to the ground. The government forces respond in kind against villages suspected of rebel sympathies.[15] The

[10] J. Kraft, *supra* n. 2 at 102.
[11] *New York Times*, Nov. 28, 1965, at 47, col. 3.
[12] J. Kraft, *supra* n. 39 at 103.
[13] *New York Times*, Feb. 4, 1971, at 13, col. 6.
[14] *Supra* n. 9.
[15] *New York Times*, June 26, 1969, at 40, col. 3.

Ethiopian government has "almost completely demolished" with air attacks the Eritrean towns of Dunkalia and Keren, where guerrillas maintained their headquarters.[16]

Men, women, and children starve. Pictures of Biafran children with bloated, distended bellies touched the conscience of mankind; yet as many as 200,000 may have starved to death.[17] The sick and wounded languish unattended. Fighting in Laos decimated the Meo tribesmen, 6,000 of whom yearly trooped through the chief Meo medical facility at Sam Thong—when it was operating.[18] Today their wounds go untreated. In Yemen, the Imam, leader of the counter-revolutionary forces, has no medical corps. Until the ICRC established field hospitals, his wounded received no care.[19] Families are dragged from their homes and interned in detention camps or "relocated" in "strategic hamlets." Those who can flee this destruction, brutality, and death do. Three hundred thousand Moslem refugees from Algeria lived in Morocco and Tunisia at the end of the Algerian civil war.[20] Two weeks after the Pakistani army swept into East Pakistan, 650,000 Bengalis were refugees in four neighboring Indian states.[21] In six years of fighting in Laos, 600,000 Laotians—one-quarter of the country's population—have become refugees.[22]

[16] *Supra* n. 4.

[17] *New York Times*, Sept. 27, 1970, at 22, col. 3.

[18] *Id.*, March 16, 1971, at 1, col. 5.

[19] The International Committee of the Red Cross, *The ICRC and the Yemen Conflict* 5 (1964).

[20] Jabhat al-Tahrir al-Quami, WHITE PAPER ON THE APPLICATION OF THE GENEVA CONVENTIONS OF 1949 TO THE FRENCH-ALGERIAN CONFLICT 7 (1960).

[21] *New York Times*, May 20, 1971, at 41, col. 1.

[22] *Cf.* D. de Huan and J. Tinker, *Refugee and Civil War Casu-*

B. The Legal Categories of Internal Conflict to Which Humanitarian Law Presently Applies

Though the preceding catalog of wanton destruction, torture, rape, pillage, and execution is in every instance but the other face of a human right ignored or violated, the traditional categories of internal conflicts to which the laws of war apply reflect more deference to the supposed jurisdictional competency of national sovereigns than concern for the human rights of those caught up in the struggle.

1. The Traditional Belligerency-Insurgency Distinction

Presently, there are only two situations of internal strife to which the law of war applies. Under traditional international law, the customary law of war applied once the rebels achieved belligerent status. Presumably, only customary law, rather than treaty law as well, came into force because the belligerent parties had not signed the latter[23] (though the distinction may be one without a difference, since much of the law of war found in treaties is either prior customary law codified or has since become customary law).

The belligerency test, discussed briefly in Chapter I, reflects the "nations rights" attitude that has long dominated international law. Many nations still insist that only those rules to which they agree bind them; and they rarely concede any international law limitations on their authority to deal summarily with domestic enemies. The doctrine of nations rights is enshrined in the United Na-

---

alty *Problems in Indochina* (1971 Staff Report of the U.S. Senate Subcommittee on Refugee Problems).

[23] *Cf. Note, The Geneva Conventions and Treatment of Prisoners of War in Vietnam,* 80 HARV. L. REV. 851 (1967).

tions Charter, which declares: "Nothing contained in the
present Charter shall authorize the United Nations to
intervene in matters which are essentially within the domestic jurisdiction of any state or shall require the Members to submit such matters to settlement under the
present Charter."[24] The language is broader than that
contained in its predecessor provision in the League
Covenant. It is true that the continuing General Assembly
consideration of racist practices in South Africa may
have established a precedent for a narrow interpretation
of the appropriate scope of exclusive domestic jurisdiction;[25] but the frequent reservations of domestic jurisdiction asserted in "acceptances" of the compulsory jurisdiction of the International Court suggest that most
states remain leery of any international interference in
what they broadly construe as their internal affairs. The
rather broad proscriptions against intervention written
into international agreements[26] and expressed in General
Assembly resolutions[27] evidence a similar attitude.

[24] Article 2(7), U.N. CHARTER.
[25] See generally, McDougal and Reisman, *Rhodesia and the
United Nations: The Lawfulness of International Concern*, 62
AM. J. INT'L. L. 1 (1968).
[26] *E.g.*, Article 18 of the CHARTER OF THE ORGANIZATION OF
AMERICAN STATES, 2 U.S.T. 2394, T.I.A.S. 2361, 119 U.N.T.S. 3,
states: "No State or group of States has the right to intervene,
directly or indirectly, for any reason whatever, in the internal or
external affairs of any other State. The foregoing principle prohibits not only armed force but also any other form of interference or attempted threat against the personality of the State
or against its political, economic and cultural elements."
[27] *E.g.*, G. A. Resolution 2131 (XX), GAOR, XX, *Supp.* 14,
A/6014, 21 Dec. 1965, states: "No state has the right to intervene, directly or indirectly, for any reason whatever, in the internal or external affairs of any other State. Consequently,
armed intervention and all other forms of interference or at-

Nations holding such beliefs would naturally reject the idea that the laws of war—international law—should dictate how they could treat insurgents. Once the rebels had achieved the status of belligerents, however, they had become in effect a *de facto* state; as a state they were entitled to all the incidents of that privileged status, one of which was being accorded the benefits of the laws of war. Once the rebels became so strong in some geographical areas that third governments found it necessary to deal with them, as well as with the established government, at least tacit recognition of rebel authority inevitably followed. The doctrine of the sovereign equality of states, which remains a fundamental building bloc of the international legal order,[28] rather than the demand of humanity, dictated applying the laws of war to belligerencies.

2. *Armed Conflict Not of an International Character*

An "armed conflict not of an international character" is the second situation of internal strife to which a portion of the laws of war apply. One frustrated scholar despairs: "One of the most assured things that might be said about the words 'armed conflict not of an international character' is that no one can say with assurance precisely what meaning they were intended to convey."[29] Consider, for example, the scale of conflicts below, arranged very roughly from left to right in order of the

tempted threats against its political, economic and cultural elements, are condemned."

[28] Friedmann, *Intervention, Civil War and the Role of International Law*, 1965 PROC. AM. SOC. INT'L. L. 67, 67-68.

[29] Farer, *Humanitarian Law and Armed Conflicts: Toward the Definition of 'International Armed Conflict'*, 71 COLUM. L. REV. 37, 43 (1971).

increasing scope and duration of the conflict, and the intensity of the threat which the dissident faction poses or posed to the established government.

Watts   Northern Ireland   Angola   Biafra   Vietnam

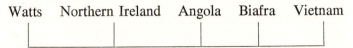

The scale illustrates how internal conflicts may range from riots to insurrections through guerrilla movements to civil wars or even mushroom into international conflicts. The problem of categorization is complicated by the non-static nature of conflict. As the fortunes of the competing parties wax or wane, the conflict may move up or down the scale.

a. LEGISLATIVE HISTORY

The legislative history of Article 3 is inconclusive. Some delegates thought they had merely incorporated the traditional doctrine that the customary laws of war governed a belligerency but not an insurgency. The United States delegation argued, for example, that the Article ought to apply only in the following circumstances:[30]

1. The insurgents must have an organization purporting to have the characteristics of a state;

2. The insurgent civil authority must exercise *de facto* authority over persons within a determinate territory;

3. The armed forces must act under the direction of an organized civil authority and be prepared to observe the ordinary laws of war; and

4. The insurgent civil authority must agree to be bound by the convention provisions.

[30] II-B FINAL RECORD OF THE DIPLOMATIC CONFERENCE OF GENEVA 12.

The identity between these criteria and those for belligerency is obvious.[31] Delegates wishing to extend Convention protection to groups who would be colored as insurgents under the traditional litmus paper tests could take little comfort in the American view, which in effect said: "Yes, insurgents should be protected, too—so long as they are belligerents." Though the conference did rebuff the American and other attempts to write these explicit limitations into Article 3, many left the Convention with the sense that it governed only civil strife in which the rebels had been recognized as belligerents. The committee report on this article states: "It was clear that this [armed conflict not of an international character] referred to civil war, and not to a mere riot or disturbances caused by bandits."[32] Even Pictet, who thinks "the Article should be applied as widely as possible,"[33] admits that the criteria embodied in the various defeated amendments "are useful as a means of distinguishing a genuine armed conflict from a mere act of banditry or an unorganized and short-lived insurrection."[34]

Pictet does contend, however, that Article 3 also governs conflicts that do not fit any of those criteria.

[31] The five requirements for belligerency are: (1) existence of a responsible government; (2) possession of territory; (3) existence of an army that follows the laws of war; (4) recognition by third states of belligerency; and (5) existence of general hostilities. H. Lauterpacht, II. OPPENHEIM'S INTERNATIONAL LAW 249 (7th ed. 1949). See also M. Greenspan, THE MODERN LAW OF LAND WARFARE 18-19 (1959).

[32] II-B. FINAL RECORD OF THE DIPLOMATIC CONFERENCE OF GENEVA 129.

[33] J. Pictet, COMMENTARY I GENEVA CONVENTION FOR THE AMELIORATION OF THE CONDITION OF THE WOUNDED AND SICK IN ARMED FORCES IN THE FIELD 50 (1952).

[34] Id.

Though he nowhere explicitly says so, he apparently believes that even one man brandishing a gun in another's face is non-international conflict within the meaning of Article 3. He, too, mines the legislative history for nuggets of proof. At the XVIIth International Red Cross Conference, which immediately preceded the 1949 Diplomatic Conference, the International Committee proposed adding a fourth paragraph to draft Article 2: "In all cases of armed conflict which are not of an international character, especially cases of civil war, colonial conflicts, or wars of religion, which may occur in the territory of one or more of the High Contracting Parties, the implementing of the principles of the present Conventions shall be obligatory on each of the adversaries."[35] After prolonged discussion, the conference deleted the phrase "especially cases of civil war, colonial conflicts, or wars of religion." Pictet concludes that "the omission of these words far from weakening the treaty enlarged its scope."[36] Article 3 as finally approved retains "the armed conflict not of an international character" language, and the conference rejection of the various amendments that would have explicitly and narrowly circumscribed its meaning by enumerating certain specific types reinforces

[35] The reference to Article 2 may be confusing. What ultimately became Article 3 was initially included in draft Article 2 as paragraph 4.

[36] J. Pictet, *supra* n. 33 at 43. Mr. Pesmazoglon of Greece feared what Pictet hoped: "I consider that the Stockholm Conference by suppressing the explicit references to 'civil war' and 'colonial war' gives too wide a scope to the text." II-B. FINAL RECORD OF THE DIPLOMATIC CONFERENCE OF GENEVA 10. Precisely because the committee shared the Greek delegate's fears, the chairman had asked a working party "to draw up a new provision of a more limited character." *Id.* at 76.

Pictet's argument that Article 3 applies to a wide range of conflicts.

Pictet finds further support for his view in the conference decision to list certain basic principles by which parties fighting each other ought to abide. Initially, the conference had weighed applying all the conventions to internal conflicts. Concerned that brigands and bandits might thus, for example, escape punishment by claiming POW status, representatives of various governments had tried—unsuccessfully, as we have seen—to limit the applicability to "conflicts which, though internal in character, exhibited the features of real war."[37] The French delegation broke the logjam over the different proposals with the suggestion that only certain principles rather than all the provisions of the conventions be applicable: "In the case of armed conflict not of an international character occurring in the territory of one of the High Contracting Parties, each Party to the conflict shall apply the provisions of the Preamble to the Convention for the protection of Civilian Persons in Time of War."[38] The Soviet Union favored an enumeration of specific convention provisions rather than a statement of general principles and therefore proposed the following text: "In the case of armed conflict not of an international character occurring in the territory of one of the states parties to the present convention, each Party to the conflict shall apply all the provisions of the present Convention guaranteeing: humane treatment for the wounded and sick;

[37] The British delegate to the Geneva Diplomatic Conference stated at the outset that he "did not believe it possible to oblige a state to apply the Conventions to situations which were not war, declared or not, as this idea was defined by international law."

[38] *Id.* at 78.

prohibition of all discriminatory treatment of wounded and sick practised on the basis of differences of race, colour, religion, sex, birth, or fortune."[39]

Although the conference adopted the French rather than the Russian approach, the final article did specify more fundamental principles than those contained in the draft preamble, which was in any case never adopted. Pictet, reflecting on the debate over Article 3, depicts the delegates as choosing between (1) applying all the convention provisions to a limited range of conflicts or (2) applying a limited number of principles to an unlimited range of conflicts. If Pictet has fairly juxtaposed the alternatives, the conference did choose the latter course.

Pictet also argues the number of applicable principles is so limited that they must be observed in all conflicts. He asks rhetorically: "What government would dare to claim before the world in a case of civil disturbances which could justly be described as mere acts of banditry, that, Article 3 not being applicable, it was entitled to leave the wounded uncared for, to inflict torture and mutilations and to take hostages?"[40] The regrettable fact is that some nations have implicitly claimed as much. Moreover, under traditional and still widely held views about the nature of international law, states are bound to observe only those rules to which they agree;[41] and they have usually resisted even minimal efforts to tie their hands in dealing with domestic enemies. All this may suggest that the delegates considered "an armed conflict not of an international character" a civil war by any other name and voted in favor of applying a limited

[39] J. Pictet, *supra* n. 33 at 47.
[40] *Id.* at 50.
[41] *The S. S. Lotus*, [1927] P.I.C.J., SER. A, NO. 10. *Cf.* J. Brierly, THE LAW OF NATIONS 45-49 (6th ed. 1963).

number of principles to a limited range of conflicts. Mounting evidence suggests that their instincts may have been sound: one of the few effective ways to deal with domestic unrest is to strike swiftly and severely.[42]

There is, however, another and to my mind more persuasive reason for taking Pictet's argument with a few grains of skepticism. While the number of principles set out in Article 3 is small, they are very general and therefore susceptible, as we will shortly see, of broad interpretation. Desirable as it may be to pour increasingly detailed content into the vague language of Article 3, one must face the dilemma that the more specific the rules he sees embodied in the Article, the less likely it is that the draftsmen ever envisioned their application to riots, insurrections, or even insurgencies. If the humanitarian must impale himself on one or the other horns of this dilemma, he may lose less blood by opting for a more definite code which extends some otherwise inapplicable rules to the most destructive kinds of internal conflicts. The alternative is to affirm the continued applicability of minimal restraints already enshrined—though admittedly not always worshiped—in the constitutions of all states. If Article 3 imposes only "a few essential rules which [the government] in fact respects daily, under its own laws, even when dealing with common criminals,"[43] then it hardly justifies the effusive praise or the desperate fears that attended its adoption.

No set of criteria for determining the type of internal conflicts to which Article 3 applies is buried in the conference committee reports. Reading through them, one

[42] See generally Pye, *The Roots of Insurgency and the Commencement of Rebellions*, 9 NAVAL WAR COLLEGE REV. 157 (1956).

[43] The exhortation is Pictet's. J. Pictet, *supra* n. 33.

nevertheless senses that the delegates intended Article 3 to apply perhaps to insurgencies (Angola), to belligerencies or civil wars (Biafra), but never to bandits or even to riots (Watts). Predictably, they showed more concern for retaining exclusive state jurisdiction than for protecting human rights.

b. STATE PRACTICE

The practice of states may often dispel the fogs of legislative history (indeed examination of state practice is to be preferred to examination of legislative history as a method of interpreting an international agreement),[44] and state practice underscores the limited range of conflicts to which authorities believe Article 3 applicable. Though there has been, as the introductory comments illustrate, no absence of opportunities for the application of Article 3 in the twenty-five years since its adoption, states have generally ignored it. So discouraging has one scholar found the record of state practice that he has concluded that governments do not regard the new rules of conventional law contained in Article 3 as obligatory.[45]

A few examples will illustrate that Mr. Siotis has ample justification for his pessimism. From 1946 until 1949, when fighting ended, the Greek government,

[44] According to the "treaty on treaties," state practice is a primary means of interpretation whereas preparatory work is a subsidiary means of interpretation, resorted to only if primary sources leave "the meaning ambiguous" or "lead to a result which is manifestly absurd or unreasonable." Articles 31 and 32, Vienna Convention on the Law of Treaties, U.N. DOC. A/Conf. 39/27, 23 May 1969, printed in 63 AM. J. INT'L L. 875 (1969).

[45] J. Siotis, LE DROIT DE LA GUERRE ET LES CONFLICTS ARMIÉS D'UN CARACTÈRE NON-INTERNATIONAL (1958).

though it permitted the ICRC to perform limited humanitarian functions, denied that it was embroiled in a civil war and refused to abide by any laws of war.[46] While Article 3 had not yet come into force, the ICRC did call the Greek government's attention to the work of the 1946 Preparatory Conference of the Red Cross Societies, which had resolved that in case of an armed conflict not of an international character each of the parties should observe the convention unless one of them explicitly refused to do so.[47] Article 3 had certainly come into force when Biafra split from Nigeria, precipitating a bloody civil war. The Nigerian government never admitted any legal obligation to adhere to its provisions though the government permitted the ICRC to perform certain humanitarian functions and itself vowed to conduct military operations humanely.[48] The widely reported "night of the long knives" suggests that the military in Indonesia did not take seriously any restraints contained in Article 3. In the recent past both Pakistan and Ceylon have had to employ regular military units against rebel forces. Neither has publicly recognized any obligations under Article 3; and press reports indicate what would appear to be widespread violations of its basic provisions.[49] Portuguese authorities have never admitted any obligation to apply the provisions of Article 3 to rebel forces in the African provinces of Mozambique and Angola even

[46] Ford, *Resistance Movements in International Law*, 7 INT'L. REV. OF THE RED CROSS 579, 585 (1967).

[47] Veuthey, *The Red Cross and Non-International Conflicts*, 10 INT'L. REV. OF THE RED CROSS 411, 412-13 (1970).

[48] Farer, *supra* n. 29 at 60. The ICRC faced many obstacles in Nigeria. See *Help to War Victims in Nigeria*, 9 INT'L REV. OF THE RED CROSS 353 (1969).

[49] *E.g.*, "Pakistan," *Newsweek* 39 (16 April 1971).

though the General Assembly has demanded the native
guerrillas be treated as prisoners of war,[50] a specific requirement quite beyond anything imposed by Article 3
itself.

In Algeria alone among contemporary internal conflicts did both sides agree to abide by Article 3.[51] Though
both sides occasionally violated it (as is perhaps inevitable in any armed conflict), they publicly and repeatedly
urged each other to respect its humanitarian provisions.
Moreover, a number of countries, such as Greece and
Nigeria, though denying the applicability of Article 3,
did permit the Red Cross to exercise humanitarian functions. In the Yemenese Civil War, the ICRC operated
field medical hospitals.[52] Following the brief 1954 revolt
in Guatemala, the ICRC inspected prison facilities and
insured proper treatment of political detainees.[53] While
these examples do not prove widespread compliance with
Article 3, they do create a less bleak picture than emerges
from analyzing foreign office statements.

Two conclusions emerge from a survey of state practice. First, states that quell riots, insurrections, or even
revolts quickly do not feel bound to respect Article 3. In
the absence of any widely held expectation that they
should conform to Article 3, they act under emergency
or martial law. The internal conflict is over before the
international community can apprize itself of the facts
and generate any pressure on the competing parties to
comply with the provisions of Article 3 or humanitarian
law in general. States do, second and nevertheless, accept

[50] General Assembly Resolution 2395, 29 November 1969.
[51] See The International Committee of the Red Cross, *The
ICRC and the Algerian Conflict* (1962).
[52] The International Committee of the Red Cross, *supra* n. 19.
[53] Ford, *supra* n. 46 at 586.

some obligation to treat opposing forces humanely if the conflict drags on beyond several weeks or months. While this recognition seldom takes the form of an explicit acceptance of Article 3, it often manifests itself in acceptance of some Red Cross initiative. The British government, for example, agreed to permit Red Cross inspections in Northern Ireland only after the conflict there had intensified and defied a quick resolution. Whatever the precise parameters of "armed conflict not of an international character," they have not proved any broader than the traditional tests for a belligerency. And they have not proved any broader for the same reason: states continue to insist that they may in internal conflicts deal with their own citizens as they wish without reference to external—that is, international—standards.

C. THE CHARACTER OF HUMANITARIAN LAW

States have, however, begun to recognize human rights legislation,[54] which establishes international standards against which they must measure their conduct toward their own citizens in peacetime. The evolving legal regime of human rights is intended to establish an international minimum standard that all states must observe in their domestic affairs. Consequently, states can no longer plausibly insist, two decades after the General Assembly issued the Universal Declaration of Human Rights, that how they treat their own citizens is solely a matter of their own sovereign concern and of no interest to the larger world community.

The proponents of human rights legislation envision

[54] Many of the human rights provisions found in national constitutions are collected in I. Brownlie, BASIC DOCUMENTS ON HUMAN RIGHTS 3-89 (1971).

it as ultimately establishing a universal, normal societal order.[55] It is their belief that the full recognition of this legal regime would prevent internal armed conflict.[56] They reason that men who enjoy all the political, social, and economic rights enumerated in the International Covenant on Economic, Social, and Cultural Rights and the International Covenant on Civil and Political Rights will have no reason to resort to arms.

Since neither the international community nor any state has yet successfully implemented a legal regime that guarantees the full range of rights accorded in these instruments, draftsmen have wisely provided in human rights conventions for the possibility of internal armed strife. Generally, these conventions permit states to ignore their obligations under these instruments, although some limit the right of derogation. Article 15(1) of the European Convention for the Protection of Human Rights, for example, permits governments to derogate from Convention rights in cases of public emergencies. In *Lawless v. Republic of Ireland*[57] the European Court construed this Article, holding that because the Irish government was fighting "a secret army engaged in unconstitutional activities and using violence to attain its purpose," it could lawfully detain Mr. Lawless without charges or trial. Though the new draft of the Inter-American Convention on Human Rights does not give governments as great a discretion to derogate from its provisions

[55] Draper, *The Ethical and Juridical Constraints in War*, 55 MIL. L. REV. 169, 181 (1972).

[56] J. Carey, U.N. PROTECTION OF CIVIL AND POLITICAL RIGHTS 2 (1971).

[57] DOC. A63.550 (1 July 1961), 1961 YEARBOOK ON THE EUROPEAN CONVENTION OF HUMAN RIGHTS.

in times of public emergency as does the European convention, it does provide: "In time of war, public danger, or other emergency that threatens the independence or security of a State Party, it may take measures derogating from its obligations under the present Convention. . . ."[58]

One can understand why the draftsmen of these instruments concluded that states need not obey rules fashioned for peacetime conditions during "public emergencies" without agreeing that states need obey no rules at all in situations of internal strife. In international conflict states have, after all, agreed to rules that protect human rights. Indeed, the theoretical rationale underlying the law of war is the same as that underlying the human rights regime.[59] While many of the specific rules of the law of war differ from human rights rules, they differ not because the two legal regimes are based on different theoretical foundations but only because they deal with very different societal conditions. Moreover, there are wide areas in which the substantive rules of the two regimes are the same or nearly so. This is particularly true of detention and confinement and trial and punishment. Their common theoretical rationale is more apparent in these overlapping areas. It would seem logical, therefore, to deduce from the common theoretical rationale a set of specific rules for situations of internal strife, which is the one societal condition in which the present international humanitarian law does not protect human rights.

[58] Art. 27, American Convention on Human Rights, reprinted in HANDBOOK OF EXISTING RULES PERTAINING TO HUMAN RIGHTS, OEA/Ser. L/V/II.23, Doc. 21 (17 Dec. 1970).

[59] For a thorough but brief sketch of the conceptual basis for the laws of war and human rights, see J. Pictet, *The Principles of International Humanitarian Law* (1970).

1. *The Theoretical Rationale for Human Rights and the Law of War*

At the most abstract level both the law of war and human rights reflect a synthesis between the requirements of necessity and humanity. Professor Baxter has succinctly delineated the tension between necessity and humanity in the former regime: "The law of war is itself a compromise between unbridled license on the one hand and, on the other, the absolute demands of humanity, which, if carried to a logical extreme, would proscribe war altogether. Stated in other terms, the law seeks to limit the measures of war to those which are necessary and to curb those activities which produce suffering out of all proportion to the military advantage to be gained."[60]

In short, the law of war insures respect for the individual and his well-being insofar as military exigencies permit. The 1961 Lagos Conference on Human Rights, sponsored by the International Commission of Jurists, similarly concluded that "the dangers of survival of the nation such as arise from sudden military challenge may call for urgent and drastic measures. . . ."[61] The conference understood that while such measures might impinge upon human rights, they could not destroy human rights altogether: "The principles [of human rights] must be maintained at all times, except in a period of national emergency declared by the state, or in exceptional circumstances and for limited periods in coping with public calamity or necessity. . . . At such times, certain of those principles may have to be temporarily relaxed. This relaxation is justified only to the extent actually required.

[60] Baxter, *The Geneva Conventions of 1949*, 9 NAVAL WAR COLLEGE REV. 59 (1956).

[61] International Commission of Jurists, THE RULE OF LAW AND HUMAN RIGHTS 13 (1966).

... In no case should fundamental human rights and the dignity of the individual be disregarded."[62]

a. NORMATIVE AMBIGUITY IN THE LAW OF WAR

The general descriptions of the tension between necessity and humanity do not indicate how one strikes a balance between the two in formulating specific rules. It has proved difficult, for example, to stake out the parameters of military necessity. German scholars formulated the most extreme modern view of military necessity.[63] The *Kriegsraison* theory equated military necessity with military benefit. Military necessity was *carte blanche* for the commander to do whatever he thought advantageous.

Though the post-World War II war crimes tribunals rejected this concept,[64] Western scholars have continued to state the doctrine of military necessity in broad terms. Professor Oppenheim, for example, characterized military necessity as "the principle that a belligerent is justified in applying any amount and any kind of force which is necessary for the realization of the purpose of the war —namely, the overpowering of the opponent."[65] Oppenheim is wrong, however. The law of war does limit the amount and kind of force a belligerent may use. Professor Greenspan does better. He defines military necessity as "the right to apply that amount and kind of force which is necessary to compel the submission of the enemy with the least possible expenditure of time, life, and money."[66]

[62] *Id.* at 14.

[63] See generally C. Clausewitz, ON WAR (Jolles trans. 1943).

[64] *U.S. v. Wilhelm List et al.*, XI TRIALS OF WAR CRIMINALS 1235 (1949).

[65] H. Lauterpacht, II. OPPENHEIM'S INTERNATIONAL LAW 336 (7th ed. 1952).

[66] M. Greenspan, THE MODERN LAW OF LAND WARFARE 314 (1959).

Although Greenspan, like Oppenheim, fails to recognize limitations on the doctrine, he does suggest some of the pragmatic motives for curtailing the use of excessive force. Deference to humanitarian principles may often facilitate accomplishment of the military mission. Discipline is the *sine qua non* of an army, and Napoleon is said to have remarked that nothing disorganized an army more or ruined it more completely than pillaging. Humanity may thus be complementary rather than contradictory to necessity.

McDougal and Feliciano contend that necessity is a function of the political legitimacy of the goals sought by the belligerent. They would thus reformulate the doctrine: "The principle of military necessity may . . . accordingly be said to permit the exercise of that violence which is indispensably necessary (proportionate and relevant) for promptly repelling and terminating highly intense initiating coercion against 'territorial integrity' or 'political independence'—indispensably necessary, in a word, for successful defense or community enforcement actions."[67] Apparently, what is sauce for the goose is not for the gander. Even if one accepts the McDougal-Feliciano denial that they thereby neither intend to exclude "aggressor-belligerents" from the benefits of the law of war nor transform their every act into a war crime, McDougal-Feliciano do not recognize limitations on the scope of necessity beyond those unspecified restraints inherent in defensive or enforcement actions.

Yet the law of war does limit the scope of military necessity. Major Downey recognizes this restriction in his definition: "Military necessity is an urgent need, ad-

[67] M. McDougal and F. Feliciano, LAW AND MINIMUM WORLD PUBLIC ORDER 528 (1961).

mitting of no delay, for the taking by a commander of measures, which are indispensable for forcing as quickly as possible the complete surrender of the enemy by means of regulated violence, *and which are not forbidden by the laws and customs of war.*"[68] The idea is not new. It was first stated in the 1862 Lieber Code[69] and is still found in American military law: "Military necessity . . . justifies those measures not forbidden by international law which are indispensable for securing the complete submission of the enemy as soon as possible."[70] Article 22 of the Hague Regulations of 1907 embodies the same view: "[t]he right of belligerents to adopt means of injuring the enemy is not unlimited."[71]

In short, there are two different kinds of rules. One kind is absolute. Military necessity can never justify disobedience because its requirements were weighed in the formulation of the rule. An example is the general prohibition on pillage or looting. The bulk of the rules are of the second kind, however. These rules are never absolutes. Rather, they prohibit only unreasonable or unnecessary acts. Consider as examples the following:

"It is expressly forbidden to destroy or seize the enemy's property, unless such destruction or seizure be im-

[68] Downey, *The Law of War and Military Necessity*, 47 AM. J. INT'L. L. 251, 254 (1953).

[69] Para. 14, *General Orders 100, Instructions for the Government of Armies of the United States in the Field* (24 April 1962) states: "Military necessity, as understood by modern civilized nations, consists in the necessity of those measures which are indispensable for securing the ends of war, and which are lawful according to the modern law and usages of war."

[70] Department of the Army FIELD MANUAL 27-10, THE LAW OF LAND WARFARE 4 (1956). Hereinafter cited as FM 27-10.

[71] Article 22, 1907 Hague Regulations.

peratively demanded by the necessities of war." (Article 23(g), Hague Regulations)

"Any destruction by the Occupying Power of real or personal property belonging individually or collectively to private persons, or to the State, or to other public authorities, or to social or cooperative organizations, is prohibited, except where such destruction is rendered absolutely necessary by military operations." (Article 53, Civilian Convention)

"It is especially forbidden to employ arms, projectiles, or material calculated to cause unnecessary suffering." (Article 23(e), Hague Regulations)

The non-absolute rules are difficult to apply. Regrettably, courts have lent a too sympathetic ear to the plea of necessity,[72] perhaps because whether destruction was unnecessary is as difficult a factual determination as whether a man has acted reasonably; and no objective standards exist by which they can measure "unnecessariness." On the other hand customary practice has transformed some of these non-absolute commands into absolute rules. Many weapons are now illegal per se because states have shown through their practice that they regard their use as always inflicting unnecessary suffering. Weapons that fall into the illegal per se category in-

---

[72] In the *High Command Trial*, for example, the Court declared: "The evidence on the matter of plunder and spoliation shows great ruthlessness, but we are not satisfied that it shows beyond a reasonable doubt, acts that were not justified by military necessity." And further: "The defendants were in retreat under arduous conditions wherein their commands were in serious danger of being cut off. Under such circumstances, a commander must necessarily make quick decisions to meet the particular situation of his command. A great deal of latitude must be accorded to him under such circumstances." XII TRIALS OF WAR CRIMINALS 125 (1949).

clude lances with barbed heads, irregular-shaped bullets, and projectiles filled with glass.[73]

There are two other explanations for the normative ambiguity of the law of war. The first is that these rules all travel, as Llewelyn taught us of the common law, in pairs of complementary opposites. Take, for example, the rule that the civilian population is never a legitimate military target. Though nowhere expressly codified in the law of war,[74] this principle was among the fundamental precepts that the 20th International Conference of the Red Cross called upon states to observe in all armed conflict.[75] Moreover, the principle is the rationale for provisions such as Hague Article 25, which prohibits "the attack or bombardment, by whatever means, of towns, villages, dwellings or buildings which are undefended. . . ."[76] The same spirit animates the entire Civilian Convention. Article 1 of the proposed draft Rules for the Limitation of the Dangers Incurred by the Civilian Population in Time of War would give concrete expression to the principle for the first time: "Since the right of Parties to the conflict to adopt means of injuring the

[73] Para. 34, FM 27-10. Although these kinds of weapons are not issued to regular troops, they are the same or are strikingly similar to the "home-made" weapons used by guerrillas.

[74] The draft preamble to the 1949 Civilian Convention did contain a statement that the civilian population was not a legitimate target, but the preamble was not adopted.

[75] The General Assembly has also affirmed the Red Cross resolution, G. A. Res. 2444, 23 U.N. GAOR Supp. 18, at 50, U.N. DOC. A/7218 (1969).

[76] Customary practice has modified this rule. Attacks upon military targets in undefended cities are legal. K. Raby, BOMBARDMENT OF LAND TARGETS—MILITARY NECESSITY AND PROPORTIONALITY INTERPELLATED (an unpublished thesis presented to The Judge Advocate General's School 1968).

enemy is not unlimited, they shall confine their operations to the destruction of his military resources, and leave the civilian population outside the sphere of armed attacks."[77] There is, however, another rule which permits incidental injury to the civilian population during attacks upon legitimate military targets.[78] As a consequence of such complementary norms, seemingly absolute rules such as the prohibition on attacking churches, schools, hospitals, and museums[79] become in fact non-absolute rules because protected institutions may be destroyed in the course of legitimate military attacks or by direct attack if they are being used for a military purpose, as, for instance, when the enemy uses a church steeple as a military observation post.

The all-too-familiar problem of rule interpretation is the second reason for normative ambiguity in the law of war. An illustrative example may be drawn from rules governing the use of particular weapons. The 1925 Geneva Gas Protocol precludes "asphyxiating, poisonous or other gases, and all analogous liquids, materials or devices."[80] The customary prohibition on poison is also now codified.[81] But what is an "asphyxiating gas" or, what is even less clear, an "analogous liquid"? What is "poison"? The attempt to categorize nuclear weapons as

[77] International Committee of the Red Cross, *Draft Rules for the Limitation of the Dangers Incurred by the Civilian Population in Time of War*, I. DOCUMENTS ON INTERNATIONAL LAW FOR MILITARY LAWYERS 61 (1969). See Appendix A.

[78] *Cf*. Article 6, *id*. at 63.

[79] See the Treaty on the Protection of Artistic and Scientific Institutions and Historic Monuments, 49 STAT. 3267; T.S. 899; 3 BEVANS 254; 167 L.N.T.S. 279.

[80] Printed in M. Hudson, III. INTERNATIONAL LEGISLATION 1670 (1931).

[81] Article 23(a), 1907 Hague Regulations.

illegal weapons because one of their three effects, radiation, constitutes poison demonstrates the interpretative difficulty.[82]

b. NORMATIVE AMBIGUITY IN HUMAN RIGHTS

An identical normative ambiguity permeates human rights. It is probably not true, as Maurice Cranston has asserted, that there are no "absolute" human rights.[83] The Universal Declaration mentions no limitations; and while it may have no binding legal force, it constitutes a persuasive statement of principles.[84] It is difficult to envision circumstances in which, for example, the law should permit torture.[85] The survival of state no more than the accomplishment of the military mission should necessitate torture. Moreover, most human rights documents also

[82] Compare N. Singh, NUCLEAR WEAPONS AND INTERNATIONAL LAW (1959) with G. Schwarzenberger, THE LEGALITY OF NUCLEAR WEAPONS (1958).

[83] M. Cranston, WHAT ARE HUMAN RIGHTS? 71 (1962).

[84] Mr. Jacob Blaustein declared in his Dag Hammarskjöld Memorial Lecture at Columbia University in December 1963: "The Declaration, which was adopted as a resolution of the General Assembly was never meant to be legally binding, but to be, as its preamble says, 'a common standard of achievement for all peoples and all nations.' Nevertheless, in the fifteen years since its adoption, it has acquired a political and moral authority which is unequalled by any other international instrument with the exception of the Charter itself." J. Blaustein, *Human Rights* 11 (1964).

[85] It need hardly be emphasized that even such absolute rules may be "interpreted" away. A British investigating team in Northern Ireland concluded that while British soldiers had subjected detainees to "ill-treatment," they had not committed "torture." "Ulster, Ill-Treatment, Not 'Torture,' " *The Washington Post*, Nov. 17, 1971, at 21, col. 1. See also Coursier, *The Prohibition of Torture*, 11 INT'L. REV. OF THE RED CROSS 475 (Sept. 1971).

limit the power to derogate from some convention obligations even in time of emergency, thereby creating absolute rights.[86]

The bulk of human rights are, however, non-absolutes. Consider the following examples drawn from the United Nations covenants on human rights. The Covenant on Civil and Political Rights permits freedom of movement within and without one's country subject to any general law of the state concerned that provides for the protection of national security, public safety, health, or morals, or the rights and freedoms of others, consistent with the other rights recognized by the covenant.[87] Another article forbids any expulsion of aliens other than that which is "lawful."[88] Few of the commands are self-defining, and the substantive content of the right of self-determination guaranteed in the Covenant on Economic, Social, and Cultural Rights is widely disputed.[89]

The complex process by which humanitarian rules evolve further complicates precise ascertainment of their doctrinal content. In a decentralized legal order like the international system, individual decision-makers necessarily determine the nature of the law. They may, of course—and often do—disagree as to the governing legal principle of its appropriate substantive content. Since they often act without articulating any legal justification, one must often speculate on what legal rationale if any underlies the action. Out of a bewildering confusion of

[86] *E.g.*, Article 4(2) of the 1966 International Covenant on Civil and Political Rights.

[87] *Id.*, Article 12.

[88] *Id.*, Article 13.

[89] Does the right of self-determination permit the Ibo's to withdraw from the Nigerian Federation? Does it authorize Warsaw Pact intervention in Czechoslovakia?

act and counteract and claim and counterclaim the observer must deduce the legal rules being applied.

Thus customary international law—viewed not only as the practice of states but more broadly as the practice of all the participants in the international legal process— plays an important role in the development of international humanitarian law. While much of the law of war is codified, only the practice of the participants in applying the conventions and other international agreements fleshes out their meaning. Particularly in an area such as internal conflict, where so little of the presently codified law of war applies (at least by its express terms), the practice of participants alone serves as a guide to the identity of the governing legal regime.

2. Policies Common to Human Rights and the Law of War

Can one then say anything more helpful than that the rules of both bodies of law are ambiguous resolutions of the competing claims of humanity and necessity? The answer is a qualified yes. While it is impossible—and probably undesirable—to eliminate all ambiguity, one can articulate underlying policies that provide guidance in the application of the rules.

a. THE PRESUMPTION AGAINST INFRINGEMENT OF HUMANITARIAN RIGHTS

First, there is a presumption against the curtailment of humanitarian rights.[90] Any infringement must be justi-

[90] The International Congress of Jurists that met in Rio de Janeiro in December 1962 resolved that "the protection of the individual from unlawful or excessive interference by government is the foundation of the Rule of Law." International Commission of Jurists, *supra* n. 61 at 68.

fied by reference to a positive legal exception. The importance of this policy is illustrated by the debate over whether the rules of aerial bombardment should specify non-military targets and by implication permit the bombing of all others or, contrariwise, specify military targets and by implication exclude as permissible targets all others.[91] The latter approach reflects the policy presumption, whereas the former does not. It would authorize bombing unless some positive law exception forbade it; yet bombing is an exercise of force justified by the principle of necessity but nevertheless an infringement of the principle of humanity. It should therefore be permitted only when explicitly authorized.

b. MINIMUM INTERFERENCE WITH
HUMANITARIAN RIGHTS

Minimum interference with humanitarian rights is the second major policy common to both the law of war and human rights.[92] The law of war frequently enjoins the commander from using any greater force than the accomplishment his mission demands. The law prohibits both unnecessary suffering and unnecessary destruction. The law also protects particular groups such as noncombatants and the sick and wounded from many infringements of their rights because their denial would not materially enhance the accomplishment of any legitimate military purpose. The provisions of the law that permit the establishment of population safety zones il-

[91] Cf. International Committee of the Red Cross, PROTECTION OF THE CIVILIAN POPULATION AGAINST DANGERS OF HOSTILITIES 51-74 (1971).

[92] The best theoretical discussion of this policy as it operates within the law of war is found in M. McDougal and F. Feliciano, supra n. 67 at 521-731.

lustrate limitations on the places in which a party may use force. The entire doctrine of neutrality may be understood as another example of this policy of minimum interference. The law also limits the period during which a party may employ force. The 1965 Human Rights Conference at Bangkok concluded that "both the declaration of public emergency and any consequent detention of individuals should, except in time of war, be effective only for a specified and limited period of time. . . ."[93] The policy of minimum interference has then at least four dimensions: it limits the amount of force that may be used; it limits the persons against whom force may be used; it limits the places where force may be used; it limits the time over which force may be used.

c. DUE PROCESS

Underlying the law of war and human rights is a third common policy: due process is required.[94] Procedural safeguards permeate these legal regimes. Property may not be confiscated arbitrarily. People may not be executed summarily. Even in the area of bombardment the law imposes some process restrictions, as, for example, the requirement that the civilian population be warned. Prior notice is also a pre-condition for resort to reprisal. In the Act of Athens, the assembled jurists declared their faith in the Rule of Law, which is due process writ large.[95]

d. RATIONALITY

The final common policy is the one that insures compliance with those preceding. Rationality in the application of the exceptional rules of necessity is the fourth policy. Although McDougal and Feliciano do not speak

[93] International Commission of Jurists, *supra* n. 61 at 14.
[94] *Id.* at 8.   [95] *Id.* at 64.

PRINCIPLES OF INTERNATIONAL HUMANITARIAN LAW

NECESSITY

Maintenance of public order legitimates the use of force; the state of war justifies resort to violence.

LAWS OF WAR

Belligerents shall not inflict harm on their adversaries out of proportion with the object of warfare, which is to destroy or weaken the military strength of the enemy.

THE LAW OF THE HAGUE

Belligerents do not have unlimited choice in the means of inflicting damage on the enemy.

PRINCIPLES PROPER TO THE RULES OF WAR

Principle of the "ratione personae" restriction

Belligerents will leave non-combatants outside the area of operations and will refrain from attacking them deliberately.

Principles of application:

1. Only members of the armed forces have the right to attack the enemy and to resist him.
2. Belligerents will take all precautions to reduce to a minimum the damage to which non-combatants will be subjected in actions directed against military objectives.

Principle of the "ratione loci" restriction

Attacks are only legitimate when directed against military objectives, that is to say whose total or partial destruction would constitute a definite military advantage.

Principles of application:

1. Belligerents will spare, in particular, charitable, religious, scientific, cultural and artistic establishments, as well as historic monuments.
2. It is prohibited to attack localities which are undefended.
3. Looting is prohibited, as is unjustified destruction or seizure of enemy property.

Principle of the "ratione condi-tionis" restriction

Weapons and methods of warfare likely to cause excessive suffering are prohibited.

Principle of application:

Warlike acts founded on treason or treachery are forbidden.

PRINCIPLES PROPER TO THE VICTIMS OF CONFLICTS

Neutrality

Humanitarian assistance is never an interference in a conflict.

Principles of application:

1. In exchange for the immunity granted to it, medical personnel should refrain from any hostile act.
2. Medical personnel are given protection as healers.
3. No one shall be molested or convicted for having given treatment to the wounded or sick.

Normality

Protected persons must be able to lead as normal a life as possible.

Principle of application:

Captivity is not a punishment, but only a means of keeping an adversary from being in a position to do harm.

Protection

The State must ensure the protection, both national and international, of persons fallen into its power.

Principles of application:

1. The prisoner is not in the power of the troops who have captured him, but of the State on which these depend.
2. The enemy State is responsible for the condition and upkeep of persons of whom it has guard and, in occupied territory, for the maintenance of order and public services.
3. The victims of conflicts shall be provided with an international protector once they no longer have a natural protector.

HUMANITY
Humanity requires action always for man's good.

HUMANITARIAN LAW
Respect for the individual and his well-being shall be assured as far as it is compatible with public order and, in time of war, with military exigencies.

HUMAN RIGHTS
The individual will see at all times guaranteed the exercising of his fundamental rights and liberties, as well as the conditions of existence propitious to the harmonious development of his personality.

THE LAW OF GENEVA
Persons placed hors de combat and those not directly participating in hostilities shall be respected, protected and treated humanely.

PRINCIPLES COMMON TO THE LAW OF GENEVA AND HUMAN RIGHTS

Inviolability
The individual has a right to the respect of his life, integrity, both physical and moral, and of the attributes inseparable from his personality.

Principles of application:
1. A man who has fallen in combat is inviolable; an enemy surrendering shall have his life spared.
2. Torture, degrading or inhuman punishment are forbidden.
3. Everyone is entitled to recognition as a person before the law.
4. Everyone has the right to respect of his honour, his family rights, his convictions and habits.
5. Anyone who is suffering shall be sheltered and receive the care which his condition requires.
6. Everyone has the right to exchange news with his family and receive relief parcels.
7. No one may be arbitrarily deprived of his own property.

Non-discrimination
Individuals shall be treated without any distinction based on race, sex, nationality, language, social standing, wealth, political, philosophical or religious opinions, or on any other criteria.

Principle of application:
Differences in treatment should however be made for the benefit of individuals in order to counter inequalities resulting from their personal situation, their needs or their distress.

Security
Everyone has the right to security of person.

Principles of application:
1. No one can be held responsible for an act he has not committed.
2. Reprisals, collective punishment, the taking of hostages and deportations shall be prohibited.
3. Each person shall benefit from legal guarantees recognized by civilized peoples.
4. No one can abrogate the rights which the humanitarian Conventions accord him.

PRINCIPLES PROPER TO HUMAN RIGHTS

Liberty
Everyone has the right to have his individual freedom respected.

Principles of application:
1. Freedom of thought, expression, association and religion is guaranteed for each one.
2. Everyone has the right to speak his own language.
3. No one can be arbitrarily arrested, detained or exiled.
4. No one can be reduced to slavery.
5. Everyone has the right to circulate freely, to leave his own country and return to it, and to seek a country of asylum.
6. Everyone is entitled to the free exercising of his political rights.

Social Well-Being
Everyone has the right to favourable conditions of life.

Principle of application:
Everyone has in particular the right to work, to just and favourable conditions of work, to the social services, free education, the cultural life and to share in the benefits of scientific advancement.

of rationality, they have identified it as an "anchor to the
search for clarification of military necessity and to stop
the indefinite regression of limits . . ."[96] by the labels of
"proportionate" and "relevant" violence. No one has to
my knowledge ever postulated the "reasonable soldier"
or the "reasonable sovereign," but both are needed if
the humanitarian objectives of the law of war and human
rights are to be achieved. How do these reasonable men
act? Primarily, they act in good faith. The necessarily
general rules of humanitarian law are swollen with the
potential for abuse and perversion. It could scarcely be
otherwise, and one cannot escape ultimate reliance upon
their good faith observance however narrowly drawn the
language of the law.

3. *The Basic Rule Structure of the
Law of War and Human Rights*

A brief description of the basic rule structure of humanitarian law will prove that both the law of war and
human rights share a common theoretical rationale that
draws its substantive life from the four policies outlined
above. Professor Jean Pictet has succinctly summarized
the rule structure of humanitarian law in the chart re-
produced above.[97] While some might question one aspect or another of his formulation, he has effectively reduced a whole body of law to readily understood form.
The chart will also serve well as a reference for our
succeeding discussion of claims to apply or not apply
particular rules in Chapter III and proposed resolutions
of those claims in Chapter IV.

From the preceding discussion one inescapable con-

[96] M. McDougal and F. Feliciano, *supra* n. 67.
[97] J. Pictet, *Principles of International Humanitarian Law* 62
(1970).

clusion emerges. The law of war and human rights are the Siamese twins of international humanitarian law, sharing a common theoretical bloodstream. Although this international humanitarian law should govern any societal condition—from domestic peace to international armed conflict—it does not. Neither of the two legal regimes, each designed with one of the two polar conditions in mind, deals effectively with the interim condition of internal conflict. Yet both their common theoretical rationale and many of their respective rules provide guidelines for the creation of a third intermediate legal regime for the regulation of internal conflict.

CHAPTER III

Trends: The Claims To Apply or Not Apply the Laws of War To Internal Conflicts

The principles just surveyed, however applicable to internal conflict, are after all only principles and not rules. While they provide guidance, they do not dictate specific answers to particular problems. The body of rules deduced from the application of humanitarian principles to the problems of international conflict is large and detailed. The question we now face is whether these rules should also govern internal conflict, or whether the problems characteristic of internal conflict differ so markedly from those common to international conflicts that the application of the same principles will yield different rules. A second question is whether some rules already proved inadequate in the context of international conflict should be revised as applied to internal conflicts.

A. THE CLAIM TO CONDUCT HOSTILITIES UNRESTRAINED BY THE RULES APPLICABLE TO INTERNATIONAL CONFLICT

As Professor Farer has pointed out, "The international legal rules governing combat operations . . . have traditionally been held to apply only to international armed conflict."[1] Even common Article 3, the "convention in

[1] Farer, *Humanitarian Law and Armed Conflicts: Toward the Definition of "International Armed Conflict,"* 71 COLUM. L. REV. 37, 40 (1971).

miniature" and the only portion of the law of war universally recognized as applicable to internal conflicts,[2] does not, it is often asserted, incorporate the Law of The Hague. The assertion is not, it should be noted, that the language of Article 3 is so general as to be meaningless, though that proposition might be argued with equal or even greater justification.[3] The belief that Article 3 does not incorporate any of the Hague rules is premised on the view that its purpose differs from that underlying the Law of The Hague. The only explicit provision in Article 3 is its statement of purpose:

"Persons taking no active part in the hostilities, including members of armed forces who have laid down their arms and those placed hors de combat by sickness, wounds, detention, or any other cause, shall in all circumstances be treated humanely, without any adverse distinction founded on race, colour, religion or faith, sex, birth or wealth, or any other similar criteria.

"To this end, the following acts are and shall remain prohibited at any time and in any place whatsoever with respect to the above-mentioned persons. . . ."

The protection of non-combatants, which, as we have seen, is widely understood to be the basic purpose of the Law of Geneva, is not so readily recognized as the animating spirit of the Hague rules. Scholars persist in char-

[2] Article 19 of the Hague Convention of May 1954 on the Protection of Cultural Property in the Event of Armed Conflict does provide that those articles of the convention which relate to the respect for cultural property apply to armed conflicts not of an international character.

[3] "It appears to us that the fundamental defect of Art. 3 . . . lies in the lack of balance between the principle figuring or heading 1 and the enumeration as examples of particular violations under sub-headings a) to d)." Scholgel, *Civil War*, 10 INT'L. REV. OF THE RED CROSS 123, 132-3 (March 1970).

acterizing the latter as "game rules," as the following passage illustrates: "The international law of war was primarily designed to govern a contest between two armed forces which carry on the hostilities in a more or less open fashion. Analogously, the rules of football were designed to govern a contest between two uniformed teams, clearly distinguishable from the spectators. How well would those rules work, however, if one team were uniformed and on the field, the other hid itself among the spectators, and the spectators wandered freely over the playing field?"[4] Analogizing the laws of war to football rules enables the author to make his point effectively; unfortunately, he reinforces the misleading and confusing idea that the purpose of the Hague rules is other than protection of non-combatants. It is not.[5] To the extent that the Hague rules are intended to protect non-combatants, they are to that same extent, as limited by reasonable interpretation, incorporated into Article 3.

Consider, for example, the following hypothesis. Government forces receive sniper fire from a small village. The village is suspected of rebel sympathies, and reliable intelligence sources report that a rebel unit has set up headquarters for its local operations in the village. The commander of the government forces calls in artillery fire on the village. A Red Cross medical unit is hit and several patients killed. Has the commander violated Article 3? As was pointed out in Chapter II, Article 25 of the Hague Regulation forbids the "bombardment, by whatever means, of towns, villages, dwellings or buildings which are undefended. . . ." Article 27 says that in

[4] Kelly, *Legal Aspects of Military Operations in Counterinsurgency*, 21 MIL. L. REV. 95, 104 (1963).

[5] Neuman, *The International Civil War*, 1 WORLD POLITICS 333, 363-4 (1949).

any attack non-military targets such as schools, hospitals, churches, and museums should be spared. We also learned, however, that damage to such institutions and loss of innocent lives does not violate the laws of war so long as it is incident to a lawful attack upon a legitimate military target. While the rebel soldiers are not protected persons within the definition of Article 3, the medical staff and patients are. They are entitled to humane treatment; and if protection of non-combatants is the underlying purpose for restricting bombardment, then the answer becomes, first, one of interpretation, and, second, of fact. The interpretative question is one we shall analyze again and again: what constitutes "humane treatment"? The general requirement of humane treatment may be too slender a basis upon which to incorporate all the rules whose purpose is the protection of non-combatants, but we also find in Article 3 the injunction that the "wounded and sick shall be collected and cared for." Like all the provisions in Article 3, this, too, is very general. At a minimum, however, one could imply that medical establishments cannot be attacked and that hospital staff must be respected. Otherwise, it is difficult to see how "the wounded and sick" can be "collected and cared for." One may then conclude that the general requirements of humane treatment and care for the sick and wounded preclude indiscriminate bombardment in the circumstances outlined above. In short, this portion of the Hague Rules is incorporated into Article 3.

The second question is the factual one: did the attack violate the rules of bombardment? was the artillery strike an excessive use of firepower? was the Red Cross unit clearly marked? was it located dangerously near a legitimate military target? It should not surprise lawyers that here, as elsewhere in the law, "the facts" are more im-

portant than the rule. One cannot determine whether
the commander violated Article 3 by shelling the village
unless he knows "the facts." Rules are not unimportant,
however; and we now turn our attention to an analysis
of more specific claims to apply or not apply particular
rules in the conduct of tactical military operations.

1. *The Claim to Use Terror Tactics*

Both the established government and the rebels have
in past internal conflicts claimed the right to use terror
tactics. Parties, of course, piously condemn their opponent's resort to such "outrageous, shocking" acts while
cloaking their own conduct in euphemisms that deceive
only those who wish to be deceived. Whatever the label,
the ingredients of a terroristic policy are the same: it is
a "symbolic act designed to influence political behavior
by extranormal means, entailing the use or threat of
violence."[6]

The guerrillas claim the right to use terror because in
the early stages of a conflict it is their only effective
weapon.[7] Sabotage and political assassination, we are
told, are "characteristically guerrilla tasks."[8] The record
justifies the assertion. The movement may begin with the
murder, beating, or kidnapping of selected government
officials, employees, businessmen or landowners.[9] Between 1956 and 1965, for example, the Viet Cong killed

[6] Falk, *Six Legal Dimensions of U.S. Involvement in Vietnam*,
II THE VIETNAM WAR AND INTERNATIONAL LAW 216, 240 (R.
Falk, ed. 1969).

[7] Thornton, *Terror as a Weapon of Political Agitation*, IN-
TERNAL WAR 71, 75 (H. Eckstein, ed. 1963).

[8] T. Farer, *The Laws of War 25 Years After Nuremberg* 42
(1971).

[9] Murray, *The Anti-Bandit War*, THE GUERRILLA AND HOW TO
FIGHT HIM, 65, 68-9 (T. Greene, ed. 1962).

over 10,000 village officials in South Vietnam.[10] One of Castro's first public acts was the execution of a large landowner in the Sierra Maestra. If the government attempts "to steal the rebel's thunder" by extending medical and educational services to the previously neglected peasants, the rebels undermine the programs by kidnapping the doctors and teachers. In the earliest phases of the revolution the rebels use terror to expose the government's weakness, intimidate its would-be supporters, and dramatize injustice and inequities.

Next the rebels raid villages, attack small military posts, and ambush patrols. The reasons for these actions are many. Guerrillas need food. In Greece the rebels not only fed themselves with stolen foodstuffs but thereby also embarrassed the government by aggravating already existing food shortages.[11] Guerrillas need weapons. One observer has calculated that the Castro forces bought or received only 15 percent of their weapons from abroad.[12] They stole the bulk of their weapons from army garrisons or captured them from defeated troops. Guerrillas need victories. Numerically inferior, they rely upon ruses and stratagems to inflict militarily insignificant but politically embarrassing defeats upon government forces.

In the last phase of their initial operations, the rebels strike at communications facilities, power plants, and other similar installations. The Algerian rebels announced their revolution with a bloody calling card: "That night (November 1, 1954) armed bands struck in fifty different actions all across Algeria. Biskra was

[10] Kelly, *Assassination in War Time*, 30 MIL. L. REV. 101, 109 (1965).

[11] Murray, *supra* n. 9 at 69.

[12] Chapelle, *How Castro Won*, THE GUERRILLA AND HOW TO FIGHT HIM, 218, 229 (T. Greene, ed. 1962).

rocked by bomb explosions. In Batna the French army barracks was attacked and two sentries killed. Two bombs exploded in downtown Algeria. Arris was besieged at Boufank. The European-owned agricultural cooperative was destroyed. In the Sighanimine Gorge armed bands stopped a bus, hauled out a caid and two Europeans, and shot them on the spot. In the Kabylia two policemen were killed and a storage depot was burned to the ground. Near Oran two settler farms were burned, a motorist killed, a power plant attacked."[13] Thus launched, the rebels continued to practice their terroristic art throughout the Algerian conflict.

The guerrillas nevertheless understand that they cannot terrorize the entire population into supporting them and their cause. Mao insisted upon "rigid discipline and scrupulously correct behavior by fully mobile guerrilla troops in order to prevent their alienating the rural population."[14] Halfway around the world and a decade later the other revolutionary hero of our age, Che Guevara, decried the use of terrorism because it "is generally ineffective and indiscriminate in its results, since it often makes victims of innocent people. . . ." He nevertheless conceded that "[t]errorism should be considered a valuable tactic when it is used to put to death some noted leader of the oppressing forces well-known for his cruelty, his efficiency in repression, or other quality that makes his elimination useful."[15] Guevara sees the guerrilla as an ascetic social reformer who must always help the peasant.[16]

Consequently, the guerrillas claim only the right to

[13] J. Kraft, THE STRUGGLE FOR ALGERIA 69 (1961).
[14] Johnson, *Civilian Loyalties and Guerrilla Conflict*, 14 WORLD POLITICS 646, 655 (1962).
[15] Che Guevara, GUERRILLA WARFARE 26 (1961).
[16] *Id.* at 43.

use terror against "the active participants in the struggle for power," not against "the more or less passive bulk of the citizenry."[17] Consider, for example, the program of the Tupamaros, the urban guerrillas of Uruguay. They robbed a bank to expose a financial scandal. They kidnapped an executive of the national power and telephone monopoly to reveal corrupt rate-fixing.[18] Each act had symbolic significance.

Government in the few instances in which it is honest enough to admit its use of terror does not so delimit its claims. French theorists, reflecting on their unhappy experience in Algeria, have concluded that terror is the essential ingredient in guerrilla wars and thus advocate its wide use. Colonel Trinquier bluntly declares: "We know that the *sine qua non* of victory in modern warfare is the unconditional support of a population. According to Mao Tse-tung, it is as essential to the combatant as water to the fish. Such support may be spontaneous, although that is quite rare and probably a temporary condition. If it doesn't exist, it must be secured by every possible means, the most effective of which is *terrorism*."[19] Professor Farer, who clucks sympathetically at guerrilla terrorism but quivers with moral indignation at the government variety, captures in a single sentence the unfortunate consequences of a government policy of terrorism. It "beaches the guerrilla fish by draining the sea."[20] Such broadscale use of terror seems almost genocidal, particularly when employed against ethnic groups such as the Kurds in Iraq or the Ibos in Nigeria.

Occasionally, governments claim rather more limited

[17] T. Farer, *supra* n. 8 at 42.

[18] See Delaney, *Reflections on Political Communication and Insurgency*, 22 NAVAL WAR COLLEGE REV. 3 (1969).

[19] R. Trinquier, MODERN WARFARE 8 (1961).

[20] T. Farer, *supra* n. 8 at 29.

rights to resort to terror. In the later stages of a guerrilla war when rebels have succeeded in occupying and administering territory, the government itself may adopt a program of political assassination. A journalist described how such a program operated in Vietnam:

"South Vietnamese government squads, generally operating in stealth at night, have begun a campaign of terror against Viet Cong officials in the Mekong River Delta.

"Small teams of commandos, armed with exact intelligence and daggers, are moving into Viet Cong hamlets in critical provinces near Saigon, assassinating key Viet Cong leaders, and slipping away.

"They are leaving calling cards on the bodies of their victims—an enormous white eye printed on a black slip of paper."[21]

This is an example of tit-for-tat terror.

The Applicable Law Does present international law permit or in any way circumscribe the use of such terror tactics in internal conflicts? Article 3 only protects those persons taking no active part in the hostilities; it does not protect combatants. But who in the context of an internal guerrilla conflict is a combatant? The traditional idea that he can be no one other than in military uniform may be inadequate. Professor Farer has, for example, asked: "Why should the guerrilla be castigated for failing to distinguish between the commander of a district paramilitary force and the civilian official from whom he receives orders? Why should the Minister of the Interior ensconced in his office be legally immune, while some wretched platoon suffocating in the scorched bush is fair

[21] Quoted in Kelly, *supra* n. 10 at 110.

game? And why distinguish between the general, directing hostilities from a command helicopter, and the same man clipping roses in the garden of his villa?"[22] Practice in World War II and after has already eroded the earlier customary rules which forbade political assassination in international conflict,[23] and some see little reason to prohibit it in internal conflicts.

Professor Farer's examples suggest that all those officials with policy-making powers can be considered legitimate assassination targets. Surely not every government employee—the schoolteacher, the clerk, the janitor—is fair game. At the same time, one need not limit assassination targets to those receiving government checks. The editor of a pro-government or pro-guerrilla newspaper, an influential private businessman, a prominent clergyman responsible for organizing rebel forces—all would seem to be legitimate targets under a broader test of combatancy.

Whether it is desirable to legitimize assassination, however, is debatable. While uniformed soldiers do not fight along fixed battle lines in a guerrilla war, they do still engage each other in fire fights—the paradigm circumstance in which the law permits one combatant to take the life of another. Assassination permits a combatant to kill another when that other poses no immediate threat to the slayer's life. Why an internal struggle for power should transform what is otherwise murder into a legitimate act of war, without the conditions that normally justify killing in war, is not clear. Selective use of assassination does not make it any less reprehensible, and one may speculate that the guerrilla's infrequent use of

[22] T. Farer, *supra* n. 8 at 43.
[23] Kelly, *supra* n. 10.

the tactic reflects, if not their deference to the norms forbidding it, at least their recognition that reciprocal assassination by the government would escalate the conflict to undesirable levels of brutality. While assassination may be an effective guerrilla weapon, effectiveness has never been the sole test of legality. The tactic seems particularly indefensible when used to disrupt the political process that might otherwise produce some compromise settlement of the problems that bred the internal conflict.

Terror tactics are not limited to political assassination or kidnapping, however. Many terroristic acts inevitably injure those who even under some broader test of combatancy are non-combatants, and Article 3 does protect non-combatants. The question is whether it protects them from terroristic acts. The answer must depend on whether the military benefit gained outweighs the harm inflicted upon innocent people. Che Guevara uses an instructive illustration in his primer on guerrilla warfare: "It is ridiculous to carry out sabotage against a soft drink factory, but it is absolutely correct and advisable to carry out sabotage against a power plant. In the first case, a certain number of workers are put out of a job but nothing is done to modify the rhythm of industrial life; in the second case, there will again be displaced workers, but this is entirely justified by the paralysis of life in the region."[24] The example not only reflects the balancing of interest suggested earlier; it suggests that an appropriate balance can be struck by distinguishing, as the law of war has always done, between military and non-military targets. Whether one can rely on a generalized rule rather than on a specific enumeration of permissible military

[24] Che Guevara, *supra* n. 15 at 27.

targets or, alternatively, a listing of those targets which should be immune from attack, is debatable; but, however formulated, such a stricture should eliminate the bomb-in-the-marketplace kind of terrorism. In attacking legitimate targets, the guerrillas should minimize the destructive impact upon the innocent population. For example, they can strike a plant after hours when the work force is absent. They can use small explosives that destroy the target without damaging surrounding buildings or homes.

There remain, of course, a wide range of legitimate activities often denominated terroristic. Ambushing a military convoy, blowing up a barracks, and robbing an arms depot are to war as dribbling, passing, and shooting are to basketball. Put another way, a convoy, a barracks, or an arms depot are legitimate military targets. The legitimacy of certain other kinds of terror tactics, particularly bombing, is analyzed below.

2. To Use Chemical or Biological Weapons

During the Yemeni civil war, royalist forces charged that the Egyptians gassed their troops and napalmed loyal villages.[25] The Egyptians denied the charge,[26] and the facts remain disputed.[27] Certainly neither side publicly claimed the right to use gas or any other chemical or biological weapons. The United States has, however, insisted that it has the right to use tear gases and herbicides and has acted upon that conviction in the Indo-

[25] Meselson, *The Yemen*, CHEMICAL AND BIOLOGICAL WARFARE 99 (1970).

[26] *Ibid.*

[27] For a history of the use of gas in warfare, see Kelly, *Gas Warfare in International Law*, 9 MIL. L. REV. 3-14 (1960).

china war.[28] Though participants have seldom invoked the right in past internal conflicts, they may, acting on the Vietnamese precedent, claim it in the future. Chemical and biological agents range from the lethal to the non-toxic, and their legality is much debated.[29]

The Applicable Law Article 3 does not explicitly limit the use of any weapon—conventional, chemical, or biological. It does, however, in addition to imposing the general requirement of humane treatment, forbid cruel treatment. One could plausibly equate "cruel treatment" with the infliction of "unnecessary suffering," the standard found in Article 23 of the Hague Rules[30] and the basis for outlawing almost all illegal weapons of war. But since Article 3 protects only non-combatants ("persons taking no active part in the hostilities"), it would not prohibit the commander from using chemical or biological weapons—not because they do not constitute cruel treatment (that is, as I have indicated, an open question), but because combatants fall outside the protective ambit of the article. Article 3 simply does not require that government forces treat resisting rebels humanely.

[28] See n. 34 *infra*.

[29] See generally, Baxter and Burgenthal, *Legal Aspects of the Geneva Protocol of 1925*, 64 AM. J. INT'L. L. 853 (1970). The twelve-member Geneva Disarmament Conference has recently agreed on a draft text prohibiting the use of bacteriological weapons. The draft text may be found 65 DEPT. OF STATE BULL. 508-510 (Nov. 1, 1971).

[30] It is almost impossible to determine what constitutes "unnecessary suffering," and some have therefore argued that it imposes no effective restraints on the use of new weapons. *Cf.* Stone, LEGAL CONTROLS OF INTERNATIONAL CONFLICT 550-551 (1959).

Chemical and biological weapons do affect the non-combatant population, however. Precisely because their effect is "blind," they may violate the Article 3 charge to treat non-combatants humanely. The World Health Organization concluded that "[c]hemical and biological weapons pose a special threat to civilians" because their effects were "indiscriminate" and could lead to "significant unintended involvement of the civilian population within the target area and for considerable distances downwind."[31] The report emphasized the "uncertainty and unpredictability" of such weapons because of "complex and extremely variable meteorological, physiological, epidemiological, ecological, and other factors."[32] If the effect of these weapons is uncontrollable, and they therefore greatly endanger the non-combatant population, Article 3 may prohibit their use—at least where the military unit has available for its use some less blind weapon with which it can eliminate or neutralize the enemy target.

The international law standard is clearer. The Geneva Protocol of 1925[33] forbids "the use in war of asphyxiating, poisonous or other gases, and all analogous liquids, materials or devices," as well as "the use of bacteriological methods of warfare." Every major state except the United States and Japan has ratified the protocol, and the President of the United States has submitted the

[31] World Health Organization, *Health Aspects of Chemical and Biological Weapons* (1970).

[32] Mirimanoff, *The Red Cross and Biological and Chemical Weapons*, 10 INT'L. REV. OF THE RED CROSS 301, 315 (June 1970).

[33] M. Hudson, III. INTERNATIONAL LEGISLATION 1670-1672 (1931).

protocol to the Senate for its advice and consent and has publicly declared that the United States will respect the principles embodied therein.[34] As Professor Baxter has pointed out: "The weight of opinion appears today to favor the view that customary international law proscribes the use of lethal chemical and biological weapons."[35]

Does customary or conventional law likewise proscribe the use of non-lethal chemical and biological weapons? Though disputed, the consensus is that it does. In the first place many scientists reject the military distinction between lethal and non-lethal agents, arguing that "the effects of a chemical warfare agent depend as much on the way it is used as on its toxicological properties."[36] A lethal agent if disseminated in small doses may cause only temporary incapacity. A non-lethal agent may kill or severely injure one exposed to an unexpectedly large concentration. Second, some scholars argue that tear gas, for example, is usually used in conjunction with other, lethal weapons whose effectiveness it enhances.[37] They add that the use of any kind of gas is repugnant to the conscience of mankind.

There is also a growing body of authoritative pronouncements that bar the use of all chemical and biological weapons. The International Committee of the

---

[34] Statement by President Nixon, *Chemical and Biological Defense Policies and Programs*, 61 DEPT. OF STATE BULL. 541 (1969).

[35] Baxter, *supra* n. 29.

[36] Mirimanoff, *supra* n. 32 at 304.

[37] Meselson, BULLETIN OF ATOMIC SCIENTISTS 31 (Jan. 1970). Much of the distaste for the use of tear gas in Vietnam stems from the critics' conviction that it is used to "flush out" suspected Viet Cong who are then machine-gunned. *Cf. New York Times*, Sept. 29, 1969, at 11, col. 1.

Red Cross has long contended that the ban was absolute.[38] To its insistent voice, the Secretary-General of the United Nations has added his.[39] The General Assembly has declared the use of chemical and biological agents "contrary to the generally recognized rules of international law . . . ,"[40] and the same sentiment is expressed in the new treaty on biological warfare.

3. To Employ Strategic Bombing[41]

The incumbent government often enjoys an advantage in firepower. The Iraqi, Cuban, Nigerian, and Pakistani

[38] International conferences of the Red Cross have repeatedly adopted resolutions condemning the use of indiscriminate weapons, as the chart below indicates.

Conference	Place	Date	Resolutions
Xth	Geneva	1921	XII
XIIth	Geneva	1925	V
XIIIth	The Hague	1928	V & VI
XIVth	Brussels	1930	V
XVth	Tokyo	1934	XXXVI
XVIIth	Stockholm	1948	XXIV
XVIIIth	Toronto	1952	XVII & XVIII
XIXth	New Delhi	1957	XVIII
XXth	Vienna	1965	XXVIII
XXIst	Istanbul	1969	XIV

[39] See Report of the Secretary-General, RESPECT FOR HUMAN RIGHTS IN ARMED CONFLICT, *Doc.* A/8052 (18 Sept. 1970).

[40] G. A. Res. 2603 A (XXIV), Dec. 16, 1969. The resolution was adopted 80-3, with 36 abstentions. The abstaining countries included the United States and most of her NATO allies who are also parties to the 1925 Geneva Protocol.

[41] Other claims are made to use firepower in particular ways, as in "free-fire" zones. The concept of free-fire zones is identified almost exclusively with American practices in Vietnam, however, and is not therefore universal enough to justify textual analysis. The term connotes a policy of authorizing troops to fire at anything and everything; and while that has never been the official

governments all struck against rebel factions from the
air. Monopolizing the skies, they strafed and bombed
villages and rural areas suspected of rebel sympathies.
The United States dropped more bombs on Vietnam
than it dropped on Germany and Japan during World
War II,[42] and it may continue to use its air power in Indo-
china long after it has withdrawn ground forces from
combat. Critics have questioned the wisdom of air strikes
in internal conflicts,[43] and the record proves that pre-
dominant air power does not insure victory;[44] but few
states with an air capability have foregone using it.

Recent advances in technology have arguably en-
hanced both the accuracy and effectiveness of strategic

---

policy of the United States, it has been her soldiers' occasional
practice—as it has occasionally been the practice of soldiers in
all conflicts—to shoot first and ask questions later. Allied Forces
do designate specified strike zones within which troops enjoy
greater than usual freedom to fire. These specified strike zones
are established in hostile areas that the government wishes to
pacify. First, the South Vietnamese government and army evacuate all innocent civilians. Second, they certify that no one other
than Viet Cong inhabit the area. Then Allied Forces operate
under relaxed rules of engagement, which, while classified, can
at least be said to give the individual soldier and unit considerable
discretion in firing.

[42] Cf. T. Taylor, NUREMBERG AND VIETNAM: AN AMERICAN
TRAGEDY 140-145 (1970).

[43] Professor Falk has challenged the legality of the bombing
as well. Falk, International Law and the United States Role in
the Viet Nam War, 75 YALE L. J. 1122 (1966). But see Moore,
International Law and the United States Role in the Viet Nam
War: A Reply, 76 YALE L. J. 1051 (1967).

[44] Batista lost in Cuba. Iraq settled for a draw in its fight
against the Kurds. Cf. New York Times, Mar. 19, 1970; at 3,
col. 2.

bombing.[45] General Westmoreland has predicted that "on the battlefield of the future, enemy forces will be located, tracked, and targeted through the use of data links, computer assisted intelligence evaluation, and automated fire control."[46] While most participants in internal conflicts will not in the foreseeable future have such sophisticated electronic weapons systems, their use would alter the nature of strategic bombing and therefore perhaps its legality.

The Applicable Law Just as Article 3 does not explicitly forbid the use of chemical and biological weapons, it does not forbid the use of air power unless its impact is so indiscriminate as to endanger protected persons. Given the precision with which bombing raids can be conducted, it is difficult to see how the Article 3 injunction to treat non-combatants humanely can be construed as an absolute bar on bombing. It may nevertheless make illegal particular raids that inflict great injury upon the civilian population without achieving commensurate military gains.

Such is often the case in internal conflicts. Since Iraqi pilots were unfamiliar with the Soviet planes they flew, they area bombed; while the government pounded Kurdish areas mercilessly, the available evidence indicates that it destroyed only homes and farmlands and killed innocent men, women, and children without inflicting heavy losses on the guerrillas.[47] The Batista air force bombed rural areas indiscriminately. Critics allege the same has been true of the American bombing policy in

[45] See generally, *The American Way of Bombing*, HARPERS MAGAZINE 55 (June 1972).

[46] Congressional Record, 511104 (July 13, 1970).

[47] Vreeland, *Iraq*, II. CHALLENGE AND RESPONSE IN INTERNAL CONFLICT 381, 399 (1967).

South Vietnam.[48] One report asserts that 80 percent of
the bombing victims in Vietnam were civilians.[49] Another
likened the Vietnamese countryside to a moonscape deso-
late and pocked with craters.[50]

The recent technological advances described earlier
may, however, enable participants to limit their air strikes
to military targets and thereby reduce the infliction of
indiscriminate destruction upon the civilian population.

It is difficult to conclude, however, that bombing raids
that inflict heavy losses on the civilian population are
illegal under Article 3, since they are arguably permissible under the relevant norms of international law
applicable to international conflicts. In the first place,
there are no codified rules of aerial warfare.[51] The rules
governing land bombardment provide some guidance
when applied analogously; but they are inadequate, as
they were drafted in 1907 before the air age began. In
the second place, state practice has imposed few limits
on bombing. The Germans launched indiscriminate V-2
rocket attacks against England. The Americans fire-
bombed Dresden and Tokyo and dropped atomic bombs
on Nagasaki and Hiroshima. The lack of authoritative
rules, coupled with the record of state practice, has led
some scholars to conclude that international law imposes
no restraints on bombing.[52]

[48] T. Taylor, *supra* n. 42.   [49] See n. 81-93, *infra.*

[50] Wulff, *A Doctor Reports from South Vietnam*, CRIMES OF
WAR 309, 309-10 (R. Falk, G. Kolko, and R. Lifton, ed. 1971).

[51] The Draft Rules of Aerial Bombardment promulgated in
1923 were never adopted. See generally DeSaussure, *The Laws
of Air Warfare: Are There Any?* 23 NAVAL WAR COLLEGE REV.
35 (1971).

[52] British Air Marshal Harris said: "In the matter of the
use of aircraft in war, there is, it so happens, no international
law at all." A. Harris, BOMBER OFFENSIVE 177 (1947). *Cf.*

In the *Shimoda case* the Japanese District Court rejected this argument and held that blind aerial bombardment was still illegal.[53] Scholars remain divided on this point[54] and are likely to remain so until the international community adopts a formal code of regulating the use of air power in armed conflict.

Increasing weapons sophistication may portend just such an international agreement. So long as states lacked confidence in the precision with which their air forces could conduct air strikes, they would not agree to any rules that narrowly limited their scope. With the development of computer-assisted target selection and the so-called smart bombs, states may feel that they can now agree to rules that circumscribe their air strikes within the capabilities of the new weaponry.

4. *To Commit Reprisals*

In the Arab-Israeli conflict both sides have justified individual raids or air strikes as reprisals.[55] Public officials in the United States have occasionally characterized particular Allied operations in Vietnam as reprisals.[56]

O'Brien, *The Meaning of Military Necessity in International Law*, 1 YEARBOOK OF WORLD POLITY 109 (1957).

[53] JAPANESE ANNUAL OF INT'L. L. 212, 240 (1964).

[54] Compare J. Spaight, AIR POWER AND WAR RIGHTS 265-81 (3rd ed. 1947) and M. McDougal and F. Feliciano, LAW AND MINIMUM WORLD PUBLIC ORDER 665-66 (1961).

[55] See the debate between Messrs. Falk and Blum in the American Journal of International Law: Falk, *The Beirut Raid and the International Law of Retaliation*, 63 AM. J. INT'L. L. 415 (1969) and Blum, *The Beirut Raid and the International Double Standard*, 64 AM. J. INT'L. L. 73 (1970).

[56] *Cf. New York Times*, July 6, 1971, at 1, col. 2. Quincy Wright questioned the validity of the Tonkin Gulf reprisals in *Legal Aspects of the Viet-Nam Situation*, 60 AM. J. INT'L. L. 750 (1966).

As internal conflicts degenerate into bloody wars, each side will likely seize upon some real or imagined excess by its opponent to justify its own excesses. Reprisal—an illegitimate act of warfare used in retaliation against a prior illegal act by the enemy for the purpose of forcing him to comply with the laws of war[57]—is always the legal rationale. Though participants in internal conflicts remain free to use reprisals, their discretion is not unlimited.

The Applicable Law Article 19 of the 1954 Hague Convention prohibits reprisals against cultural or artistic property in any armed conflict. Article 3 explicitly forbids "the taking of hostages," a frequent reprisal tactic in an earlier era. The question is whether its grant of general protection to the non-combatant population insulates them from any other kind of reprisal. Pictet argues that the humane treatment requirement excludes reprisals against protected persons as individuals or as members of a community.[58] Mr. Kalshoven thinks the answer less certain and therefore urges amending Article 3 to prohibit all forms of reprisals.[59] If Article 3 prohibits all reprisals, as Pictet contends, it goes further than do the present rules of international law applicable to international conflicts. While they enumerate many specific prohibitions, they do permit reprisals against innocent

[57] M. Greenspan, THE MODERN LAW OF LAND WARFARE 407-8 (1959).

[58] J. Pictet, I. COMMENTARY ON THE GENEVA CONVENTIONS 55; II. COMMENTARY ON THE GENEVA CONVENTIONS 36; III. COMMENTARY ON THE GENEVA CONVENTIONS 40; IV. COMMENTARY ON THE GENEVA CONVENTIONS 39.

[59] Kalshoven, *Human Rights, The Law of Armed Conflicts, and Reprisals*, 11 INT'L. REV. OF THE RED CROSS 183 (April 1971).

persons outside the control of the reprising power. There
is no control criterion included in Article 3; but it would
be anomalous if a single provision, thought to embody
to minimum protections of the larger agreement, in fact
extended greater protections than the parent instrument.
The unmistakable trend in international law is toward
limiting the right of reprisal.[60] Although the Belgian delegate to the 1874 Brussels Conference felt there was some-
thing "odious" about the principle of reprisal,[61] the rapporteur of the 1899 Hague Peace Conference commented
that the provision in Article 50 prohibiting collective
punishment had been drafted "without prejudice to the
question of reprisal."[62] Not until the 1929 Geneva Prisoner of War Convention did international law include
an express prohibition on reprisals against prisoners.[63]
The 1949 Geneva Conventions expanded that prohibition. Now all persons and property protected by the four
Conventions are also protected from reprisals.[64]

International law also prohibits the use of particular
weapons as reprisals. Many states that ratified the 1925
Geneva Protocol reserved the right to use the prohibited
weapons if another party first used them. It is difficult
to imagine states agreeing to anything more than a no-
first-use prohibition on most such weapons, although
states have done so in the new treaty on biological weapons. One must keep in mind, however, that such reserva-

[60] But see Lillich, *Forcible Self-Help Under International Law*,
22 NAVAL WAR COLLEGE REV. 56, 58-60 (1970).

[61] Quoted in Kalshoven, *supra* n. 57 at 185.

[62] *Id.* at 184.

[63] Art. 2, 1929 Geneva Prisoner of War Convention.

[64] Reprisals would constitute "a grave breach" of the Conventions. See Article 50, GWS; Article 51, GWS (Sea); Article 130,
GPW; and Article 147 (GC).

tions do not entitle a state to use such weapons in retaliation for any infringement of the laws of war other than use of the proscribed weapon.[65]

B. THE CLAIM TO INTERFERE WITH THE CIVILIAN POPULATION

More than a century ago Abraham Lincoln asked: "Must a government of necessity be too strong for the liberties of its people or too weak to maintain its own existence?" It was Mr. Lincoln who established the first modern precedent for suspending democratic guarantees during a civil war; and today free societies usually confer dictatorial powers on their war leaders, confident that their Cincinnatus will vanquish the enemy, restore the sacrificed freedoms, and return to his plow. Emergency government is a normal response to either external or internal crises; whatever its precise form, emergency government claims the right to intensify its regulation and supervision of the community. Whether such claims are legally permissible within the domestic constitutional framework of any given country is beyond the purview of this book.[66] What is relevant is the compatibility of such claims with the applicable rules of international law.

1. To Relocate Citizens

Most frequently, governments combatting an internal guerrilla movement assert the right to relocate citizens in "fortified," "strategic," or "pacified" villages or hamlets. In Malaya the British uprooted hundreds of thousands of Chinese squatters living in remote jungle villages that

[65] Kalshoven, *supra* n. 57 at 188.

[66] See generally C. Rossiter, CONSTITUTIONAL DICTATORSHIP 77-129 (1948).

the army and police could not protect and resettled them on new land within effective British control.[67] They deeded land to these peasants, who henceforth lived in one of 600 new villages enclosed in barbed wire and lighted at night.[68] The British thus severed the lifeline between the guerrillas and the civilian community while improving the living conditions of the poorest and most vulnerable portion of the population.[69] One observer analogized the British effort to pest control: "to destroy the enemy, [they] are breaking up the nesting places of the pests."[70]

In Cambodia the government resettled approximately 600,000 Khmers in rectangular, stockaded villages that the native population could defend. As in Malaya, the motive was the same: to snatch "a malleable and easily terrorized population from the enemy grasp." The result, again, was an improvement in the economic life of the relocated peasant.[71]

The French emulated the British practice in Algeria, where they moved nearly two million Moslems into fortified villages. One of the principal theoretical architects of French strategy commented upon its historical roots: "In effect, we are re-establishing the old system of medieval fortified villages, designed to protect the inhabitants from marauding bands."[72] Some no doubt came voluntarily to escape the rebels. Others were forced to protect

[67] Linebarger, *They Call 'em Bandits in Malaya*, MODERN GUERRILLA WARFARE 293, 296-7 (F. Osanka ed. 1962).

[68] Dougherty, *The Guerrilla War in Malaya*, MODERN GUERRILLA WARFARE 298, 303 (F. Osanka ed. 1962).

[69] *Id.* at 304.

[70] Linebarger, *supra* n. 65 at 296.

[71] Kelly, *Revolutionary War and Psychological Action*, MODERN GUERRILLA WARFARE 425, 438 (F. Osanka, ed. 1962).

[72] R. Trinquier, *supra* n. 19 at 74.

themselves.[73] The army, which operated this system of *quadvillages*, imagined itself building a new Algeria.[74]

To salvage the old Algeria, however, the French intensified their supervision of the "pacified" population. In Algiers, for example, they issued identification cards and consistently checked Moslems. They also established the *ilot* system: one person in each family was responsible to a floor chief, who was responsible to a building chief, who was responsible to a block chief. Through this system the French administrator could and did reach into every Moslem home. A French military magazine described the mission: "The population must be cleaned up, assisted, helped, organized, administered."[75]

The Portuguese in their African provinces, the Ethiopians, the Israelis in the occupied territories, the South Vietnamese and Americans in Vietnam have used the same or similar techniques. While these relocation programs do differ in scope and detail, they remain identical in the broad outlines. The old, the young, men, women, and children are removed from their homes and resettled in areas that the government can defend. The government extends medical, educational, and other social services to the villages while closely watching the native population. The educational program usually includes political indoctrination.

The Applicable Law Article 3 does not prohibit resettlement programs. Since all those involved would fall within its protective ambit, they are, of course, entitled to "be treated humanely, without any adverse distinction founded on race, colour, religion or faith, sex, birth, or wealth." Though some might argue that resettlement programs for

[73] J. Kraft, *supra* n. 13 at 101.
[74] *Id.* at 107.   [75] *Id.* at 103.

specific groups such as the Moslems in Algeria, the Chinese in Malaya, or the blacks in Angola and Mozambique represent impermissible discriminations based on religion, color, and race, the government can reply that Article 3 prohibits only adverse distinctions on those grounds. From its point of view, the resettlement program is in the best interests of the people relocated. Furthermore, the government could contend that so long as its motives were other than bias or prejudice against particular ethnic groups, it cannot be barred from taking legitimate steps to secure itself and its citizens simply because the burdens of defense fall more heavily on one group than another.

More specific guidelines for the operation of resettlement programs may be found in the international law applicable to international conflicts, particularly the law of belligerent occupation. Article 49 of the Civilian Convention is the key article.[76] While prohibiting "[i]ndivi-

---

[76] Article 49 of the Geneva Civilian Convention states:

"Individual or mass forcible transfers, as well as deportations of protected persons from occupied territory to the territory of the Occupying Power or to that of any other country, occupied or not, are prohibited, regardless of their motives.

"Nevertheless, the Occupying Power may undertake total or partial evacuation of a given area if the security of the population or imperative military reasons so demand. Such evacuations may not involve the displacement of protected persons outside the bounds of the occupied territory except when for material reasons it is impossible to avoid such displacement. Persons thus evacuated shall be transferred back to their homes as soon as hostilities in the area in question have ceased.

"The Occupying Power undertaking such transfers or evacuations shall ensure, to the greatest practicable extent, that proper accommodation is provided to receive the protected persons, that the removals are effected in satisfactory conditions of hy-

dual or mass forcible transfers," it does authorize the "total or partial evacuation of a given area if the security of the population or imperative military reasons so demand." The article admonishes the Occupying Power to transfer "[p]ersons thus evacuated . . . back to their homes as soon as hostilities in the area . . ." cease, as the Vietnamese do once Allied forces have pacified the area. During the evacuation and relocation, members of a family may not be separated. The government must also insure "satisfactory conditions of hygiene, health, safety, and nutrition";[77] and most governments try although not all succeed. While some provisions of Article 49 would make little sense in the context of an internal conflict in which both sides consider themselves citizens of the same country (secessionist wars excepted), it does set out some standards that could be used to implement the Article 3 requirement of humane treatment.

Other Civilian Convention articles raise disquieting questions about other aspects of relocation programs. Article 51 prohibits the occupying power from "compelling protected persons to serve in its armed or auxiliary forces." It furthermore forbids "pressure or propaganda

---

giene, health, safety and nutrition, and that members of the same family are not separated.

"The protecting Power shall be informed of any transfers and evacuations as soon as they have taken place.

"The Occupying Power shall not detain protected persons in an area particularly exposed to the dangers of war unless the security of the population or imperative military reasons so demand.

"The Occupying Power shall not deport or transfer parts of its own civilian population into the territory it occupies."

[77] See also Article 55, which provides that "the Occupying Power has the duty of ensuring the food and medical supplies of the population. . . ."

which aims at securing voluntary enlistment." The Vietnamese "Chieu Hoi" program is a typical example of government efforts to re-educate disaffected citizens; and if the principle of Article 51 were applicable to internal conflicts, the program would be illegal.[78] The French infused a great deal of political indoctrination into the curriculum in the schools that they established in camps and villages.

Article 78 permits the occupying power to "subject [protected persons] to assigned residence or internment . . . for imperative reasons of security." The article specifies, however, that protected persons should have the right to appeal the decision and to periodical review if the decision is upheld. Few countries have established judicial procedures for the review of relocation decisions.

The Civilian Convention also contains over twenty separate articles on places of internment and the rights of internees.[79] Many requirements parallel those found in the POW Convention. Generally, Chapter II insures that the internee is safely housed, well-fed and treated, and otherwise protected. Few internment camps would meas-

[78] But see Wosepka, *Repatriation and the Chieu Hoi Amnesty Approach in Vietnam: Consequences and Prospects*, 5 INT'L. LAWYER 637 (1971).

[79] See Chapter II, Places of Internment, Arts. 83-88; Chapter III, Food and Clothing, Arts. 89-90; Chapter IV, Hygiene and Medical Attention, Arts. 91-92; Chapter V, Religious, Intellectual and Physical Activities, Arts. 93-96; Chapter VI, Personal Property and Financial Resources, Arts. 97-98; Chapter VII, Administration and Discipline, Arts. 99-104; Chapter VIII, Relations with the Exterior, Arts. 105-16; Chapter IX, Penal and Disciplinary Sanctions, Arts. 117-26; Chapter X, Transfers of Internees, Arts. 127-28; Chapter XI, Deaths, Arts. 129-31; and Chapter XII, Release, Repatriation, and Accommodation in Neutral Countries, Articles 132-35.

ure up to the Chapter II standards were they applicable
to internal conflicts.

2. To Defoliate Farm and Forest Lands and Destroy Food Stores

In most third world countries the majority of the population lives outside the cities. Rural and poor, they sub-
sist on the land. They till a few acres, raise a few chick-
ens. Meager though their stores be, it is from them that
the rebels sustain themselves. The thick jungle and tropi-
cal rain forests that flourish in many of these lands protect the guerrilla forces. They provide shelter, conceal
their movements, and prevent effective pursuit. In Malaya
the jungle is so thick, for instance, that a man disappears
from view six feet off the road.[80] In Cyprus and in the
Philippines the mountain forests offered refuge to insurgent forces.[81] In such circumstances it is only natural that
government forces would try to cut off rebel food supplies
and destroy their natural cover, as the English did during the Boer war.[82]

The Allied program in South Vietnam is an illustration
of such an effort. It is unclear when Allied planes began
flying crop destruction missions, and how many arable
acres they destroyed is disputed. Perhaps as early as
1962, certainly no later than the spring of 1965, the
Allies had launched a crop destruction program.[83] A De-

[80] Dougherty, *supra* n. 66 at 302.

[81] See Gourlay, *Terror in Cypress*, THE GUERRILLA—AND HOW
TO FIGHT HIM 232 (T. Greene, ed. 1962) and Hammer, *Huks in
the Philippines*, MODERN GUERRILLA WARFARE 177 (F. Osanka,
ed. 1962).

[82] The tactic is not new to the American army either. Union
forces used it during the Civil War.

[83] S. Hersh, CHEMICAL AND BIOLOGICAL WARFARE: AMERICA'S
HIDDEN ARSENAL 151 (1968).

cember *New York Times* dispatch reported: "Crop destruction missions are aimed only at relatively small areas of major military importance where the guerrillas grow their own food or where the population is willingly committed to their cause."[84] A 1967 Japanese study concluded that Allied spraying had ruined more than 3.8 million acres of arable land.[85] The United States dismissed such claims as propaganda. It once conceded destroying 20,000 acres, or one-third of one percent of the land being cultivated. However great the acreage destroyed, the United States, as Major General Davison insisted, claimed that "great care has been taken to select areas in which most harm would be done to the Viet Cong and the least harm to the local population."[86]

Allied ground forces also destroyed crops and killed livestock. The journalistic accounts of the war are replete with examples of units pouring gasoline on rice stores and torching them or shooting livestock.[87] Again one hears, at least occasionally, the legal justification for the destruction: the food was intended for or was being used by the Viet Cong.[88] Frequently, Allied forces commandeered the rice supplies rather than destroy them.[89]

"Only We Can Prevent Forests" sloganeered the men who ran the Allied defoliation program, and they lived up to their motto. Though effective defoliation posed great-

---

[84] *Ibid.*   [85] *Id.* at 152.   [86] *Id.* at 156.

[87] *Cf.* J. Schell, THE MILITARY HALF (1968).

[88] An American pilot is quoted as saying, "We bomb the paddies by day to deny food to the VC . . . as a matter of fact we destroy pretty much anything that might be useful" in Mirsky, *The Tombs of Ben Suc,* CRIMES OF WAR, 363, 367 (R. Falk, G. Kolko, and R. Lifton, eds. 1971).

[89] Bertolino, *Report on American Conduct of the War in the South,* CRIMES OF WAR, 319, 328 (R. Falk, G. Kolko, and R. Lifton, eds. 1971).

er problems than did crop destruction,[90] the Allies persisted. They wished to strip off the forest cover above rebel supply routes and expose concentrations of guerrilla units. They did.[91]

The Applicable Law Article 3 does not explicitly forbid crop destruction or defoliation programs. Unless they generally or in particular instances produce inhumane side effects upon the protected population so great as to offset the legitimate military advantage thereby gained, they are legally permissible. Critics of United States policies in Vietnam decried the cruel impact of crop destruction and defoliation programs on what they described as the innocent civilian population. The chemicals used in crop spraying are toxic,[92] and they can and sometimes do adversely affect men. The same Japanese study charged that the herbicides used in crop destruction programs had caused over 1,000 peasant deaths.[93] Others have attributed blindness and premature or stillborn births to exposure to the chemicals used.[94] Defoliation seldom causes any such immediate effect because few people other than transient guerrillas inhabit the forested areas. It may nevertheless cause untoward ecological im-

[90] S. Hersh, *supra* n. 81 at 155 quotes Secretary McNamara as telling Congress that "defoliation is still a rather primitive technique. . . . It depends for its effectiveness on the time of year, the type of foliage and on wind and other conditions in the area."

[91] Allied spraying, it is estimated, destroyed 20 percent of Vietnam's forest land. One-half billion dollars of prime hardwood was destroyed.

[92] The level of toxicity to man is, however, low and the chemical dissolves in the soil quickly. It can nevertheless cause eye irritation and gastro-intestinal upset.

[93] S. Hersh, *supra* n. 81 at 152.

[94] *Id.* at 157.

balances whose total effect is as yet unrealized. The chemicals do affect livestock and other animals.[95]

Under the more detailed norms of the law of war applicable to international conflicts, defoliation and crop destruction would remain legitimate military tactics. Article 23(g) of the Hague Regulations simply formalizes the "balancing test" outlined above: ". . . [I]t is especially forbidden to destroy or seize the enemy's property, unless such destruction be imperatively demanded by the necessities of war."[96] As one post-World War II war crimes judge lamented: "The rule is clear enough but the factual determination as to what constitutes military necessity is difficult."[97] Some courts have lent a sympathetic ear to the plea of military necessity; others, a deaf one.[98] In the Hostages Trial the court suggested that a retreating army could destroy public and private property "which would give aid and comfort to the enemy."[99] The Allies in Vietnam denied villages to the Viet Cong by destroying them, and former Secretary of the Navy Paul Nitze's justification echoes the Court's judgment: "Where neither the United States nor Vietnamese forces can maintain con-

[95] *Ibid.*

[96] Article 46 says that private property must be respected, and subsequent articles whose provisions were repeated and expanded in the Civilian Convention delineate the rights of the Occupying Power vis-à-vis property owners. These and other articles dealing with property seem inappropriate in the context of internal conflict.

[97] The German High Command Trial, XII. LAW REPORTS OF TRIALS OF WAR CRIMINALS 1, 93-94 (1949).

[98] Courts have been less sympathetic to the plea in non-property cases. E.g., *The Peleus Trial,* I. LAW REPORTS OF TRIALS OF WAR CRIMINALS 1, 15-16 (1947).

[99] *The Hostages Trial,* VIII. LAW REPORTS OF TRIALS OF WAR CRIMINALS 34, 67-9 (1949).

tinuous occupancy, it is necessary to destroy those facilities."[100] The tribunal in the High Command case felt
that "a great deal of latitude" should be given the commander who must decide whether to destroy enemy
property. It, too, emphasized the importance of the factual determination: "What constitutes devastation beyond
military necessity in these situations requires detailed
proof of an operational and tactical nature."[101] The hard
hand of war can be just that—hard, terribly hard.

C. The Claim to Treat Captured Personnel as
Common Criminals or Traitors Rather Than as
Prisoners of War

The rebel presently fights in a twilight zone between
lawful combatancy and common criminality.[102] Governments are, as we saw in Chapter II, loathe to recognize
the captured or surrendered rebel as a POW, particularly
in the insurgent stage of the revolution. The Russian
delegate to the 1912 International Conference of the Red
Cross denounced the proposal to extend convention protections to participants in civil wars: "I consider that the
Red Cross Societies should have no duty towards insurgents or bands of revolutionaries whom the laws of my
country regard as criminals."[103]

The guerrilla himself was initially regarded even in

[100] Norden, *American Atrocities in Vietnam*, crimes of war
265, 276 (R. Falk, G. Kolko & R. Lifton, eds. 1971).

[101] The German High Command Trial, *supra* n. 95 at 123-6.

[102] Greenspan, *International Law and Its Protection for Participants in Unconventional Warfare*, 341 annals of the american
academy of political and social sciences 30, 33 (1962).

[103] Schlogel, *supra* n. 3 at 125.

international conflicts as a violator of the law of war;[104] and though the 1949 Geneva Conventions granted him legal status in certain limited circumstances, he remains an outcast.[105] The British in Malaysia and the French in Algeria, for example, initially prosecuted captured rebels in criminal courts. The Portuguese have consistently treated captured rebels as criminals. Even the South Vietnamese, though they treated the bulk of captured personnel as POW's, prosecuted some persons for treason and sabotage in their criminal courts.

Indeed, a country's initial reaction is usually to decree martial rule, expand the reach of the criminal law, and increase the punishment for offenses endangering national security.[106] In the Philippines, for example, the government suspended the right of habeas corpus for all those detained for the crimes of "sedition, insurrection, or rebellion" and for "all other crimes . . . committed . . . in furtherance . . . thereof."[107] In Thailand the government conferred upon military courts the jurisdiction to try "offenses against the Sovereign . . . the security of the state . . . public peace and order."[108] These examples demonstrate that states, far from recognizing rebels as legitimate combatants, will first pursue extraordinary criminal remedies against them.[109]

[104] Baxter, *So-called "Unprivileged Belligerency": Spies, Guerrillas, and Saboteurs,* 28 BRIT. YB. INT'L. L. 323, 334 (1951).

[105] Professor Farer refers to the guerrilla as the "stepchild of the laws of war" and characterizes him as "grudgingly recognized and poorly treated." *Supra* n. 8 at 36.

[106] See J. Kelley and G. Pelletier, LEGAL CONTROL OF THE POPULACE IN SUBVERSIVE WARFARE 336-339 (1966).

[107] *Id.* at 104.   [108] *Id.* at 105.

[109] For an analysis of a specific case, see Dugard, *South West Africa and the "Terrorist Trial,"* 64 AM. J. INT'L. L. 19 (1970).

The record of state practice also demonstrates, however, that governments may eventually treat captured persons as prisoners of war. France finally abandoned its effort to prosecute the Algerian rebels as criminals. In March 1958 General Salan ordered that military prisoners be held in special camps rather than in prisons; and the International Committee of the Red Cross, which had been permitted to inspect the French prison and detention camps, "construed these actions to mean that the French government intended to accord to FLN militants treatment 'closely related' to that governing prisoners of war in international conflicts."[110] The Algerian rebels had said from the beginning that they treated captured French soldiers as prisoners of war.[111] Though both factions in the Congo mistreated captured personnel, one student nevertheless concluded: "Most captives in the Congo civil war were detained under acceptable conditions and exchanged or released in the course of hostilities. The International Committee of the Red Cross visited prisons representing all factions during the crisis in an effort to insure that prisoners received treatment in accordance with the Geneva Conventions."[112] Similarly, the Nigerian government did not prosecute Biafrans in her criminal courts but agreed to treat them humanely.

The Applicable Law This confusing pattern of state practice reflects the confused state of present law. Article 3

---

[110] Fraleigh, *The Algerian Revolution as a Case Study in International Law*, THE INTERNATIONAL LAW OF CIVIL WAR 179, 196 (R. Falk, ed. 1971).

[111] Jabhat al-Tahrir al-Quami, *White Paper on the Application of the Geneva Conventions of 1949 to the French-Algerian Conflict* 15-18 (1960).

[112] McNemar, *The Post-Independence War in the Congo*, THE INTERNATIONAL LAW OF CIVIL WAR 244, 264 (1971).

does not confer POW status upon anyone although it does charge the captor to treat a prisoner humanely. Even if the POW convention were itself applicable, many combatants in internal conflicts would not qualify as POW's. Basically, Article 4 of the POW Convention says that one is a POW if (1) he is a member of a national armed force or (2) if he is a member of a group that fulfills the following four conditions:

(a) that of being commanded by a person responsible for his subordinates;

(b) that of having a fixed distinctive sign recognizable at a distance;

(c) that of carrying arms openly;

(d) that of conducting their operations in accordance with the laws and customs of war.

No guerrilla is likely to qualify for POW status under such conditions. While the guerrilla force will probably have a hierarchical command, its members are not likely to wear a "fixed distinctive sign recognizable at a distance"; nor will they always bear arms openly.[113] Whether or not they obey the laws of war seems an irrelevant criterion. Desirable as it might be for all parties to a conflict to obey the laws and customs of war,[114] why should one's failure to do so affect his status or even his subsequent treatment other than the severity of punishment should he be prosecuted for violating the law of

[113] Kelley, *supra* n. 4 at 99.

[114] The theoretical difficulty of making international law binding on guerrillas and other insurgent groups is explored in *Note, The Geneva Conventions and the Treatment of Prisoners of War in Vietnam*, 80 HARV. L. REV. 851 (1967). Among recent groups only the Algerians claimed to follow the law of war. The Viet Cong, for example, rejected the idea that it was bound "by the international treaties to which others besides itself subscribed." 5 INT'L. REV. OF THE RED CROSS 636 (1965).

war? In our criminal law the man charged with the most reprehensible crime is still submitted to the reasoned judgment of the law. The absurdity of the last of the four conditions is not the point, however; it is that many participants in an internal war would not be entitled to POW status even if international law standards were applicable.

On the other hand, there is, as Professor Baxter has pointed out, a trend toward extending "the protection of prisoner of war status to an ever-increasing group. . . ."[115] Free World Forces in Vietnam, for example, treat as prisoners of war large numbers who do not satisfy the Article 4 criteria. Moreover, the General Assembly has repeatedly called upon governments to treat captured insurgents as prisoners of war;[116] and the International Committee of the Red Cross has intervened with varying degrees of success in numerous internal conflicts to insure humane treatment of prisoners.[117]

The answer may well be that a combatant in an internal conflict is and should be neither fish nor fowl. Rather than trying to determine whether or not he is a prisoner of war with all the legal consequences such a status entails, one might more fruitfully reflect upon whether different kinds of participants in internal conflicts should be entitled to different rights. Such a classification scheme would reflect the functional necessity and wisdom of treating one kind of participant differently from another. Within certain categories one might then look to particular provisions in the Geneva Conventions for authoritative standards of humane treatment. Assimilating a

[115] Baxter, *supra* n. 102 at 343.

[116] E.g., Gen. Ass. Res. 2396 (2 Dec. 1968); Gen. Ass. Res. 2395 (29 Nov. 1968); and Gen. Ass. Res. 2446 (19 Dec. 1968).

[117] Veuthey, *The Red Cross and Non-International Conflicts*, 10 INT'L. REV. OF THE RED CROSS 411, 416 (Aug. 1970).

rebel to a prisoner of war for one purpose would not dictate assimilating him to a prisoner of war for all purposes. Some provisions of the POW Convention might prove unworkable in the peculiar context of internal war. It is far more difficult, for example, to determine "the combat zone" in a guerrilla conflict than in a World War II-type war, which was the paradigm in the draftsmen's minds. Others may be incompatible with specific Article 3 provisions. There is, for instance, the clause in Article 3 that seemingly permits prosecution and execution of rebels even though prisoners of war could not be under the terms of the POW Convention. A functional analysis also requires concentration on the more specific claims to treat captured personnel in particular ways.

1. To Try and Execute Summarily

A news photo flashed around the world during the 1968 Tet offensive in Vietnam showed the Saigon chief of police blowing out the brains of a suspected Viet Cong with his hand gun. It dramatically demonstrated the frequently asserted claim regarding executing captured foes summarily. Journalists reported that some commanders in the Nigerian army similarly disposed of captured Ibo tribesmen fighting for Biafra. Both sides in the Congolese war occasionally indulged their taste for summary justice. Following an attack upon a United Nations mess at Kindu, Congolese soldiers arrested thirteen Italian airmen, shot them, dismembered their bodies, and passed the pieces out to onlookers.[118] A year before, a Liberian contingent had herded ninety-two arrested Baluba tribesmen into unventilated railroad cars. They suffocated.[119]

Guerrilla forces often dispense summary justice because they control no territory and lack the facilities in

[118] McNemer, *supra* n. 110.   [119] *Id.* at 265.

which to house prisoners. One should hardly expect a
small mobile unit to drag handcuffed prisoners through
the jungle with them on their way to the next ambush.
The policy of taking no prisoners is a reasonable one;
unfortunately, it is often translated into a policy of executing all captured personnel. The practice of the Castro
forces demonstrates, however, that "taking no prisoners"
need not be a euphemism for murder. A journalist who
trudged through the mountains with Castro quotes his
brother Raoul, talking to captured Batista soldiers:

"We hope that you will stay with us and fight against
the master who so ill-used you. If you decide to refuse
this invitation—and I am not going to repeat it—you will
be delivered to the custody of the Cuban Red Cross.
Once you are under Batista's orders again, we hope that
you will not take up arms against us. But, if you do, re-
member this. We took you this time. We can take you
again. And when we do we will not frighten or torture or
kill you, any more than we are doing to you at this moment. If you are captured a second time or even a third
by us, we will again return you exactly as we are doing
now."[120]

Enlightened though such a policy be, it is not usually
followed.

The Applicable Law In fact, there are really two separate
claims being made here: the first, to forego any trial at
all; the second, to execute. As to the first, there can be
little doubt but that international law requires trial before the imposition of punishment, whether capital or
otherwise. Article 3 forbids: ". . . the passing of sentences
and the carrying out of executions without previous judgment pronounced by a regularly constituted court afford-

[120] Chapelle, *supra* n. 12 at 223.

ing all the judicial guarantees which are recognized as indispensable by civilized peoples." This simple prohibition reflects a principle of criminal justice common to all domestic legal systems: every man is entitled to his day in court. The specific application of that principle as dictated by the language of Article 3 is not so simple. What is a "regularly constituted court"? What "judicial guarantees" are recognized as "indispensable by all civilized peoples"?

The "regularly constituted court" requirement should not be construed too literally. Guerrillas, after all, are not apt to carry black robes and white wigs in their back packs. Any proceeding they convoke will necessarily be ad hoc. While the government will have a system of established courts, they may not be open for business—at least not for the business of trying rebels. Operating under martial rule, the government may have created special courts or conferred jurisdiction on military tribunals. Precedent justifies characterizing such tribunals as "regularly constituted courts."[121] The test is authoritativeness; that is, whether the appropriate authorities, acting under appropriate powers, created the court according to appropriate standards.

There is today a consensus that certain specific rights are fundamental to trial in any such court. Among these are prompt notice of charges, adequate time and facilities to prepare defense, right to counsel, and the assistance of an interpreter. This list of rights appears in such diverse agreements as the NATO Status of Forces Agreement,[122] the POW Convention,[123] the Civilian Conven-

[121] J. Kelly and G. Pelletier, *supra* n. 104 at 303-05.
[122] Art. VII(9), 62 STAT. 1681; T.I.A.S. 1838; 4 BEVANS 559; 21 U.N.T.S. 77.
[123] Arts. 84, 99, 103-06.

tion,[124] the European Convention For the Protection of Human Rights and Fundamental Freedoms,[125] and the draft Inter-American Convention for the Protection of Human Rights.[126] The right to a speedy trial and the right to appeal are also important, though less universally conceded rights. The "judicial guarantees . . . recognized as indispensable by all civilized peoples" do not include a jury or a ban on hearsay evidence—unless one takes the rather parochial view that only the United States is civilized. There are almost no rules of evidence in civil law countries,[127] and they do not require jury trials in some criminal cases.[128] These are indeed minimum standards, but it is difficult to imagine guerrilla forces being able to comply with even them; and there is substantial precedent for the proposition that the government may suspend at least some among them during public emergencies.[129]

[124] Arts. 68-75 and 123.

[125] Art. 6, 213 U.N.T.S. 221 (1950).

[126] Art. 8, *Handbook of Existing Rules Pertaining to Human Rights* 50-70 OEA/Ser. L/V/II. 23, Doc. 21 (17 Dec. 1970). The Convention is also reprinted in 65 AM. J. INT'L L. 679 (1971).

[127] J. Merryman, THE CIVIL LAW TRADITION 1 (1969). The civil law tradition is the most influential legal tradition in the world.

[128] *Id.* at 139. Professor Merryman does argue that the equivalent of a jury exists, but he admits that it "may not consist of twelve persons, it may frequently take the form of lay advisors who sit on the bench with the judge, and even where it looks like ours, it may not have to render a unanimous verdict of guilty in order for the accused to be convicted." At some point differences of degree become differences of kind, and the professor's conclusion from the preceding recital is an understatement: "These are, particularly when they accumulate, important differences between our conception of a jury and theirs."

[129] Article 15 of the European Convention, for example, explicitly states: "In time of war or other public emergency threat-

Article 3 is silent as to the scope of permissible punishments, though it impliedly sanctions executions, only conditioning their imposition upon a prior judicial determination of guilt. States have repeatedly used the firing squad, the rope, or the gas chamber to silence once and for all those who opposed them, though both the Iraqi and Nigerian governments declared a general amnesty at the end of hostilities between them and their defeated secessionist foes. Those who oppose capital punishment concede that "there is nothing [in Article 3] to prevent the execution of such combatants merely for having borne arms against the enemy."[130] Since "the slaughter of prisoners with or without legal proceedings can hardly satisfy humanitarian conscience," they argue for either (1) deferment or (2) annulment of capital punishment during hostilities. Mr. Veuthey argues: "Any capital punishment in time of conflict, in relation with the conflict, cannot fail to bring about an increase in tension, vigorous reaction from the enemy and even reprisals."[131] The problem of capital punishment is but one aspect of the problem. The black militant demand in this country to be treated as a POW illustrates the complexity of the issue because the reverse side of the coin that he may not be punished for "offing a pig" is that he may be held for

---

ening the life of the nation any High Contrasting Party may take measures derogating from its obligations under this Convention. . . ." The European Court of Human Rights has upheld detention without trial under the Article 15 exception by the Republic of Ireland in its suppression of the outlawed Irish Republican Army. *"Lawless" Case*, Europ. Court of Human Rights (1961), 4 YRBK. EUROP. CONVENTION ON HUMAN RIGHTS 438, 474.

[130] Veuthey, *supra* n. 115 at 416.

[131] *Supra*, n. 55.

the duration of the conflict. The indeterminate sentence is widely used because otherwise a rebel tried in a civil court must be released and may then return to the streets or jungles to continue the revolution, a prospect that can hardly delight authorities.[132] Attempts to "re-educate" confined rebels or loyalists may also violate their rights if they are analogized to POW's. Participation in a "Chieu Hoi"-like program arguably constitutes a renunciation of rights not permitted by the Geneva Convention. Present international law provides almost no guidelines as to the permissible kind and form of punishment beyond Article 5 of the Universal Declaration of Human Rights, which prohibits "cruel, inhuman or degrading treatment or punishment."

2. *To Detain Arbitrarily*

The problem of detention is multifaceted, and the claim to detain arbitrarily is but a general one embracing many specific, related claims. There are, for example, claims to detain incognito without charges; claims to hold in solitary confinement; claims to bar visits by relatives, friends, ministers, or representatives of relief organizations; and claims to deny, regulate, or censor correspondence. Beyond these claims there is the problem of housing and feeding those detained. While no government explicitly claims the right to hold persons in unsanitary camps and feed them a less-than-subsistence diet, governments do hold people in just such conditions daily.

---

[132] Consequently, the South Vietnamese review all defendants immediately prior to their release and may extend their confinement. T. Mien, Vietnam: NATIONAL SECURITY NEEDS IN A CONSTITUTIONAL GOVERNMENT 16 (an unpublished thesis, The Judge Advocate General's School, 5 February 1971).

A few examples will put flesh on this skeletal outline
of claims. In 1955 the Singapore Legislative Assembly
passed legislation permitting authorities to detain persons for as long as two years on the mere suspicion that
the detainee might commit an act "prejudicial to the
security of Malaya."[133] The act also authorized the imposition of house arrest, police supervision, and curfews
on suspected individuals. Both government and rebel
groups have refused inspections by agencies such as the
International Committee of the Red Cross, even though
its reports are never made public. North Vietnam did not
permit any Red Cross visit to a POW camp. The Red
Cross never inspected rebel prison facilities in Algeria.[134]
South Vietnamese citizens demonstrated against their
government's refusal to permit visits to friends and relatives incarcerated in Vietnamese jails.[135] The press descriptions of the so-called "tiger cages" revealed shocking
conditions in what had been trumpeted as model facilities.[136] One can only deplore the practice of throwing
people of different ages and sexes into deep, windowless,
concrete pits.

The problem is partially one of resources and priori-
ties. One can hardly expect a small, underdeveloped
country whose government is fighting for its existence to
devote substantial of its precious resources to building
and maintaining model penal colonies. One can expect
even less of the guerrillas. But the problem is exacerbated

[133] Several hundred persons were detained under this act. See
Hidseing, *The First Five Years of the Federation of Malaya
Constitution*, 4 MALAYA L. REV. 183 at 184-185 (1962). The act
is analyzed in Davis, *Prevention of Crime Ordinance*, 1959, 1
MALAYA L. REV. 163 (1959).
[134] Farleigh, *supra* n. 108.
[135] *New York Times*, Jan. 1, 1971, at 1, col. 5.
[136] *Cf. New York Times*, July 14, 1970, col. 3 at p. 1.

by the lack of authoritative international law standards
for detention applicable to internal conflicts. In their
absence it is not surprising that conditions should have
tended toward the lowest common denominator.

The Applicable Law Article 3, whose protective ambit
embraces all those detained for any reason, imposes only
the general requirement of humane treatment, which is
amplified by prohibitions on "cruel treatment and torture"
and "outrages upon personal dignity, and in particular,
humiliating and degrading treatment." These general
standards do not constitute a set of specific rules and
regulations for detention. They do provide guidance for
the establishment of one, particularly if interpreted in the
light of the detailed provisions of the POW and civilian
conventions, which are, after all, designed to implement
the same standards.

The POW Convention sets out very specific rules for
detention.

Medical care: Prisoners of war "may be interned only
in premises located on land and affording every guarantee of hygiene and healthfulness."[137] They are entitled to
free medical care as needed[138] and should be medically
examined monthly.[139]

Housing: Generally, prisoners cannot be held in "close
confinement."[140] They must be housed in barracks "protected from dampness and adequately heated and lighted"
and allotted at least the minimum "surface and cubic
space. . . , bedding and blankets" given "forces of the
detaining power who are billeted in the same area."[141]
The detaining authorities are obligated "to take all sani-

---

[137] Article 22.   [138] Article 15.   [139] Article 31.
[140] Article 21.   [141] Article 25.

tary measures necessary to insure the cleanliness and healthfulness of camps and to prevent epidemics."[142]

Food: Prisoners are entitled to "daily food rations . . . sufficient in quantity, quality, and variety to prevent loss of weight or the development of nutritional deficiencies."[143]

Communication privilege: Within a week of capture, the prisoner is entitled to write his family,[144] and he may continue writing no less than two letters and four cards monthly.[145] Moreover, "prisoners of war shall be allowed to receive by post or by any other means individual parcels or collective shipments containing, in particular, foodstuffs, clothing, medical supplies and articles of a religious, educational, or recreational character. . . ."[146]

It is unrealistic to expect that participants in internal conflicts will build and maintain such model detention facilities, desirable as that might be. There is nevertheless one recurrent standard in these provisions not found in Article 3, and adherence to it might insure more humane detention conditions than now generally prevail. The standard is that prisoners are entitled to the same general treatment accorded members of the captor's armed forces or his nationals, as, for example, in Article 49, which specifies that those prisoners who are required or who elect[147] to work are entitled "to suitable working conditions not inferior to those enjoyed by nationals of the Detaining Power employed in similar work, especially as regards accommodations, food, clothing, and equip-

---

[142] Article 29. [143] Article 26. [144] Article 70.

[145] Article 71. [146] Article 72. But see Article 76.

[147] Article 49. Officers cannot be required to work, though they may volunteer. Non-commissioned officers can be given only supervisory jobs.

ment."[148] Given the often disparate conditions in which guerrillas operate and the poverty that afflicts most third-world countries, the similar treatment standard will not insure anything like ideal treatment. The ideal is seldom a viable alternative, however; and so long as the participants feed, house, and care for their prisoners no less well than they do for their own forces, they may have conceded as much to the demands of humanity as the necessity of their circumstances permits.

3. *To Use Coercive Means of Interrogation*

Intelligence information is vital to both sides in an internal conflict. Superior intelligence often proves the critical factor in a successful revolution. It is important to the guerrilla because he must know when to strike and when to flee. It is even more important to the government, however, because it must pierce the veil of secrecy behind which the rebel conceals his operations. A military correspondent for *Le Monde* said of the need for intelligence in Algeria: "The search for information, once the concern of general staffs, has become for everybody a question of life or death."[149] Consequently, both sides may claim the right to use coercive methods of interrogation to obtain intelligence data. Laotian Major Generals Vang Pao and Kouprasith Abkay conceded to newsmen "that prisoners who had refused to cooperate in interrogations . . . were subjected to deprivation of food and drink, to beatings and electrical shock torture."[150] Concerning one man, starved for four days despite a shoulder wound, beaten and tortured by shocks administered through electrodes fixed to two fingers of his left

[148] Article 51.
[149] Quoted in J. Kraft, *supra* n. 13 at 102.
[150] *New York Times*, Oct. 20, 1970, at 27, col. 3.

hand, General Vang Pao shrugged: "He does not want to tell the truth, so he was forced a little." Such callous observation proves Professor Farer's assertion that "since in guerrilla war the most serious problem facing incumbents is a lack of intelligence, the military if not the political, leaders may regard any inhibitions on intelligence-gathering techniques with surly apprehension."[151]

The Applicable Law Article 3 does not forbid interrogation, but it does prohibit "torture." There may well be a distinction between "coercion" and "torture"; but while the former is not specifically forbidden, its use may be circumscribed by the prohibitions on inhumane, humiliating, or degrading treatment. It should also be clear that most of the standard techniques—applying electrical shocks, driving splinters under fingernails, dunking in water—constitute torture rather than coercion under any reasonable definition of those terms.

Were the entire POW Convention applicable, authorities could still interrogate prisoners. Article 17 does not bar all questioning. It does, however, forbid "any physical or mental torture" as well as "any form of coercion." While requiring prisoners to give their "surnames, first names and rank, date of birth, and army, regimental, personal or serial number," it specifies that "prisoners of war who refuse to answer may not be threatened, insulted, or exposed to unpleasant or disadvantageous treatment of any kind." Again, terms such as "disadvantageous treatment" are not self-defining; but Article 17 would appear to preclude the common practice of denying food and medical attention to captured persons until they "talk." This view is reinforced by the frequent charge to treat the sick and wounded "without any adverse distinc-

[151] Farer, *supra* n. 1 at 64.

tion founded on sex, race, nationality, religion, political, or other similar criteria."[152] Refusal to answer questions should not preclude care, since "only urgent medical reasons" determine priority of treatment.[153] Other Convention articles point to the same conclusion. Captors must evacuate the prisoner from "the combat zone" as quickly as possible.[154] One could imply that beyond ascertaining identity, any questioning must be delayed until the prisoner is interned in "camps situated in an area far enough from the combat zone to be out of danger."[155] The latter implication is practically sound because most violations occur within a very short time after capture when line personnel interrogate for "combat" intelligence. The line officer, untrained in the art of questioning and lacking the time to "soften" the prisoner, too often resorts to intimidation or torture.[156]

The prohibition on coercion does not tie the hands of the skilled interrogator. He can exploit the understandable fears of the prisoner through a variety of standard psychological techniques of interrogation. As one scholar has put it: "Article 17 . . . does not protect the prisoner against the wiles and cunning of enemy interrogators."[157] There are no international "Miranda" rules, and the captor has no duty under the convention to reassure, calm, or put the enemy prisoner at ease.

[152] E.g., common Article 3; Article 12, GWS; Article 12, GWS (Sea); Article 16, POW; Article 13 (GC).

[153] Article 12, GWS and GWS (Sea).

[154] Article 19, POW.   [155] Ibid.

[156] Moreover, the officer is probably unfamiliar with the native language. The U.S. Army trains its soldiers to segregate prisoners and send them to the rear immediately so that trained interrogators can question them.

[157] Glod and Smith, Interrogation Under the 1949 Prisoners of War Convention, 21 MIL. L. REV. 148 (1963).

D. THE CLAIM TO BAR HUMANITARIAN RELIEF

Humanitarian relief efforts are not new. During the 18th-century wars between France and England, Samuel Johnson organized a committee in London to supply clothing to French prisoners of war held in England.[158] What is new is the capacity of the international community to mobilize large-scale sustained relief efforts. The United Nations and the International Committee of the Red Cross maintain trained staffs and can tap substantial resources. The Red Cross, particularly, can draw upon its considerable experience in organizing and carrying out relief efforts.[159] A host of other private organizations such as church groups also run humanitarian relief programs and often participate in joint efforts.[160]

Unfortunately, governments sometimes decline offers of humanitarian relief or diminish its impact by interfering with shipments. The attitude of the Nigerian government during the recent civil war in that country is a case in point. They declared the first executive of the relief effort "persona non grata" after ten months because they felt he favored the Biafrans.[161] They authorized only perilous nighttime flights to rebel-held territory.[162] They insisted that flights to Biafra land at the Uli airfield, which

[158] Such efforts are seldom popular.

[159] E.g., *Relief in 1967*, 8 INT'L. REV. OF THE RED CROSS 407-15 (Aug. 1968).

[160] Freymond, *Aid to the Victims of the Civil War in Nigeria*, 10 INT'L. REV. OF THE RED CROSS 65, 76-77 (Feb. 1970).

[161] *Help to War Victims in Nigeria*, 9 INT'L. REV. OF THE RED CROSS 353, 356 (July 1969).

[162] *Id.* at 355. The Nigerian air force had no night fighters but did use anti-aircraft guns. As guns were flown into Biafra under cover of darkness, government forces were apt to shoot at anything in the air.

Biafra used for military purposes. Biafran authorities refused to permit the neutralization of the base.[163] When
Biafrans and federal authorities finally agreed upon a
neutral base, Nigerian pilots strafed it.[164] An ICRC DC-
7B flying to Biafra was shot down on 5 June 1969, and
the ICRC felt obliged to suspend further relief flights for
several weeks.[165] The Nigerian government insisted on
inspecting shipments.[166] It would not permit the ICRC to
send food through a land corridor, which the head of the
relief operation in Biafra insisted was necessary if adequate foodstuffs were to be supplied.[167]

Countries other than the Nigerian federal government
blocked relief efforts. On several occasions the government of Equatorial Guinea, from whose Santa Isabel base
the ICRC flew its relief planes to Biafra, jeopardized the
airlift. It forbade transportation of fuel that the ICRC
used to generate electricity in its hospitals and to run the
trucks delivering food and medicine.[168] It once forbade
any flights at all for two weeks.[169]

The attitude of the federal government was understandable if not commendable. In the first place, it was
legitimately concerned that rebel supporters might conceal military supplies in the relief shipments. Secondly, it
feared that the relief supplies would strengthen the rebels
and thereby prolong their resistance. In an internal con-

[163] *Help to War Victims in Nigeria*, 8 INT'L. REV. OF THE RED
CROSS 516, 517 (Oct. 1968).

[164] *Help to War Victims in Nigeria*, 8 INT'L. REV. OF THE RED
CROSS 455, 461 (Sept. 1968).

[165] *Help to War Victims in Nigeria, supra* n. 159 at 353.

[166] Freymond, *supra* n. 158 at 67.

[167] *Help to War Victims in Nigeria, supra* n. 161 at 518.

[168] *Help to War Victims in Nigeria*, 10 INT'L. REV. OF THE RED
CROSS 81, 84 (Feb. 1969).

[169] *Id.* at 86.

flict it is difficult to ascertain whether one is feeding an innocent civilian or a soldier. A wounded soldier whom an ICRC medical team heals may return to the battlefront. For all these difficulties, starvation cannot be recognized as a legitimate means of waging war even though the Tribunal in the High Command Case held:

"A belligerent commander may lawfully lay siege a place controlled by the enemy and endeavour by a process of isolation to cause its surrender. The propriety of attempting to reduce it by starvation is not questioned. Hence the cutting off of every source of sustenance from without is deemed legitimate. It is said that the commander of a besieged place expels the non-combatants, in order to lessen the number of those who consume his stock of provisions, it is lawful, though an extreme measure, to drive them back, so as to hasten the surrender."[170]

The Applicable Law Article 3 does not oblige the warring factions in an internal conflict to accept or permit humanitarian relief. It does, however, permit "[a]n impartial body, such as the International Committee of the Red Cross [to] offer its services to the Parties to the conflict." The draftsmen undoubtedly assumed that a party that accepted such an offer would respect the Red Cross symbol and its personnel because Article 3 does not specifically require respect for the emblem, Red Cross hospitals, or Red Cross personnel. Yet some states have agreed to Red Cross efforts at the organization's own peril. Red Cross hospitals have been attacked and doctors slain. Consequently, national societies have often hesitated to act.[171]

[170] *The German High Command Trial, supra* n. 95 at 84. See Mayer, *Starvation as a Weapon*, CHEMICAL AND BIOLOGICAL WARFARE 76 (S. Rose ed. 1968).

[171] Veuthey, *supra* n. 115 at 416.

Even under the broader rules of the Geneva Conventions, states have not obligated themselves to accept offers of humanitarian assistance. Several Convention provisions nevertheless subsume the compatibility of private relief efforts with Convention obligations. Common Article 9 of the Geneva Conventions, for example, states: "The provisions of the present Convention constitute no obstacle to the humanitarian activities which the International Committee of the Red Cross or any other impartial humanitarian organization may, subject to the consent of the Parties to the conflict concerned, undertake for the protection of prisoners of war and for their relief."[172] This provision expands Article 88 of the 1929 Geneva Conventions, which limited the right of humanitarian initiative to the International Red Cross. The Hague Regulations of 1907 also permitted approved relief agencies to carry out their charitable activities, and the ICRC during World War I opened a Prisoners of War Agency and sent delegates to inspect internment camps.[173] The right of humanitarian initiative is thus a well-established principle and codified in prior international agreements based on past practice.

The rules governing the kind of relief a charitable group may offer, the persons whom it may aid, and the procedures by which it dispenses assistance are less clear. Since the present Conventions mention the Red Cross in connection with a number of specific humanitarian responsibilities,[174] any initiative in one of those areas would be legitimate. Beyond that Pictet categorizes authorized activities into three kinds: (1) representations, interven-

[172] It is Art. 10 in the Civilian Convention.
[173] J. Pictet, III. COMMENTARY ON THE GENEVA CONVENTIONS 104 (1960).
[174] *Id.* at 106.

tions, suggestions, and practical measures affecting the protection accorded under the Convention; (2) the sending of medical and other personnel and equipment; and (3) the sending and distribution of relief (foodstuffs, clothing, and medicaments).[175] The only test is whether the activity is "purely humanitarian in character."[176] The concept of appropriate relief has gone far beyond Article 24 of the 1909 London Declaration, which declared that food, clothing, clothing material, and footwear suitable for military use were conditional rather than absolute contraband. Unfortunately, one man's humanitarianism may be another's political maneuvering; and even the ICRC has been accused of favoritism.

Pictet implies that eligible recipients include all those to whom the Conventions are applicable. That criterion, broad as it is, may still be too narrow. There are unfortunate gaps in Convention coverage;[177] and the range of conflicts to which it is applicable is, as we have seen, uncertain. The Civilian Convention, for example, often refers only to children, expectant mothers, and the wounded and sick. They are not likely to constitute the bulk of any civilian population. Scholars who support the right of humanitarian intervention built into the norm a shock-the-conscience test: intervention was justified only when the target state violated some minimum international law standard.[178] It would seem that any group whose human

[175] *Id.* at 108.   [176] *Id.* at 107.

[177] See Bond, *The Protection of Non-Combatants in Guerrilla Conflicts*, 12 W&M L. REV. 787 (1971).

[178] One example of humanitarian intervention was the joint Belgian-American airlift in the Congo, where the rebels held as hostages two thousand Europeans whose hearts they threatened to wear as fetishes and with whose skin they vowed to clothe themselves.

rights are endangered is a legitimate object of humanitarian concern.

Disputes over the appropriate nature of relief as the eligibility of recipients have not usually proved insurmountable as have, too often, questions about procedures for supplying the aid. Time and again the ICRC effort to help war victims in Nigeria collapsed because the parties quibbled over where, when, and how goods were to be shipped. The frustrating fact is that states may take away with the left hand what they give with the right by permitting in principle humanitarian relief but insisting upon procedures that negate its impact.

In an international conflict a state may blockade its enemy. In an internal conflict a state retains its right to inspect shipments, regulate commerce, or close its ports. It, too, may blockade rebel-held territory, as the Union did during the American Civil War. International law does not permit a state to cut off all shipments to the blockaded country, however. Article 23 of the Civilian Convention guarantees free passage for humanitarian shipments.[179] The right of free passage is couched in very

[179] Article 23 states:

"Each High Contracting Party shall allow the free passage of all consignments of medical and hospital stores and objects necessary for religious worship intended only for civilians of another High Contracting Party, even if the latter is its adversary. It shall likewise permit the free passage of all consignments of essential foodstuffs, clothing and tonics intended for children under fifteen, expectant mothers and maternity cases.

"The obligation of a High Contracting Party to allow the free passage of the consignments indicated in the preceding paragraph is subject to the condition that this Party is satisfied that there are no serious reasons for fearing:

"(a) that the consignments may be diverted from their destination,

"(b) that the control may not be effective, or

restrictive language. First, the article limits the kind of relief. Only "medical and hospital stores," "objects necessary for religious worship," and "essential foodstuffs, clothing, and tonics" are entitled to free passage. Second, the article limits the persons entitled to relief—in the first instance, to civilians; in the second instance, to children under fifteen and expectant mothers. This limitation cannot be read to exclude the sick and wounded, since Article 38 of GWS (Sea) authorizes free passage for such consignments.[180] Third, the article conditions free passage of such limited relief to such limited categories of persons on several factors, the chief being that no "definite advantage" will "accrue to the military efforts or economy of the enemy" upon receipt of the goods. Pictet urges a reasonable interpretation of the "definite advantage" condition: "It will be agreed, generally speaking, that the contribution represented by authorized consignments should be limited: in the majority of cases, such consign-

---

"(c) that a definite advantage may accrue to the military efforts or economy of the enemy through the substitution of the above-mentioned consignments for goods which would otherwise be provided or produced by the enemy or through the release of such material, services or facilities as would otherwise be required for the production of such goods.

"The Power which allows the passage of the consignments indicated in the first paragraph of this Article may make such permission conditional on the distribution to the persons benefited thereby being made under the local supervision of the Protecting Powers.

"Such consignments shall be forwarded as rapidly as possible, and the Power which permits their free passage shall have the right to prescribe the technical arrangements under which such passage is allowed."

[180] J. Pictet, IV. COMMENTARY GENEVA CONVENTIONS 180 (1958).

ments will be hardly sufficient to meet the most urgent needs and relieve the most pitiable distress; it is hardly likely, therefore, that they would represent assistance on such a scale that the military and economic position of a country was improved to any appreciable extent."[181]

The article also gives the blockading power the right to supervise shipments: "the power which permits their free passage shall have the right to prescribe the technical arrangements under which passage is allowed." How else could the blockading power quiet its fears "that the control [might] not be effective." The blockading power may, of course, rely upon a disinterested organization such as the International Committee of the Red Cross to supervise distribution. Still, it will wish to set the times, places, and means of delivery. These arrangements, which are necessary to insure the safety of the personnel distributing the goods, as well as to protect the interests of the blockading power, should not negate the impelling requirement that "[s]uch consignments shall be forwarded as rapidly as possible."

[181] *Id.* at 182.

CHAPTER IV

Recommendations: Proposed Revisions in the Law of War Applicable to Internal Conflict

A. SUBSTANTIVE REFORMS

International law can responsively order internal conflict only if it, first, provides uniform rules for the conduct of military operations therein and, second, provides rules for the classification and treatment of non-combatants. Although the 1949 Geneva Diplomatic Conference rejected the notion that all the laws of war should apply to internal conflict, the International Committee of the Red Cross and others have recently proposed draft protocols that would extend a part of the law of war to internal conflict. As early as 1956 the ICRC published a draft convention entitled "Rules for the Limitation of the Dangers Incurred by the Civilian Population in Time of War,"[1] which recapitulated and modernized much of the Hague law and made it applicable to all armed conflict, internal as well as international.[2] Governments generally ignored the proposal, and the ICRC has recently suggested several modifications that it hopes will "make the medicine go down."

The ICRC presented to the 1972 Geneva Conference a draft "Additional Protocol to Article 3 Common to the Four Geneva Conventions of August 12, 1949,"[3] which included a chapter on the protection and care of the sick and wounded. The United States proposed a "Conven-

---

[1] See Appendix A.   [2] Article 2(b).   [3] See Appendix B.

tion Relative to the Protection of Human Rights in Internal Armed Conflict."[4] The Canadian delegation to the
1971 Geneva Conference submitted a draft "Protocol to
the Geneva Conventions of 1949 Relative to Conflicts
not International in Character,"[5] which incorporates the
key humanitarian provisions of Geneva law. Other significant proposals include the "Minimum Rules for Non-
delinquent Detainees,"[6] drafted by the Medico-Legal
Commission of Monaco and the Standard Minimum
Rules for Delinquent Detainees,[7] produced by the United
Nations Economic and Social Council. These proposals
are all based on the same fundamental humanitarian
spirit that permeates such documents as the Universal
Declaration of Human Rights and the Covenant of Civil
and Political Rights.

The urgent need now is to analyze and integrate these
various proposals. In many cases they deal with a particular subject in virtually identical language; in others, with
markedly divergent language. Some address themselves
to Hague problems; others, to Geneva problems. Even
taken all together, they do not mend all the gaps in humanitarian protection for those caught up in internal conflicts. What follows is a coherent critique. It is an attempt
to view these proposals from a broader perspective—one
that encompasses the entire range of law of war problems
characteristic of internal conflicts.

1. *Limitations Should Be Imposed on the
Participant's Conduct of Hostilities*

Drafting a uniform set of rules for the conduct of military operations in internal conflicts is difficult even

---

[4] See Appendix C.   [5] See Appendix D.   [6] See Appendix E.
[7] *Cf.* J. Carey, U.N. PROTECTION OF CIVIL AND POLITICAL RIGHTS
106 (1970).

though there is wide agreement on two principles: (1) that the civilian population should be spared insofar as possible the sufferings of war and (2) that attacks cannot be launched against them as such.[8] The difficulty is that in internal conflicts there is no sharp distinction between those taking part in the hostilities and members of the civilian population, and a convention that premises its provisions on the viability of such a distinction will inevitably leave major gaps or prove unenforceable. Nevertheless, even in these wars the law must continue to distinguish between what a soldier can do, for example, to the enemy firing a weapon at him and what he can do to an old man plowing a rice paddy. The customary distinc-

[8] ". . . the United Nations itself—and, consequently, the member states—has repeatedly expressed the idea that the civilian population is not a lawful objective. Three important resolutions must be mentioned here: Resolution 1653 (XVI) of 24 November 1961 on the legality of the use of nuclear weapons, which in its preamble deduces the illegality of these weapons from the prohibition against unnecessary human suffering and from the fact that these weapons cause indiscriminate suffering and destruction to mankind; Resolution 2162 B (XXI) of 5 December 1966 on chemical and bacteriological weapons (the question of the Geneva Protocol), which states in its preamble that weapons of mass destruction are 'incompatible with the accepted norms of civilization' and asserts 'that the strict observance of the rules of international law on the conduct of warfare is in the interest of maintaining these standards of civilization'; and finally, Resolution 2444 (XXIII) of 19 December 1968 with respect to human rights in armed conflicts, which 'adopts as its own' resolution XXVIII adopted by the XXth Conference of the Red Cross (Vienna, 1965) and which reiterates the following principles: the choice of means for injuring the enemy is not unlimited, attacks against the civilian population as such are prohibited, and a distinction must be made at all times between combatants and the civilian population. . . ." D. Bindschedler-Robert, THE LAW OF ARMED CONFLICT, 19 (1971).

tion between combatants and non-combatants remains valid because it is functional: it defines the attitude and the action of one party to the other at the moment of their contact with each other. For instance, if "Charlie" is firing at an American soldier, he is a combatant; if he is waving a white flag, he is a non-combatant. The cruel battlefield reality of self-defense and survival dictates that a soldier can act differently toward a combatant and a non-combatant. The rules must be so fashioned as to enhance the soldier's effectiveness vis-à-vis the combatant enemy without unnecessarily endangering the non-combatant, whether he be friend or foe.

a. USE OF WEAPONS SHOULD BE RESTRICTED

The 1956 ICRC draft thus bans only those weapons "whose harmful effects—resulting in particular from the dissemination of incendiary, chemical, bacteriological, radioactive or other agents—could spread to an unforeseen degree of escape, either in space or time, from the control of those who employ them, thus endangering the civilian population."[9] This does not necessarily constitute an absolute ban on fire, chemical, biological, or atomic weapons; nor should it be interpreted as such. It does reflect the widely held view, reaffirmed by the International Law Institute at Edinburgh in 1969, that "international law prohibits the use of all weapons which by their nature affect indiscriminately both military objectives and non-military objects . . . or [are] otherwise uncontrollable."[10]

But the effects of some of these weapons are controllable. Moreover, although the 1968 Teheran Interna-

[9] Article 14.
[10] Para. 7, Resolution 1, Fifth Commission (9 September 1969).

tional Conference on Human Rights declared that "the use of chemical and biological warfare, including napalm bombing, erodes human rights and engenders counter-brutality,"[11] some of these weapons may inflict less suffering than do ordinary weapons. An incapacitating tear gas could, for example, render an enemy force temporarily helpless without permanent injury to anyone. The United Nations Secretariat concedes that chemical weapons could be used within the zone of contact of opposing forces; against military targets such as airfields, barracks, supply depots, and rail centers well behind the battle area itself; or against targets that have no immediate connection with military operations, such as centers of population, farm land, and water supplies. The circumstances in which they could be used within a zone of contact are many and varied—for example, to achieve a rapid and surprise advantage against a poorly trained, ill-equipped military force that lacked chemical protective equipment; to overcome troops in dug-outs, foxholes, or fortifications where they would be otherwise protected against fragmenting weapons and high explosives; to remove foliage, by means of chemical herbicides so as to improve visibility and to open up lines of fire, and to prevent ambush; to create barriers of contaminated land on or in the rear of the battlefield to impede or channel movement; or to slow an enemy advance by forcing them to use protective clothing and equipment.[12] While their use in any of the above circumstances might endanger a portion of the civilian population, it need not.

[11] See Chapter III, FINAL ACT OF THE INTERNATIONAL CONFERENCE ON HUMAN RIGHTS, A/Conf. 32/41 (1968).

[12] United Nations Office of Public Information, *The Dangers of Chemical and Bacteriological (Biological) Weapons* 7-8 (1969).

Since some of these weapons have legitimate military uses, it would probably be futile to ban them entirely. It is, moreover, unrealistic to expect that nations would agree in the context of a convention on internal conflict to more restrictive provisions than are presently embodied in international agreements. Nations are more likely to limit their use of nuclear, chemical, and biological weapons in separate treaties—a fact that the ICRC implicitly notes in the disclaimer that the Article 14 restriction is "[w]ithout prejudice to the present or future prohibition of certain specific weapons. . . ."[13] Finally, these are not the weapons most frequently used in internal conflicts. Nuclear and biological weapons have never been used, and chemical weapons have been used rarely (though that use has been accompanied by great publicity and has occasioned great concern). There is little to be gained by outlawing weapons that have never been and are not likely to be used in internal conflict while permitting the unregulated use of common but deadly weapons.

Consider, for example, punji sticks. Punji sticks are wooden poles whose ends have been sharpened to a point and covered with excrement. They are placed in a hole that is then covered with ground camouflage. It gives way as soon as someone steps on it. The unlucky man plunges onto the poles, which pierce him. He may be impaled and slowly die. Even if he is rescued, serious infection sets in, causing great suffering and perhaps death. Punji sticks have taken a far greater toll in the Vietnam war than have nuclear or biological weapons. And yet the ICRC draft does not outlaw such weapons.

[13] The Salt talks and the new draft convention on bacteriological weapons are contemporary proof that the greatest hope for limiting weapons use lies in multilateral treaties negotiated among the major powers.

That is why it is to be regretted that the ICRC draft on air bombardment does not incorporate the "unnecessary suffering" standard, which is the basis for most of the present weapons law. The ICRC does correct this defect in its draft protocol to Article 3 by including the unnecessary suffering prohibition in Article 18(2). The unnecessary suffering standard protects combatants as much or more than it does non-combatants, of course; and so long as the sole aim is to insulate non-combatants from the effects of blind weapons, its omission is understandable. Difficult as it is to apply the standard, it is an explicit recognition that "[t]he right of belligerents to adopt means of injuring the enemy is not unlimited."[14] One could even add to the general language—"it is expressly forbidden to employ arms, projectiles, or material calculated to cause unnecessary suffering"—a non-exhaustive list of particular illegal uses. In this way one might specifically prohibit weapons such as punji sticks, as well as the most objectionable uses of fire and chemical weapons. For example, the convention could forbid the use of napalm against troops or individuals in the open. It could also forbid the destruction of food stores or farming areas by herbicides where their destructive impact impinges largely upon the non-combatant population.[15] Professor Westing pointed out that in Vietnam "enormous amounts of food must be destroyed in order to create a hardship for the Viet Cong."[16] He added: "In fact, classified studies

[14] Article 22 of the Hague Regulations. The same language is repeated in Article 1 of the ICRC draft on air bombardment.

[15] In its alternative proposals for Article 16 of the draft Article 3 protocol, the ICRC would insulate "objects indispensable to the survival of the civilian population." The U.S. draft sidesteps these controversial questions but at least includes a paraphrase of Article 23 of the Hague Regulations.

[16] *New York Times*, July 12, 1971, at 27 col. 3.

performed for and by the U.S. in 1967 and 1968 revealed that food destruction has had no significant impact on the enemy soldier. Civilians, in contrast, did and do suffer. Estimates in these studies varied between 10 and 100 for how many civilians have to be denied food in order to deny it to one guerrilla."[17] The imposition of such unnecessary suffering should be forbidden. If parties cannot restrict the flow of food to the civilian population through a blockade, they should not be able to accomplish the same result through the use of herbicides. A flat prohibition on starvation as a weapon of war is needed.

b. CHOICE OF TARGETS SHOULD BE LIMITED

The civilian population has suffered far more greatly from indiscriminate aerial bombardment than it has from the misuse of weapons systems. Not surprisingly, the ICRC draft on air bombardment devotes ten articles to bombardment, only two to weapons. The inadequate state—some would say absence—of international law governing aerial bombardment makes it difficult if not impossible to draw analogies from present Conventions. The ICRC proposals are not without precedent, however. They reflect a mixed parentage: the draft Rules of Aerial Bombardment, the practice of states, the principles underlying the law of land bombardment, and the insight of scholars.

First, the draft rules flatly forbid area bombardment: a single attack upon an area "including several military objectives at a distance from one another where elements of the civilian population or dwellings, are situated in between the said objectives."[18] Even when attacking a mili-

[17] *Id.*
[18] Article 10. Article 24(3) of the 1923 draft rules also forbade area bombardment.

tary objective "in towns and other places with a large civilian population,"[19] the bombadier must conduct the strike "with the greatest degree of precision."[20]

Second, the draft rules, while permitting strategic bombing, specifically confine legitimate targets to "military objectives."[21] Even targets that fall within one of the enumerated categories of military objectives cannot be considered such "where their total or partial military destruction, in the circumstances ruling at the time, offers no military advantage."[22] The draft rules do not, as do the rules of land bombardment, specifically exempt some buildings (such as churches, schools, hospitals, or museums) from attack. Rather, they identify permissible military targets.

Clearly, the civilian population is not a military target; and, third, the draft rules bar "[a]ttacks directed against the civilian population."[23] The frequent—and reprehensible—tactic of terror bombing is thus forbidden. The rules nevertheless recognize that "should members of the civilian population . . . be within or in close proximity to a military objective they must accept the risks resulting from an attack directed against that objective."[24]

[19] Article 9.   [20] Ibid.

[21] Article 7. Article 24(2) of the 1923 draft rules limited military objectives to "military forces; military works; military establishments or depots; factories constituting important and well-known centres engaged in the manufacture of arms, ammunition or distinctively military supplies; lines of communication or transportation used for military purposes."

[22] Id. The same principle was embodied in Article 24(1) of the 1923 draft rules.

[23] Article 6. Article 22 of the 1923 draft rules prohibited "aerial bombardment for the purpose of terrorizing the civilian population."

[24] Article 6. Cf. Article 24(4) of the 1923 draft rules.

Generally accepted customary international law has always permitted incidental injury to the civilian population. The draft rules carefully circumscribe this exception, however. The ban on area bombardment and the consequent emphasis upon precision strikes have already been noted. If the "person responsible for ordering or launching an attack" can choose one among several objectives, any of whose destruction would render the same military advantage, "he is required to select the one, an attack on which involves the least danger for the civilian population."[25] Furthermore, he must "refrain from the attack if . . . the loss and destruction [inflicted upon the civilian population] would be disproportionate to the military advantage anticipated."[26] He must insure that "no losses or damage are caused to the civilian population" or "are at least reduced to a minimum."[27]

Fourth, the draft rules seek further to protect the civilian population by imposing warning requirements. Article 8(c) states that "whenever the circumstances allow . . . the civilian population in jeopardy" should be warned "to enable it to take shelter."[28] It is not clear what "circumstances" would preclude warning, though one would surely be that the warning would alert enemy forces who could then frustrate the attack. In most internal conflicts the government retains air superiority and can attack

[25] Article 8.   [26] *Ibid.*

[27] Article 10. The 1923 draft rules did not impose such stringent duties. Nevertheless, Article 25 ordered the commander "to spare insofar as possible buildings dedicated to public worship, art, science, or charitable purposes, historic monuments, hospital ships, hospitals, and other places where the sick and wounded are collected. . . ." The language was lifted almost verbatim from Article 27 of the Hague Regulations.

[28] The 1923 draft rules did not require any warning.

rebel areas from the air with impunity. In those "circumstances," excusing a failure to warn on such grounds sounds disingenuous. It becomes a subterfuge behind which the government may strike directly at the civilian population.

Fifth, and finally, the draft rules encourage the parties to broaden the categories of exempt targets. They may declare "open towns."[29] The rules carefully define the "conditions" that a town must "satisfy" to be declared an open town and authorizes verification inspections. "In order to safeguard the civilian population from the dangers that might result from the destruction of engineering works or installations . . . the States of Parties concerned are invited" to agree upon their immunity where the installations are "intended essentially for peaceful purposes" or have no "connection with the conduct of military operations."[30] Parties to a conflict are always free to conclude such agreements, of course. They rarely do, and it is doubtful that these provisions will prove any more effective in inducing wartime agreements than have similar provisions in current treaties. Parties to the Geneva Conventions have never, for example, heeded the Article 3 suggestion that they "endeavor to bring into force, by means of special agreements, all or part of the other provisions of the present Convention."

The ICRC has included a number of target limitations in its draft protocol to Article 3 so that the protection of the civilian population would not necessarily depend on adoption of the 1956 Draft Rules. Chapter IV of the

[29] Article 16. The 1923 draft rules did not speak of "open towns," but Article 26 authorized the creation of "zones of protection" for historical monuments.

[30] Article 17.

draft protocol prohibits terror bombing, excludes as legitimate targets "objects indispensable to the survival of the
civilian population," and requires where possible warn-
ings.[31]

c. other restraints should be imposed

The non-combatant population may suffer as much or
more from the participant's irresponsible conduct of
ground operations as from their indiscriminate aerial
bombardment. Indeed, many common battlefield practices victimize the non-combatant population far more
than they do combatants, and their prohibition in the
Hague Regulations underscores the common purpose it
shares with the Geneva Conventions: protection of non-
combatants. Fortunately, the Canadian draft incorporates
some of the most basic Hague restrictions. It reaffirms
the Article 3 prohibition against taking hostages.[32] It also
forbids pillage and "reprisals against persons and property. . . ."[33] The U.S. draft includes similar prohibitions.[34]

The Hague prohibitions on pillage are absolute. While
other provisions permit the destruction of property when
required by military necessity, it can never justify pillage.
In other words, the draftsmen weighed whatever military
benefit might accrue from pillage against its impact on
the population and concluded that it should never be
permitted. It is difficult to see why the law should strike
a different balance in internal conflict. Although indiscriminate looting may demoralize the pillaged population,
it may also demoralize the soldiers. They may degenerate
into "hyenas of the battlefield." Since a pillaging force
thereby gains no significant military advantage, an absolute prohibition is desirable.

[31] Articles 14-17.   [32] Article 12(1).
[33] Article 12(3).   [34] Article 14.

The Canadian draft also absolutely forbids reprisals. Moreover, it does not limit the ban to "protected" persons or property, as does Article 33 of the Civilian Convention upon which, the draftsmen assure us, they modeled Article 12.[35] The omission is an important one, as earlier discussion has indicated. It means, quite simply, that reprisals are outlawed. A party to the conflict may henceforth never resort to them, whatever the opposing party's conduct. The draft thus goes far beyond present law, which still permits reprisals against unprotected persons and property.

Finally, the Canadian draft imposes, like Article 3, a general requirement of humane treatment "with respect to persons belonging to it or under its control."[36] In amplifying language it includes a prohibition on "medical or scientific experiments not necessitated by the medical treatment of such persons." This specific prohibition, though common to all four Geneva Conventions,[37] is not found in Article 3. While experiments such as those conducted by German scientists upon Jews in World War II have fortunately not plagued internal conflicts, one can scarcely object to the inclusion of the prohibition.

One other provision, not found in either draft but that should be included, is the Secretary-General's proposal for the establishment of safety zones.[38] These zones might, for example, embrace farm areas or population relocation centers. The idea of safety zones is not new, of course;[39] but their use in internal conflicts could minimize destruc-

[35] Explanatory Notes—Draft Protocol Presented by the Canadian Expert, 3 *Doc. CE Com.* II/7 (27 May 1971).

[36] Article 13.   [37] Articles 12, 12, 13(1), 32 respectively.

[38] Para. 45-87, RESPECT FOR HUMAN RIGHTS IN ARMED CONFLICT, REPORT OF THE SECRETARY-GENERAL Doc. A/8052 (18 Sept. 1970).

[39] *Cf.* Articles 14 and 15, GC.

tion and suffering. Such zones would facilitate humanitarian relief efforts. The general guidelines for the establishment of "open towns" would serve equally well as criteria for the creation of safety zones. It is also crucial to emphasize that the creation of special zones does not reduce the parties' obligation to conduct military operations responsibly elsewhere. The U.S. draft encourages and authorizes the parties to agree on the establishment of safety zones.[40]

None of the drafts clearly outlaws the use of terror tactics, though several proscribe the use of terror. Difficult as they would be to proscribe entirely, inclusion of the Hague prohibition on treacherously wounding "individuals belonging to the hostile army or nation"[41] as in the U.S. draft would be helpful. Any convention should also forbid assassination.

The ICRC draft, when merged with Chapter 4 of the Canadian draft, would nevertheless provide substantial protection to the non-combatant population in internal conflicts. The minimal restraints embodied in the drafts would not impede either side from effectively waging war. They would, however, reduce those excesses which inflict great suffering upon the non-combatant population without achieving any proportionate military advantage.

2. *The Law Should Protect Non-Combatants*

a. THE NEW RULES SHOULD PROVIDE FOR THE DETERMINATION OF THE STATUS OF VARIOUS PARTICIPANTS IN INTERNAL CONFLICTS

A wide variety of individuals and groups participate in internal conflicts in a wide variety of ways. Since the

---

[40] Article 16.

[41] Article 23(b) of the Hague; Article 14(b) of the U.S. draft.

humanitarian rights to which they are entitled should depend upon the nature of their participation, international law should establish appropriate categories—statuses—that reflect the different kinds of participation. Traditionally, international law has identified two broad groups of participants in internal conflict: combatants and the civilian population.

The traditional categorization has two major defects. The first is that it is often difficult to distinguish between combatant rebel forces and the civilian population. Men, women, and children who ostensibly appear civilians often assist guerrilla forces by providing food, shelter, and/or information. Or they may aid rebel forces by simply refusing to cooperate with government authorities or giving them misinformation. These people may act out of fear or sympathy or even indifference, but they do thereby aid rebel forces. Traditional international law never identified the point at which the civilian passes beyond the pale of "innocence"; but surely at some point along the continuum of increasing involvement in the rebellion he becomes more a rebel than a civilian.

And what of the "Sunshine Patriots"—loyal citizens by day but rebels during the hours of darkness? These patriots hide behind the mask of civilian innocence. While this disguise makes the government job of identifying and apprehending the rebels much more difficult, it also greatly endangers the civilian population because the government may feel compelled to cast a broad net. Unable to distinguish between rebels and the civilian population, it may lump them all into one. The result is indiscriminate bombardment, mass arrests, searches, detentions, and forced resettlement programs. Regrettably, it is sometimes difficult to tell the sheep from the goats.

The second defect in the traditional categorization is

that it ignores major differences among participants within each category. When the International Committee of the Red Cross asked experts whether international humanitarian law protected combatants in international conflicts, it specified twelve different classes of combatant: "(1) regular armed forces of the established government; (2) rebel armed forces; (3) mercenaries; (4) infiltrators; (5) governmental special anti-guerrilla forces; (6) guerrilleros complying with Article 4 of the POW Convention; (7) guerrilleros not complying with some of the conditions of that article; (8) guerrilleros operating on the territory of neutral states; (9) deserters and 'transfugees'; (10) saboteurs; (11) spies and informers; (12) terrorists."[42]

Similarly, the ICRC divided the civilian population into nine groups: "(1) political opponents; (2) senior politicians and civil servants; (3) those providing administrative services; (4) police; (5) displaced and resettled persons; (6) population subject to intermittent control by the guerrilla forces; (7) population constantly subject to control by guerrilla forces; (8) persons passively (not denouncing) or actively (transport, shelter, information, etc.) assisting guerrilla forces; (9) persons refusing to obey guerrilla forces."[43]

Regardless of whether one subscribes to the particular classification scheme (and, as I shall presently show, I think it is seriously flawed), the International Committee has conclusively demonstrated that sheep and goats do not constitute the bulk of the herd.

There is, however, as great a danger in drawing too

[42] International Committee of the Red Cross, REPORT ON THE CONSULTATION OF EXPERTS CONCERNING NON-INTERNATIONAL CONFLICT AND GUERRILLA WARFARE 18 (1970).
[43] *Id.* at 28 and 6-9.

many lines too finely as in drawing too few too crudely. Sabotage, spying, treason, and terrorism may well be defined, for example, in separate criminal statutes and different punishments meted out to the perpetrators thereof. But there is little reason why the conditions of their detention or their rights to and in a judicial proceeding should vary. Similarly, the government's regular forces and its special guerrilla forces, while of course performing different military tasks, should be subject to the same laws and entitled to the same rights. The need is to define those broad categories of persons entitled to the same or similar treatment.

The little-known classification procedures used by Allied forces in Vietnam provide a good starting point for discussion of possible classification schemes.[44] Generally,

[44] ANNEX A—*MACV DIR* 381-46 (27 December 1967) states: CRITERIA FOR CLASSIFICATION AND DISPOSITION OF DETAINEES

1. PURPOSE. To establish criteria for the classification of detainees which will facilitate rapid, precise screening, and proper disposition of detainees.

2. DEFINITIONS.

a. *Detainees. Persons who have been detained but whose final status has not yet been determined. Such persons are entitled to humane treatment in accordance with the provisions of the Geneva Conventions.*

b. Classification. The systematic assignment of a detainee in either the PW or Non-Prisoner of War category.

c. *Prisoners of War. All detainees who qualify* in accordance with paragraph 4a, below.

d. Non-Prisoners of War. All detainees who qualify in accordance with paragraph 4b, below.

3. CATEGORIES OF FORCES.

a. *Viet Cong (VC) Main Force (MF).* Those VC military units which are directly subordinate to Central Office for South Vietnam (COSVN), a Front, Viet Cong military region, or subregion. Many of the VC units contain NVA personnel.

the aim in Vietnam was to separate from all others those
foreign soldiers and domestic citizens who took up arms
against the government. The former were treated as
POW's even though many could not meet the Geneva
Convention criteria for the POW status. "All others" were
further subdivided into three groups: civil defendants,
returnees, and innocent civilians. Those classified as in-

---

b. *Viet Cong (VC) Local Force (LF)*. Those VC military units
which are directly subordinated to a provincial or district party
committee and which normally operate only within a specified
VC province or district.

c. *North Vietnamese Army (NVA) Unit*. A unit formed,
trained and designated by North Vietnam as an NVA unit, and
composed completely or primarily of North Vietnamese.

d. *Irregulars*. Organized forces composed of guerrilla, self-
defense, and secret self-defense elements subordinate to village
and hamlet level VC organizations. These forces perform a wide
variety of missions in support of VC activities, and provide a
training and mobilization base for maneuver and combat support
forces.

(1) *Guerrillas*. Full-time forces organized into squads and
platoons which do not necessarily remain in their home village
or hamlet. Typical missions for guerrillas include propaganda,
protection of village party committees, terrorist, and sabotage
activities.

(2) *Self-Defense Force*. A VC paramilitary structure responsible for the defense of hamlet and village in VC controlled
areas. These forces do not have their home area, and they perform their duties on a part-time basis. Duties consist of con-
structing fortifications, serving as hamlet guards, and defending
home areas.

(3) *Secret Self-Defense Force*. A clandestine VC organization which performs the same general function in Government
of Vietnam (GVN) controlled areas. Their operations involve
intelligence collection, as well as sabotage and propaganda activities.

nocent civilians were promptly released and returned to their homes. Returnees—those previously disaffected who agree to support the government—were sent to Chieu Hoi centers, where they were rehabilitated. Civil defendants were prosecuted in the local Vietnamese courts for whatever crime they were alleged to have committed.

---

4. CLASSIFICATION OF DETAINEES.

a. Detainees will be *classified PW's when determined to be qualified under one of the following categories:*

(1) A member of one of the units listed in paragraph 3a, b, or c, above.

(2) A member of one of the units listed in paragraph 3d, above, who is captured while actually engaging in combat or a belligerent act under arms, other than an act of terrorism, sabotage, or spying.

(3) A member of one of the units listed in paragraph 3d, above who admits or for whom there is proof of his having participated or engaged in combat or a belligerent act under arms other than an act of terrorism, sabotage, or spying.

b. Detainees will be *classified as Non-Prisoners of War when determined to be one of the following categories:*

(1) *Civil Defendants.*

(a) A detainee who is not entitled to PW status but is subject to trial by GVN for offenses against GVN law.

(b) A detainee who is a member of one of the units listed in paragraph 3d, above, and who was detained while not engaged in actual combat or a belligerent act under arms, and there is no proof that the detainee ever participated in actual combat or belligerent act under arms.

(c) A detainee who is suspected of being a spy, saboteur or terrorist.

(2) *Returnees (Hoi Chanh).* All persons regardless of past membership in any of the units listed in paragraph 3, above, who voluntarily submit to GVN control.

(3) *Innocent Civilians.* Persons not members of any units listed in paragraph 3, above, and not suspected of being civil defendants.

On the whole these distinctions make sense. The government has an obvious interest in separating out innocent civilians caught in its nets and returning them to their homes. A brief detention and interrogation, while an inconvenience to the citizen, is not too great an infringement on his rights. It is difficult to see how the government could with any lesser interference ascertain the status of the non-combatant.

At the other polar extreme it is also easy enough to understand why foreign soldiers are treated as POW's. They, of all participants in guerrilla conflicts, fit most neatly into the regular Geneva Convention categories. One of the strengths of the latest ICRC draft is that it provides: "Members of regular armed forces and members of those armed forces which have fulfilled the conditions stipulated in Article 4A(2) [of the POW Convention] shall receive after having fallen into the power of the adversary, a treatment similar to that provided for prisoners of war in the said Convention."[45] While the

---

5. DISPOSITION OF CLASSIFIED DETAINEES.

a. Detainees who have been classified will be processed as follows:

(1) *US captured PW's* and those PW's turned over to the US by FWMAP will be retained in US Military channels until *transferred to the ARVN PW Camp.*

(2) *Non-Prisoners of War* who are *suspected as civil defendants* will be released to the appropriate GVN civil authorities.

(3) *Non-Prisoners of War* who qualify as *returnees* will be transferred to the appropriate Chieu Hoi Center.

(4) *Non-Prisoners of War* determined to be *innocent civilians* will be released and returned to place of capture.

b. Responsibilities and procedures for evacuation and accounting for PW's are prescribed in MACV Directive 190-3 and USARV Regulation 190-2.

[45] Article 25.

government could arguably treat them as spies and saboteurs, policy reasons dictate extending POW status to them. Trying and executing foreign nationals unnecessarily inflames passions and may frustrate the possibility of a negotiated settlement, the usual outcome of these conflicts. The North Vietnamese government, for example, prudently dropped its plans to try U.S. airmen as war criminals when the United States and other countries raised strenuous protests.

The reasonableness of classifying one's own nationals as POW's is less obvious. In most cases those who have taken up arms against their government will have violated its criminal laws and could therefore be tried as common criminals. Most states have adopted such a policy, particularly in the initial stages of the insurgency. There is, however, one advantage to treating captured rebels as POW's: a POW may be interned for the duration of the conflict. Contrariwise, treating all rebel citizens as POW's would arguably preclude an effort like the Chieu Hoi program. But so long as the government is dealing with its own citizens rather than with foreign nationals, the Chieu Hoi program may be defended as an act of amnesty or pardon, powers traditionally held by all governments.

The government should be permitted discretion in choosing among these alternate methods of handling its dissident citizens so long as it treats all humanely. The government cannot be scored for enforcing its criminal laws against those it calls citizens. The citizen-turned-rebel can little complain if his former government takes him at his word, accepts his renunciation of allegiance, and treats him as it would any other foreign enemy. Furthermore, there is no reason why the government must treat all citizens either as POW's or as civil defendants so long as it uses a rational basis for distinguishing those

against whom it pursues the normal criminal process from
those it interns as POW's. In Vietnam, for example, the
government separated its citizens into three groups:
POW's, civil defendants, and returnees. It is important
that the government retain its flexibility in dealing with
rebels. Yet it is also essential that it act within the law.
Thus, Kelley and Pelletier conclude: ". . . a firm yet
flexible system of law is required so as to permit the government to act effectively to meet this threat while at the
same time establishing limits and protections for the nationals of the country to insure their individual rights."[46]

While countries may, as have the U.S. and its allies,
voluntarily adopt classification schemes, nothing in international law presently insures their adoption. Moreover,
a state may adopt a classification scheme considerably
less rational and just than minimum standards of humanity would dictate. While sovereign states should retain
considerable discretion in dealing with their domestic and
foreign enemies, international law must circumscribe
their exercise of an otherwise unfettered discretion. Prisoners of war, returnee, civilian defendant, and innocent
civilian constitute functional categories that wisely reflect
the need to treat different kinds of participants differently.
Since some states object to calling captured nationals
POW's (though not necessarily to treating them as such),
"detained combatant" might prove a more acceptable
name.[47]

[46] Kelley & Pelletier, *Legal Control of Populations in Subversive Warfare*, 5 VA. J. INT'L. L. 175 (1965).
[47] The United States, for example, objected to the use of
"Prisoners of War" in the ICRC draft protocol on care for the
sick and wounded in non-international conflict, as implying that
combatants may have POW status. The objection received unanimous support.

There are two other categories of individuals who deserve particular protection: the sick and wounded, and medical personnel. The sick and wounded may, of course, also fall within one of the other previously enumerated classes and may ultimately derive their rights and obligations from their "other" status; but their medical condition entitles them initially to special treatment. Medical personnel may also fall within other categories; and to the extent that they participate as combatants, for example, they must lose whatever immunity they otherwise enjoy in the discharge of their medical services.

The Canadian draft contains several articles that deal with the problems of the sick and wounded, and the ICRC draft protocol includes seven articles devoted to the same purpose. The U.S. draft has eight articles dealing with protection of the sick and wounded. The Canadian draft singles out the wounded and sick for "particular protection and respect" and provides that they "shall receive the care necessitated by their condition without any adverse distinction" and "with the least possible delay."[48] It imposes the obligation "to search for and collect the wounded and sick" and "to communicate to each other all details on persons who are wounded, sick, or who have died. . . ."[49] Finally, a separate article urges the parties "to conclude local arrangements for the removal [of the sick and wounded] from areas where hostilities are taking place. . . ."[50] Article 7 of the ICRC draft protocol likewise emphasizes that the wounded and sick deserve

[48] Article 2(2). Article 12, the "keystone" provision common to the two Geneva Conventions for the Protection of the Sick and Wounded, embodies the same principles.
[49] Article 3(2). Cf. Articles 16-17, GWS, and 19-20 GWS (Sea).
[50] Article 7.

"special protection and respect," but it further stresses
that military persons who are sick and wounded fall within that category. Although the ICRC draft imposes an
obligation to search for and collect the wounded and
sick, it does not require that the parties communicate information about them. The U.S. draft, like the Canadian
draft, does impose a communication duty.[51]

If the wounded and sick are to be nursed effectively,
those who care for them must also enjoy special protection. The Canadian, ICRC, and U.S. drafts all contain a
provision immunizing any member of the population who
nurses the wounded and sick from molestation or conviction.[52] This is an important provision in the context of
internal conflicts because individuals—peasants, farmers
—will often care for the sick and wounded, particularly
among the guerrillas. Similarly, all three drafts guarantee
medical personnel respect and protection and specify that
"[t]hey shall receive all facilities to discharge their functions and shall not be compelled to perform any work
outside their mission."[53]

The proposed protocols and conventions would also
protect medical establishments and transports from attacks.[54] The language of the respective articles is nearly
identical, but the Canadian draft includes a third para-

[51] Article 6(2).

[52] Article 4(2) in the Canadian draft; Article 7(2) in the
U.S. draft and Article 9(2) in the ICRC draft. *Cf.* Article 18,
GWS.

[53] Article 5 in the Canadian draft, Article 8 in the U.S. draft,
and Article 10 in the ICRC draft. The Geneva Conventions
clothe medical personnel with extensive protections. See Articles
24-32, 36-37, 33 and 20 respectively.

[54] Article 6 in the Canadian draft, Article 9 in the U.S. draft,
and Article 11 in the ICRC draft. *Cf.* Articles 19-23, 33-37,
GWS; and 22-35, 38-40, GWS (Sea).

graph that authorizes use of the Red Cross emblem when the medical facilities are being used solely for that purpose. This is a sound addition and is a useful implementation of the common article that makes the Red Cross emblem "the distinctive emblem of the medical services of the Parties to the conflict."[55] Its usefulness depends upon universal adherence to the closing reminder: "It shall not be used for any other purposes and shall be respected in all circumstances."[56] The drafts thus breathe life into the simple Article 3 command to collect and care for the sick and wounded.

Chaplains, priests, and others who minister to the spiritual needs of the community should enjoy an immunity analogous to that given medical personnel. They are thus in all drafts included alongside medical personnel as persons entitled to special respect and protection. They must be permitted to "discharge their functions,"[57] an indispensable right if detained persons are "to receive spiritual assistance from ministers of their faith."[58]

The key to any sound classification system is rationality, and it thus becomes important to insure that rationality by specifying how classification decisions are to be made. The who, how, and why of decision-making can either frustrate or implement the formal classification scheme; and yet none of the current draft protocols or conventions establishes any procedural guidelines.

(1) *The rules should specify who is entitled to make*

[55] Article 9 in the Canadian draft, Article 12 in the U.S. draft, and Article 13 in the ICRC draft.
[56] *Ibid.*
[57] Article 5 in the Canadian draft, Article 8 in the U.S. draft, and Article 10 in the ICRC draft. *Cf.* Articles 34-38, POW.
[58] Article 19(b) in the Canadian draft. See also Article 26(3)(c) of the ICRC draft protocol.

these status determinations. The front-line soldier must necessarily make the initial classification decision during the conduct of tactical operations. It is important, however, to insure that his initial decision be neither final nor prejudicial. In the first place, the category into which the non-combatant fits is not always readily apparent. Peasants, for example, do not wear placards identifying themselves as "rebel sympathizers" or "government loyalists." They look discouragingly alike. In such circumstances, classification becomes a complex political-legal judgment, which the average soldier is ill-equipped to make. Quite aside from the fact that he is not trained to interrogate or classify, he will rarely have the time to question extensively; nor will he have access to other information that would enable him accurately to evaluate responses. About the most he can do is make rough judgments based on the facts as they appear to him and perhaps a brief interrogation. It is thus important to require that a soldier who detains an individual must either free him promptly or as soon as possible evacuate him to a safe area where his status can be finally determined.[59] The prompt evacuation requirement also insures that detained people are removed from the area of hostilities and thereby reduces the likelihood that the capturing force will misuse them as hostages or shields.

Ideally, a three-man panel composed of judicially qualified individuals should determine the status of de-

[59] The necessity to evacuate all captured personnel to the rear for classification is a basic point stressed in all army instructional programs. The recently revised *Army Subject Schedule 27-1, The Geneva Conventions of 1949 and Hague Convention No. IV of 1907*, states: "Combat soldiers do not determine the status of any captured person. All persons captured or detained should be evacuated to the detainee collecting point where proper authorities can classify them."

tained individuals. The ideal is seldom an alternative, however; and many governments lack the personnel to staff such tribunals. At a minimum a senior military officer or civil servant should be charged with the responsibility for making status determinations. Appeal from his decision should be permitted as a matter of right in any case in which the senior official classifies a citizen as a "combatant-detainee" or POW. The decision to deprive a citizen of his right to trial in civil courts and to confine without a judicial determination of guilt for an indefinite period is so extraordinary that it should be made only in a judicial forum.

(2) *The new rules should set out the procedure by which the determination must be made.* What rules should govern such proceedings? Again, Allied practice in Vietnam is instructive. In cases in which the status of a detainee is doubtful, his case was referred to a tribunal,[60] which, according to applicable Army regulations,[61] consists of three or more officers who, where practicable, should be judge advocates or other military lawyers familiar with the Hague and Geneva Conventions. An army directive establishes very specific procedures for the hearings.[62] It specifies, for instance, that the individual has a

---

[60] The United States and South Vietnam were obligated by their view that the conflict was an international one to which all the Geneva Conventions applied to determine the status of persons before "a competent tribunal." Article 5, POW. Nothing in Article 3, were it alone applicable, would require a government to submit doubtful cases of status to any tribunal. This is a major gap in Convention protection.

[61] Military Assistance Command Vietnam Directive 20-5, *Inspections and Investigations of Prisoners of War-Determination of Eligibility* (15 March 1968), reprinted in 62 AM. J. INT'L. L. 768 (1968).

[62] *Id.*, para. 7.

right to an interpreter and to counsel with whom he may be present at all open sessions of the court.[63] Counsel must be informed of the tribunal procedures and have free access to his client. He can call, examine, and cross-examine witnesses.[64] While the tribunal is not bound by the Uniform Code of Military Justice rules of evidence, it must follow specified procedures[65] that insure that the defendant has his day in court. While it would probably be unwise to set out in the Conventions such a detailed tribunal procedure, a model set of procedures could be annexed to the Convention. While its procedures would probably differ from those observed in a civil court trial, the minimum standards of due process and fairness should govern any hearing.

(3) *The rules should set out the criteria upon which the classification decision must be made.* Any new convention must define the status categories specifically enough to enable the authorities to classify accordingly. It must do better than the old Oklahoma statute which said that for its purposes anyone who looked like an Indian was an Indian. Unfortunately, the present drafts imply that anyone who looks like a civilian is one and must be treated as one both during the conduct of tactical military operations and thereafter. Much of the futile and often circular argument over the appropriate definition of the civilian population stems from a failure to analyze the point in time and the purpose for which the definition is sought. As has already been pointed out, the functional distinction during military operations is between the combatant and the non-combatant, not between the combatant and the civilian population. No reason requires that the soldier initially treat one non-

[63] *Id.*, para. 9.   [64] *Id.*, para. 11.   [65] *Id.*, para. 14.

combatant differently from another. The non-combatant poses no immediate threat. He has surrendered or is offering no resistance or, to use the quaint language of the Geneva Conventions, is in "the hands of" the soldier. What action the soldier may take against non-combatants during the conduct of military operations should depend on a balancing of military necessity against the human rights of the individual—and not on whether they are citizens, enemy aliens, guerrilla sympathizers, or loyal supporters.

These differences are relevant in determining the *subsequent* treatment to which the non-combatant is entitled. A government fighting for its survival may legitimately distinguish between those among its citizens who support it and those who oppose it in according civil and political rights. It may punish the latter—swiftly and severely—so long as it does so in accordance with minimum legal standards of justice. It may intern them, confiscate their property, deprive them of their right to vote. It may, as all governments do, try, convict and jail, or execute those who violate its laws. Even in peacetime governments distinguish between citizens and aliens; *a fortiari*, a government may in wartime greatly curtail the civil and political rights of aliens. But while governments may thus accord different types of non-combatants different civil and political rights, they cannot authorize soldiers to treat the different types of non-combatants differently during the conduct of tactical military operations.

A combatant may be defined as one who resists the opposing force by directly participating in military operations. All others would be non-combatants. A POW or "detained combatant" is a former combatant: that is, one who has resisted the capturing force by directly participating in military operations. This definition eliminates the restrictive and excessively formal Article 4 criteria, which denied prisoner of war status to guerrillas. Some may fear that the broadened definition, while including guerrillas, would embrace too many others, such as sympathizers and collaborators. An entire people might thus become a legitimate military target. The scope of the category depends, of course, on the interpretation of "directly participating" and "military operations." The use of the term "directly" implies some degree of causality. The individual's act must cause in some immediate sense the military damage inflicted upon the adversary. "Military operations" connote tactical maneuvers and should not be confused with the broader concept of "military effort," which necessarily includes many non-combatants whose work, however, does not directly inflict damage upon the enemy.

A returnee is a citizen combatant who elects to reaffirm his former allegiance. It is important to emphasize his native citizenship because the government should not include foreign nationals in such a category. On the other hand, the government must have the discretion to offer this opportunity to rebel citizens if it is to "win their hearts and minds." Alternatively, it will either incarcerate or exterminate them, neither of which seems more humane.

A civil defendant is one who has violated the criminal law of the country. Sympathizers and collaborators who do not directly participate in military operations and therefore do not qualify as POW's usually violate domestic criminal law. They may be tried in the ordinary criminal courts and punished accordingly. Interestingly enough, aliens remain equally subject to the domestic criminal law and could thus be prosecuted in the ordinary criminal courts for aiding the revolutionary effort.

b. THE NEW RULES SHOULD SPECIFY THE TREATMENT
TO WHICH PARTICIPANTS IN EACH STATUS CATEGORY ARE
ENTITLED

The recently proposed draft protocols and conventions
deal most effectively with the general problem of insuring
humane treatment for non-combatants. Perhaps the
plight of non-combatants touches more deeply the collective conscience of mankind; perhaps the law of Geneva
solutions furnish more useful analogs to the problem of
treating non-combatants in internal conflicts humanely;
perhaps the minutely detailed provisions of the Geneva
Conventions provide a basis for deducing generalized
norms applicable to non-international conflicts. Whatever the reason, these new proposals all flesh out the
skeletal command in Article 3 to treat non-combatants
humanely by (1) specifying the nature of detention facilities; (2) establishing minimum standards for shelter,
food, and medical care; (3) listing the fundamental rights
to which any defendant in a judicial proceeding is entitled; and (4) imposing limitations on the kind and
length of sentences.

(1) *The nature of detention facilities.* The U.S. draft
contains the general and important provision that the
"parties to the conflict shall not force the displacement
of any portion of the population except if the security
of the population on imperative military reasons so demand."[66] Chapter 6 of the Canadian draft protocol deals
generally with the rights of "persons in restricted liberty."
Internment camps may not "be set up in areas particularly exposed to dangers arising out of the conflict."[67]
And if the "area in which [such persons] are confined,
detained, interned, or restricted becomes particularly ex-

[66] Article 17(1).   [67] Article 21(1).

posed to dangers arising out of the conflict," they must
be removed.[68] These provisions reflect analogous provisions in both the Civilian and Prisoner of War Conventions.[69] The draft convention also requires that the internment camps and only internment camps be marked
as such.[70] The Geneva Conventions require similar marking for POW camps[71] and civilian detention facilities.[72]
Finally, the same article obligates parties to advise each
other of the location of internment camps as states are
required to do under the Civilian Convention.[73]

Unfortunately, the Canadian draft does not specify
that internment camps be built in healthful areas and
maintained in sanitary conditions, as does the U.S.
draft.[74] The Geneva Conventions offer the model upon
which to fashion these minimal assurances of decent detention facilities.[75] Regrettably, too, neither the Canadian
nor U.S. draft defines internment camps. The Canadian
delegation's explanatory notes do not illuminate their
concept of an internment camp, and one suspects from
the absence of any discussion that they used the term as
it is used in the Civilian Convention. It is thus unlikely
that the restrictions upon internment camps apply to
either penal institutions or resettled villages or that the
occupants of either enjoy the same rights as internees.

The Minimum Rules for the Protection of Non-Delinquent Detainees drafted by the Medico-Legal Commission of Monaco establish more detailed and thorough
criteria for any institution or place of detention than does

[68] Article 19(e).
[69] *Cf.* GC Articles 83 and 38(4); POW Article 19.
[70] Article 21(2).   [71] Article 23.   [72] Article 83.
[73] *Ibid.*   [74] Article 25.
[75] *Cf.* GC Article 85 and POW Articles 22, 25 and 29.

the Canadian draft protocol.[76] Though the ICRC has
recommended even more detailed standards,[77] the rules
seem as vigorous as could be reasonably demanded.
Moreover, the rules are applicable to a wider range of
detention facilities than are those contained in the Canadian draft. They are intended to compliment the minimum rules drawn up by the United Nations Social and
Economic Council for detained delinquents[78] and thus
insure the same fundamental protections for all persons
howsoever detained.

The Monaco Medico-Legal rules prescribe "adequate
space, ventilation, lighting and heating for each detainee. . . ."[79] Each detainee is entitled to "an individual
bunk or bedding" which must be "properly maintained
and changed often enough to ensure its cleanliness."[80]
The detention facility must have baths and toilets.[81] The
Geneva Conventions impose similar and more extensive
requirements.

(2) *Minimum standards for shelter, food, and medical
care.* The Canadian draft requires that all persons in restricted liberty "be adequately fed, clothed and sheltered . . ."[82] and receive necessary medical attention including periodical medical examinations and hospital
treatment.[83] Article 19(a) and (c) must be read in conjunction with Article 2, which guarantees "the care neces-

[76] See Articles 10-15.
[77] Graven, *Minimum Rules for the Protection of Non-Delinquent Detainees,* 8 INT'L. REV. OF THE RED CROSS 59, 63 (February 1968). The ICRC draft protocol, however, is roughly similar
to the U.S. and Canadian provisions. See Article 26.
[78] *Id.,* at 59.   [79] Article 11.   [80] Article 14.
[81] Article 15.
[82] Article 19(c). *Cf.* Articles 25-27, POW; 85, 89-90, GC.
[83] Article 19(a). *Cf.* Articles 30-31, POW; 91-92, GC.

sitated by their conditions" to "[a]ll persons who are wounded or sick as well as the infirm, expectant mothers, maternity cases and children under fifteen. . . ." The U.S. list of rights to which interned persons are entitled unfortunately omits the right to medical care, though such a right may be implied from general injunctions to treat such persons humanely.[84] The language that accords protections to the sick and wounded parallels that found in Article 7(1) of the ICRC draft.

One important shelter provision is Article 19(f), which requires that women "be confined in separate quarters under the supervision of a woman." The U.S. draft also specifies separate quarters under female supervision.[85] The Medico-Legal rules echo the separate quarter provision[86] and further specify that "children less than six years of age shall in no case be separated from their mothers." All three drafts contain provisions stressing the importance of communal housing in cases of interned families although none requires it.[87] The Medico-Legal rules also guarantee separate housing for "civilian or military detainees belonging to countries which are hostile to each other" and proscribes confining non-delinquent detainees with "penal law detainees and convicted prisoners."[88]

The Medico-Legal Institute draft is much more detailed in other aspects as well. It devotes one article to clothing, which must be appropriate to the climate,

[84] Article 25.   [85] Article 27.

[86] Article 6. The separate quarter provision is an example of a non-adverse discrimination. *Cf.* Articles 25, POW; GC.

[87] Article 20 in the Canadian draft, Article 28 in the U.S. draft, and Article 6 in the Medico-Legal draft. *Cf.* Article 82, GC.

[88] Article 9. *Cf.* Article 84, GC.

"clean and well maintained," and cannot be "degrading or humiliating."[89] Another article is devoted to food. All detainees are entitled to "decently served . . . wholesome meal(s) of nutritious value" whose "calorific value and vitamin content shall be consistent with acknowledged standards appropriate to age and work performed."[90] Detainees may under certain circumstances prepare their food or "obtain extra food at their own expense or at the expense of their family, friends, or of a relief society. . . ."[91] The provisions on medical care are extensive. Detention facilities must have a resident doctor and access to the services of a psychiatrist.[92] The doctor must "examine detainees on arrival and whenever necessary thereafter."[93] He must also "advise the director of the institution on matters of hygiene and cleanliness. . . ." The detention facilities must be well-equipped.[94] Wherever women are housed, "suitable provision for pre- and post-natal treatment of maternity cases, . . . maternity cases, . . . and nurseries" must be made.[95] Other articles in the draft supplement those contained in Chapter VII. Work harmful to health is prohibited.[96] Detainees are entitled to an hour's physical exercise daily.[97] Living and

[89] Article 17. The U.S. draft simply requires "adequate" clothing. See Article 25(c).

[90] Article 20(1). The Geneva Conventions require authorities to consider "the habitual diet of the prisoners" in preparing meals. See also Article 25(b) of the U.S. draft.

[91] Article 20(2).   [92] Article 21(1).

[93] Article 23(a). The Geneva Conventions require monthly inspections.

[94] Article 21(1).   [95] Article 22.

[96] Article 19. The Geneva Conventions closely regulate work. Cf. Articles 49-57, POW; 95-96, GC.

[97] Article 18. Cf. Article 38, POW; 94, GC.

working conditions must be healthful.[98] The Medico-Legal draft thus incorporates more of the Geneva Convention protections than do any of the other drafts except for the "special cases" provided for in the annex to the ICRC protocol. In civil wars or in conflicts where the armed forces of other states participate on either or both sides, the whole of the Geneva Conventions apply.

(3) *Other protected rights.* Among the other protected rights to which any detainee should be entitled are the rights to communicate with family and friends and to practice his religion. The Canadian draft guarantees both[99] though it deletes without explanation the category of "objects necessary for religious worship" from the otherwise transplanted language of GC Article 23.[100] It nevertheless assures the detainees' freedom of worship. It also permits them freedom of correspondence; and while it does grant authorities the power to restrict the flow of correspondence from a detainee, they can never limit it to less than two letters and four cards monthly. The rights guaranteed in the U.S. draft are much less specific. Interned persons may practice their religion. They may receive "individual or collective relief sent to them."[101] It does not confer upon them the right to send or receive mail, and it is silent as to their right to receive visitors! The Monaco draft does guarantee these rights. The correspondence provision is however, more vague than Article 19(g) in the Canadian draft. It permits the exchange of letters with "[the detainees'] families and relatives as well as with the legal representatives, agents or advisors whose services they require . . ." but only "to an extent compatible with the maintenance of good order,

---

[98] Articles 11-12.   [99] Article 19(b) and (g).
[100] Article 10(1).   [101] Article 25(d) and (e).

administrative needs and security requirements."[102] On
the other hand, the same article permits visits which the
Canadian draft does not authorize. It also obligates the
camp officials to keep detainees "regularly informed of
major current events."[103] Article 29 states that "[d]e-
tainees shall as far as possible be provided with spiritual
or religious comfort." It also adds that no detainee may
be compelled to worship.

The draft conventions do not guarantee any right to
work. Rather—and with good reason—they restrict the
circumstances in which a detainee may be forced to
work. One can scarcely quarrel with the regulation that
"detainees shall be responsible for keeping rooms, premises and beds neat and tidy."[104] But just as the Geneva
Conventions have exempted POW's and others from
dangerous or unhealthy work, the Monaco Medico-Legal
draft prohibits compelling detainees to perform harmful
or degrading work.[105] This simple restriction is unfortunately not contained in either the Canadian or U.S.
drafts. The ICRC draft protocol is particularly vague in
its provisions for "treatment of persons whose liberty has
been restrained."[106]

(4) *Fundamental rights to which defendant is entitled
in any judicial proceeding.* The Canadian draft repeats
the language of Article 3 but inserts as one judicial guarantee recognized as indispensable by all civilized people
the right to be represented by counsel.[107] The Canadian
delegation did not explain why it selected for specific

[102] Article 26(1). The Red Cross has suggested a much narrower exception. *Supra* n. 73 at 66.
[103] Article 27.
[104] Article 13, Medico-Legal draft.
[105] Article 19.   [106] See Article 26.
[107] Article 15.

enumeration only the right to counsel. Although the draft does impliedly guarantee a right of appeal, it also impliedly permits its suspension.[108] On the other hand, the U.S. draft singles out only the right to appeal and indeed specifies in a separate article that the detained person must be informed of his right to appeal.[109]

It is to be regretted that Article 15 of the Canadian draft does not include at least the right to have an interpreter and to call and examine witnesses. The phrase "all the judicial guarantees which are recognized as indispensable by civilized peoples" is unnecessarily general, and these specific rights should be enumerated within the appropriate section of Article 3 as examples of judicial guarantees. Retaining the general phrase allows the expansion of these rights as the international consensus on "judicial guarantees" evolves; listing the specific rights insures present adherence to minimum standards of justice.

The draft does authorize a trial observer. This important provision requires authorities to notify the National Red Cross and the International Committee whenever "an accused is to be tried for an offense arising out of his participation in the conflict. . . ."[110] Representatives of these societies "shall have the right to attend the trial of any accused person, unless the hearing is, as an exceptional measure, to be held *in camera* in the interests of security."[111] The Geneva analog to this provision is found in Article 74 of the Civilian Convention.

The Medico-Legal draft rules, which are designed to govern detention of non-delinquent detainees, nevertheless contain provisions regulating punishment of detainees for offenses committed subsequent to detention

---

[108] Article 16.   [109] Article 22.
[110] Article 17(2).   [111] Article 17(1).

(e.g., a violation of camp regulations).[112] "Except in very minor cases," a detainee cannot be punished without "being informed of the accusation against him and his being given the possibility of presenting his defense, if necessary through an interpreter, and without a full and impartial inquiry by the director."[113] While the draft does not specify what legal regulations the camp director must promulgate, it does enjoin any punishment—presumably even in very minor cases—"otherwise than in conformity" with such regulations.[114]

These rules, like those in the Canadian and U.S. drafts, seem unnecessarily vague. And the ICRC draft protocol does not address itself to the problem at all. The draftsmen of the Prisoner of War Convention specifically enumerated many rights to which prisoners were entitled in circumstances analogous to those governed by Article 31 of the Medico-Legal draft.[115]

(5) *Limitations on the kind and length of punishment.* One of the major defects of common Article 3 is that it does not advert specifically to the problem of punishment. The Canadian draft at least forbids collective penalties, since one could be punished only for offenses he personally committed;[116] and the ICRC draft protocol contains a similar clause.[117] The Canadian draft also limits imposition of the death penalty. A convicted person could not in any case be executed "until [he] has exhausted all means of appeal and petition for pardon or reprieve."[118] Furthermore, it forbids the carrying out of

[112] The Geneva Conventions are considerably more detailed. See Articles 82-98, POW and 100, GC.
[113] Article 31(1).   [114] *Ibid.*
[115] See generally Part III of Chapter III, "Judicial proceedings" and Article 105 in particular.
[116] Article 14.   [117] Article 27.   [118] Article 18(2).

any "death sentence imposed upon persons whose guilt
arises only by reason of having participated as combatants . . . until after hostilities have ceased."[119] The ICRC
draft protocol echoes this latter sentiment.[120] While there
may be sound policy reasons for exempting from capital
punishment those soldiers who have not committed war
crimes, the draft language would exempt all—even those
who violated the law of war. While the draft does not
require a general grant of amnesty, as some delegates
urged, it does suspend capital executions until the end of
hostilities, at which time amnesty is a likelihood. The
U.S. draft states that "at the conclusion of the hostilities
the parties to the conflict should endeavour to grant amnesty to as many as possible of those who have participated in the conflict or have been convicted of offenses
or deprived of liberty in connection with the conflict."[121]
Some delegates argued for the abolition of capital punishment; others pointed out that states are not likely to
smile so benignly on what after all is treason.

Considering the nature of much non-capital punishment, one may wonder whether incarceration for the
duration of the conflict is to be preferred to execution.
Although neither the Canadian nor U.S. draft imposes
any restrictions on non-capital punishment, the Medico-
Legal draft rules do. Article 31(2) prohibits "corporal
punishment, confinement to cells which are dark or too
small to permit normal posture, blows, and all cruel or
degrading treatment. . . ." The draft rules also limit the
imposition of solitary confinement which would impair
the detainee's physical or mental health. A doctor should
certify in writing that such punishments are "bearable
and without danger."[122] These more explicit restrictions

[119] Article 18(1).   [120] Article 28.   [121] Article 23.
[122] Article 31(2).

are not startlingly new. They are found in the present Geneva Conventions,[123] and there is little reason why they should not apply with equal force to internal conflict.

3. Humanitarian Relief Should Be Allowed

The right of humanitarian initiative presently contained in Article 3 is, as we have seen, an insufficient guarantee that suffering innocents will receive humanitarian aid. The Canadian draft Convention would remedy this defect (1) by explicitly authorizing the activities of the Red Cross and other relief societies "subject to temporary and exceptional measures imposed for reasons of security,"[124] and (2) by incorporating the principles of Article 23 of the Civilian Convention into Chapter 3 of the draft instrument.[125] The ICRC draft protocol contains very similar provisions,[126] but while the U.S. draft also recognizes the right of humanitarian relief, it does so in more general terms.[127]

Under Article 23 of the Canadian draft Convention, parties to the conflict in effect give an advance or prior permission to their national Red Cross societies and other relief organizations to provide humanitarian assistance. Significantly, the article neither confines this permission to the carrying out of normal services nor authorizes the parties to the conflict to establish criteria and conditions for the distribution of aid (other than those required "for reasons of security"). Rather, the article states that the Red Cross Societies shall "pursue [their] activities *in accordance with Red Cross principles*

---

[123] One must read Article 89 with Articles 25, 29, 87, 88, and 98; POW. The consequence, as some government experts pointed out, is that confinement is not a very effective penalty.

[124] Article 23.   [125] Articles 10-11.

[126] Articles 29-31.   [127] Article 19.

as defined by International Red Cross Conferences."[128]
It is not clear whether the following statement that
"[o]ther relief societies shall be permitted to continue
their humanitarian activities under similar conditions"
means that they, too, must conform to the guidelines
established by International Red Cross Conferences or
that they need simply act in accordance with the authoritative pronouncements of their respective policy-making
organs.

The Red Cross "principles" referred to must constitute more than technical guidelines for the acquisition
and distribution of goods and services. These would more
properly be denominated rules or regulations and are in
any case seldom the concern of International Conferences, which articulate broad humanitarian principles.[129]
Their inclusion by reference is extraordinary, for it permits a private organization to establish standards binding
upon signatory states. This provision also allows for the
future expansion and development of the concept of
humanitarian assistance as new Red Cross Conference
declarations reflect evolutions in the humanitarian conscience.

Since the draft article is a nearly verbatim transplant
from Article 63(a) of the present Civilian Convention,
the legislative history of that article and its subsequent
application may provide some insight into the usefulness
of draft Article 23. First of all, the delegates to the
Geneva Diplomatic Conference agreed that authorities
could not use the security exception as an excuse for
suspending all humanitarian activities.[130] As Pictet ob-
serves in his commentary: "The Occupying Power may

[128] Emphasis provided.
[129] *Cf.* J. Pictet, RED CROSS PRINCIPLES (1955).
[130] J. Pictet, IV COMMENTARY 333 (1958).

not use the reservation lightly. Its security must be threatened by some real danger."[131] The parties' general obligation to facilitate rather than frustrate relief efforts is underscored by the injunction in draft Article 22 to "encourage the work of organizations engaged in this task [reuniting families] provided they conform to security regulations." Article 11(2) also requires that parties grant to relief organizations "all facilities for carrying out their purposes within the bounds set by military or security considerations." Finally, Article 19(d) specifies that all confined, detained, or interned persons "be enabled to receive individual or collective relief. . . ." Secondly, the legislative history reinforces the broad scope of permissible humanitarian activities. Again, one cannot improve upon Pictet's succinct statement: "This conception of the mission of the Red Cross implies a very broad interpretation of the word 'activities.' Whether the activities in question are the traditional activities of the Red Cross or some entirely new task, the only condition set by the Convention—and it is an essential one—is that it should be in accordance with the true Red Cross spirit."[132]

Articles 10 and 11 contain even more expansive guarantees. Although the draftsmen contend that they have merely adapted Article 23 of the Civilian Convention "to non-international situations,"[133] even their frequent use of language lifted from that article cannot obscure their deletion of several of its restrictive provisions. One, the draft article permits shipments to all non-combatants, not just to "children under fifteen, expectant mothers and maternity cases." Two, it reduces the number of conditions justifying interference with the shipments while pre-

[131] *Ibid.*   [132] *Id.*, at 332.
[133] *Supra* n. 33 at 16.

serving the party's right "to prescribe under what reasonable technical arrangements the passage is to be made." Even the right reserved is a narrower one, since the standard of reasonableness is not found in the present Article 23. More significantly, the draft article does not include the objectionable provision that authorizes a state to forbid shipments if they would produce "a definite advantage . . . to the military efforts or economy of the enemy. . . ." The draft article, like GC Article 23, obligates the parties to forward all consignments "as rapidly as possible." Since incumbent governments have proved sensitive about any implied recognition of rebel forces, the draft article wisely specifies that "[a]n offer of supplies . . . shall not be considered as an unfriendly act or have any effect on the status of the Parties to the conflict." Governments have also refused proffered relief shipments, perhaps resenting the implication that they could not care for their own. Article 10 would not permit states to sacrifice their helpless citizens on the altar of chauvinism. Paragraph 5 states: "The Party to the conflict to whom a consignment has been made may not refuse it unless the consignment is not needed to meet the needs of those persons for whose benefit it was intended." The draft article, tailored to the peculiarities of internal conflict, thus incorporates the basic principles of GC Article 23 while eliminating some of its restrictive provisions which have often frustrated humanitarian relief efforts.

The second article of Chapter 3 introduces into the draft convention the concept presently embodied in Article 30 of the Civilian Convention: the individual right to seek assistance from relief societies. The rapporteur of the Committee which considered Article 30 thought it important that the Convention confer individual rights upon persons as well as lay general responsibilities on states.[134] Pictet concurs.[135]

4. Criteria for the Determination of Non-International Conflict Should Be Specified

Though the meaning of the phrase "non-international conflict" is, as we have seen, uncertain, all the drafts repeat it without specifying any criteria by which to determine its existence. The U.S. has proposed an alternative article that would enumerate certain conditions as evidence of such a conflict, but it carefully and narrowly concludes that "the present Convention has no application to situations of internal disturbance or tension."[136] As a general guideline, one might more reasonably conclude that a non-international conflict is any internal conflict that endangered those rights normally protected by the law of war. There are, however, more specific criteria.

a. USE OF REGULAR COMBAT TROOPS

The use of regular combat units in tactical operations would be the most important criterion for the application of the laws of war.[137] Both because of the weapons soldiers are likely to use and the probable scope of any military operation (the use of air cover or support, for

[134] II-A. FINAL RECORD OF THE GENEVA DIPLOMATIC CONFERENCE 822.

[135] J. Pictet, *supra* n. 117 at 215.

[136] Article 2(2). The enumerated criteria in Article 2 would justify application of all the Geneva Conventions under the Annex provision in the ICRC draft!

[137] Professor Farer has focused on this single fact as the test for impermissible intervention. Farer, *Intervention in Civil Wars: A Modest Proposal*, I THE VIETNAM WAR AND INTERNATIONAL LAW 518 (R. Falk, ed. 1968).

example), the threat from such tactics to those human rights normally protected by the laws of war is great.

b. DURATION OF THE CONFLICT

Another criterion for the application of the laws of war is duration of the conflict. As the fight drags on, the disruption of normal life intensifies. The sick and wounded demand treatment; the hungry, food; the homeless, shelter. The number of prisoners grows, and difficult questions about their classification, punishment, detention, and care must be answered. All of these problems are common to international conflicts, and large portions of the laws of war were designed to provide humanitarian solutions.

c. FOREIGN TROOP PARTICIPATION

Foreign troop participation in tactical combat operations is a third criterion for the application of the laws of war. There is no litmus-paper test by which one can distinguish an internal war from an international war; and while one can imagine an internal conflict in which foreign troops participate on either side without thereby internationalizing it, their presence creates conditions that demand application of the laws of war. Foreign assistance may augment native firepower and thereby increase the potential destructiveness of their operations. Foreign advisors may organize and lead guerrilla strikes against the opposing force. Their capture and subsequent treatment, if not in accord with the minimum standards of the laws of war, may exacerbate tensions and produce a spiraling wave of inhumane reprisals.

d. INTENSITY OF THE CONFLICT

What may be called the "intensity" of the conflict for want of a more descriptive term is a final criterion for the application of the laws of war. Sporadic raids and fire-fights do not greatly endanger large numbers of people, nor are they apt to provoke government use of combat troops. They may entail an occasional violation of a human right normally protected by the laws of war; unfortunately these violations often proliferate as the fighting intensifies. It is precisely at the point when the fighting becomes the bloodiest that the laws of war should be applied to prevent wholesale slaughter and destruction. Neither side wins if it inherits only the wind. A stable government rests upon a loyal people, and one does not induce loyalty by raping and pillaging. A viable economy requires productive farms and industries. Little can be reaped from the salted earth or defoliated forests; neither can wares be conjured from the rubble of bombed factories. An efficient state needs doctors, engineers, lawyers, scientists. Whichever side wins will need their professional skills and can ill afford their loss through mass executions or indiscriminate bombardment.

e. IMPOSITION OF EMERGENCY MEASURES

A group of distinguished scholars have identified several other criteria which would indicate a need to apply the laws of war to an internal conflict:

"It is submitted that even though governments fighting insurgents generally refuse formally to recognize the 'belligerency,' they acknowledge the seriousness of the insurgency rather clearly through alterations in their normal domestic laws and institutions. Some of the signs that internal strife ought not to be considered as purely domestic are the following:

"a. Imposition of martial law or state of siege generally or in certain areas over a long period of time;

"b. organization of emergency military or para-military security agencies, inter-departmental committees or councils operating with extraordinary powers similar to those exercised in wartime;

"c. enforcement of laws and institutions commonly associated with wartime such as high draft calls, extraordinary measures with respect to food and other necessities, transportation and the like;

"d. drastic increase in detentions and other deprivations of civil rights for political or security reasons, detentions over long periods without trial, increase in trials not characterized by minimal due process, or at least, due process as it was supposed to exist in the state in normal times."[138]

These suggested tests reflect the insight of an old adage: what one does speaks louder than what one says.

The criteria outlined above are nothing more than contextual factors that provide a sounder index to the applicability of the laws of war than do the traditional categories of riot, insurrection, insurgency, and belligerency. It is true that these categories reflected roughly differences in duration, troop involvement, and the intensity of the conflict. That is, riots or insurrections seldom lasted long. Moreover, military combat operations —particularly those involving foreign troops—usually occurred only during insurgencies or belligerencies. One might therefore conclude that the rights protected by the laws of war are far more likely to be denied during an insurgency or belligerency than during a riot or insurrection because, when combatting the former, the government will usually conduct the kind of operations that often generate law of war violations. Policies adopted to control riots and put down insurrections may, of course, also violate certain human rights; but to the extent that

[138] Institute of World Polity, THE LAW OF LIMITED INTERNATIONAL CONFLICT 48-9 (1965).

the rights violated are other than those guaranteed in the laws of war, they have no application. The point is that the traditional categories do not invariably reflect accurately the duration, troop involvement, and intensity of an internal conflict.

B. INSTITUTIONAL REFORMS

Important as is substantive reform of the law, institutional reform must accompany it if it is to prove successful. Throughout the international legal process the institutional framework is weak and inadequate. Nowhere is this more true than in the law of war area. States retain almost exclusive unilateral authority to decide how to characterize the conflict and therefore what laws to respect. They decide, again unilaterally, how to classify other participants and therefore what treatment to accord them. No international body possesses the authority to review these decisions. Neither can any observe the parties' discharge of their responsibilities. In such circumstances it is not surprising that states keep the promise of humanitarian treatment to the ear but break it to the hope.

1. Procedures Should Be Established for Reporting Status Determinations and for Periodic Reports on All Persons Held in Custody

The Canadian draft wisely imposes reporting requirements. It says that the parties shall endeavor to exchange reports on all "who are wounded, sick or who have died while in their hands."[139] The Canadian draft does not limit the reporting to "enemy" or "adverse party" dead as does the U.S. draft.[140] In the context of an internal conflict it

[139] Article 3(2).   [140] Article 6(2).

may be difficult to determine the loyalty of a corpse. Still, the family will want to claim the body, and they need to know. It is unfortunate that only the U.S. draft imposes a flat obligation to publish the information when the identity of the dead cannot be determined and communication is therefore impossible.[141]

These provisions are adequate insofar as they go, but they do not go far enough. In the first place only the status of the sick, wounded, and dead need be reported. The same humanitarian reasons require reports on all detained persons. Their family and friends are equally interested in knowing their whereabouts and the condition of the confinement. No possible military advantage can accrue to a party who conceals the identity of detained persons.

Secondly, the drafts require that parties need only report data to the enemy. The parties should also submit similar reports to the International Committee of the Red Cross or whatever other international body assumes supervisory powers under point 2 below. The ICRC could not, for example, discharge its Article 17 responsibility to attend trials if it lacked adequate information on detained persons. Should it be given expanded investigatory and supervisory powers, it would need such information. A model report form should be annexed to any draft convention.

2. *The Filing of Military Manuals and Directives Should Be Required*

To a great extent there is no law of war except what the soldier does in the field. He does not read the Geneva Conventions before he acts. He may recall his training.

[141] *Ibid.*

He may consult field regulations or field manuals. The soldier thus inevitably makes law on the battlefield. If he has received sound instruction in his responsibilities and if he has been issued directives that embody sound principles, he will usually make good law. The quality of the directives is all-important because every army runs on directives. States should file all unclassified manuals and directives that include guidance on the law of war with an international organization. The ICRC or other supervisory body could review all these and offer appropriate suggestions. This is preventive law. The Geneva Conventions require that signatories instruct their soldiers in their convention responsibilities. The proposed drafts do not impose a similar responsibility. They should. Moreover, states should be required to file reports outlining the substance of such instruction and specifying the dates and places it is given. It would also be desirable if an international observer attended such instructional classes.

3. *Procedures Should Be Established for Inspecting a Party's Compliance with the Relevant Laws*

Professor Levie scores as one of the four major inadequacies in the present law of war the absence of an " 'umpire' with sufficient authority to oversee application of the law, to investigate alleged or possible violations, to determine the facts with respect thereto, and to take the necessary action to ensure the correction of the fault."[142] Although the "protecting power" was intended to serve this purpose, Professor Levie points out: ". . . although there have probably been close to one hundred armed

[142] Levie, *Some Major Inadequacies in the Existing Law Relating to the Protection of Individuals During Armed Conflict,* HAMMARSKJÖLD FORUM 19 (1970).

conflicts of various sorts and sizes since the end of World
War II, the institution of the Protecting Power has not
once during that period been called into being."[143] It takes
no more than a keen eye for the obvious to agree with the
Secretary-General, who has admitted: ". . . there would
be pressing need for measures to improve and strengthen
the present system of international supervision and assistance to parties to armed conflicts in their observance
of humanitarian norms of international law. . . ."[144]

Resuscitation of the protecting power concept is one
solution. Though the Canadian draft does not use the
term "protecting power," it does authorize other states
"to receive wounded, sick or infirm persons, children
under fifteen, expectant mothers and maternity cases on
its soil."[145] This provision, however, is not mandatory.
Moreover, it is excessively narrow, as is the traditional
scope of a protecting power's authority. As Professor
Levie reminds us: ". . . it should be borne in mind that
nowhere in either customary or conventional international law is there any rule which would authorize the Protecting Power, even if it were designated and functioning,
to supervise the compliance of a belligerent with that
area of the law of armed conflict governing the conduct of
hostilities."[146] A government that is suppressing a rebellion will not look kindly upon the nationals of third-party
states operating on its territory. The protecting power is
a moribund institution whose revival would still not solve
the general problems of inspection.

Another alternative is reliance upon some present or
future United Nations agency. Ad hoc U.N. fact-finding
groups have often worked well in the past, and the Neth-
erlands has proposed the creation of a permanent U.N.

[143] *Id.*, at 20.
[145] Article 8.

[144] *Supra* n. 38 at para. 215.
[146] Levie, *supra* n. 124 at 22.

fact-finding agency.[147] One should keep in mind, however, that previous fact-finding commissions have worked well only when welcomed by the host state. Any effective agency must possess mandatory powers of inspection, and it cannot always anticipate an open arms greeting. Moreover, the United Nations is an intensely political body; and subjective disagreements about the justice of the respective participants' causes will inevitably complicate problems that are difficult enough to resolve from an impartial perspective. The United Nations efforts in Egypt and the Congo illustrate the detrimental impact of political disagreements within the organization upon permanent U.N. missions.

Professor Levie has suggested a third alternative: the creation of a twenty-five-member "International Commission for the Enforcement of Humanitarian Rights during Armed Conflict" (hereinafter referred to as ICEHRAC): "Thus the convention creating that institution could provide that, when the existence of a state of armed conflict is acknowledged by the states involved, or when a decision to that effect has been reached by ICEHRAC in accordance with the other provisions of the convention, and no Protecting Powers have been designated in accordance with customary international law within one week thereafter, ICEHRAC would automatically begin to function in the capacity of a substitute for the Protecting Power, with all the rights and duties which have been, or which may be granted to such powers."[148]

Professor Levie does not specifically suggest how the agency should conduct its inspection and supervisory

[147] The General Assembly has also encouraged the use of fact-finding procedures. G.A. Res. 2329, 22 GAOR, *Supp.* 16 (A/6716) at 84 (1967).

[148] Levie, *supra* n. 124 at 23.

functions beyond analogizing its role to that of a protecting power, whose authority he describes as vague. The frequency and nature of investigations, the conditions under which they will be undertaken, and the kind and identity of recipients of any report issued are all key unanswered questions.

ICEHRAC could retain wide discretion as to the appropriate response to some of these questions. As to others, however, it could not. The parties to a conflict could not tolerate investigations that interfered with the conduct of military operations. Bearing responsibility for the safety and welfare of the Commission staff on the scene (as they undoubtedly would), parties to the conflict would insist on reserving the right to deny approval to any mission that exposed them to grave dangers.

The unresolved problems that the creation of any new body generates may persuade observers to expand the power of the International Committee of the Red Cross. This fourth alternative has numerous advantages. The ICRC has already acted successfully on many occasions as a substitute protecting power. It has a rich backlog of experience upon which to draw. It knows what to look for and how to find it. The International Committee enjoys great prestige and would not have to prove either its competence or its impartiality.

There are nevertheless disadvantages to the proposal. Chief among them is the fear that the ICRC in the exercise of its mandatory functions would embroil itself in enervating disputes with parties to the conflict. Consequently, it might compromise the effectiveness of its voluntary assistance programs and all would be lost. Half a loaf may indeed be better than none at all. Professor Levie discounts similar fears about the viability of his

proposed agency.[149] The answer to those critics who believe that the reach of mandatory powers may exceed
their grasp is "or what's a heaven for?"

4. *Other Proposed Institutional Reforms*

Professor Levie has suggested still another institutional reform: the creation of an independent international
body with the authority to decide when conflicting parties must observe the laws of war.[150] Indeed, this is to
be the principal function of the previously mentioned
ICEHRAC. Any party to the Convention establishing
ICEHRAC could ask that body to decide whether a particular conflict required application of the laws of war.
The parties involved would have an opportunity, if they
wished, to argue their cases. Any ICEHRAC decision
would bind all parties to the Convention; and should it
subsequently determine that one of the parties ignored
its decisions, all members would automatically be obligated to impose "complete economic and communications sanctions" against the non-complying state.

Existing organizations such as the Security Council
could perform a similar function; but their politicization,
which we have already discussed, would impede their effectiveness. Conferring such authority on the ICRC might
indeed undermine it as even those who oppose giving it
mandatory inspection powers fear. So long as a state retains the power to characterize the conflict, it will probably not balk at the mandatory activities of the ICRC,
whose intercession it may anticipate among the consequences of its own unfettered decision to consider the
conflict one calling for ICRC action. Put another way,

[149] *Id.*, at 16-18. [150] *Id.*, at 10.

the state can still determine when the ICRC may act by reserving the unilateral authority to characterize the conflict. Were the ICRC instead vested with the authority to decide when to exercise its mandatory powers, states might well object and refuse to cooperate with the organization at all. South Africa and Southern Rhodesia are proof enough that sovereign states can still thumb their noses at the international community.

States are not likely to consent to the creation of some independent third body such as ICEHRAC, desirable as it might be. The 1949 Geneva Diplomatic Conference rejected similar proposals,[151] and Professor Levie must take pride in his masterful understatement that its creation now "would entail a somewhat broader delegation of authority than States have heretofore been willing to make."[152] A clause permitting voluntary acceptance of the organization's compulsory powers might make the proposal more palatable, but only because none would partake of the bitter fruit. The unhappy history of voluntary acceptances of the World Court's jurisdiction would undoubtedly repeat itself.

States would certainly not accept any such proposal unless the Convention articulated specific standards that would circumscribe the committee's discretion to denominate a conflict one to which the laws of war applied. Thus, one comes full circle again to the importance of substantive reform. Acceptance of this procedural innovation would depend—partially, at least—upon adoption of some of the substantive reforms urged above.

[151] II-B. FINAL RECORD OF THE GENEVA DIPLOMATIC CONFERENCE 11, 16.

[152] Levie, *supra* n. 124 at 14.

CONCLUSION

One can draw many conclusions from the preceding chapters. First, the incidence of internal conflict has increased, is increasing, and will continue to increase throughout the coming decades. The conditions that breed domestic violence in the Third World persist and will not likely disappear in the near future. Although internal conflict will plague underdeveloped countries, it will also occasionally erupt in the more advanced northern industrial societies. The Irish Catholic in Ulster and the French Separationists in Quebec may be but harbingers of the winter of our discontent. Some predict that widespread urban guerrilla warfare will shortly break out in the United States, and even the more repressive Soviet government may be unable to suppress ethnic demands for greater autonomy within the Soviet Union or even independence without using armed force. In short, internal conflict is spreading like an epidemic throughout the world.

The second conclusion is that the international community has done little to check its advance. Cure is always better than treatment, of course. But since we do not yet clearly understand the causes of internal conflict, we can scarcely attempt any cure with confidence. And if the causes are what they appear—poverty, illiteracy— we cannot anticipate an early cure, since the industrial nations have shown little interest in mounting the necessary assistance program. Isolation of the disease is always a helpful measure, and the recent efforts to develop normative and institutional restraints on intervention could reduce its spread by inhibiting one nation from peddling its revolution elsewhere or escalating and prolonging the conflict by introducing combat forces. Unfortunately, scholars have concentrated on the problem of armed intervention rather than on the more subtle forms of intervention such as propaganda and training students; and through these means "revolutionary" states will still foment rebellion and "establishment" governments will buttress their status quo brethren.

Even if the international community were successful in isolating internal conflict, it remains violent; and international law has not, thirdly, reduced its ravages by regulating the conduct of participants therein. While Article 3 does make certain basic principles of the law of war applicable to "conflicts not of an international character," their substantive content, as well as the range of internal conflicts to which they apply, is uncertain. Even under the most imaginative interpretation this "convention in miniature" is inadequate as a source of regulative rules for internal conflict.

What, then, would be an adequate code of conduct for internal conflict? The fourth conclusion is that one cannot simply swab on the present law of The Hague and Geneva Conventions. In the first place, it is often unneeded medicine. In the second place, it is often too weak. In other words, parts of the present international law of war deal with problems peculiar to international conflict or are outmoded and therefore ineffective.

One necessarily comes to the fifth conclusion: the international community needs a new Convention that synthesizes and modernizes the principles of the law of war for internal conflict. A new Convention is needed because customary law develops too slowly and, since traditionally international law has not regulated internal conflict, in this area not at all. A Convention would provide explicit standards by which the international community could judge the conduct of participants. While the new Convention must embody the humanitarian principles common to present international humanitarian law, it must apply exclusively to internal conflicts because they present peculiar problems. The various proposals reviewed in Chapter IV are all welcome suggestions. We can and should, however, integrate their separate provisions into a single Convention.

Though less apparent than these, several other conclusions follow from the first five. One, adoption of some of the recommended rules would necessitate amending the present international law of war. Consider, for example, the suggested rules of aerial bombardment. This is an instance in which present international law is outdated; and though the problems of aerial bombardment are, roughly, similar in any kind of conflict, adoption of the recommended rules would mean that international law imposed greater restraints on the conduct of aerial warfare in internal conflicts than in international ones. To the extent that the recommended rules only modernize existing law, the revised rules should also apply to international conflict. Thus, for instance, the provisions I have suggested outlawing specific weapons or particular weapons use should apply *a fortiari* to international conflicts.

There is, finally, the challenge of integrating any new Convention with existing human rights law applicable during peacetime or in times of internal "disturbance or tension." One must see humanitarian law as a whole. Each separate part must dovetail with the other, and a common skein of concern should run through the law applicable to the lowest levels of unrest to the highest levels of violence.

Perhaps this is to expect too much. The law of war is proof that Holmes' aphorism about the common law is true of all law: its life force has been experience, not logic. Surely, however, our present experience with internal conflict will produce some reform. Indeed, as I have remarked elsewhere, law reform is one of the few beneficial consequences of war. We can, like civilized men in all ages, seek to preserve and strengthen those qualities of reason and charity which led Camus to conclude that in times of pestilence we learn that there is more to praise in men than to despise. Extending the basic protections of the law of war to internal conflicts is an act of reason and charity in a time of pestilence.

Appendices

Rules for the Limitation of the Dangers Incurred by the Civilian Population in Time of War (1956)

Preamble

All nations are deeply convinced that war should be banned as a means of settling disputes between human communities.

However, in view of the need, should hostilities once more break out, of safeguarding the civilian population from the destruction with which it is threatened as a result of technical developments in weapons and methods of warfare,

The limits placed by the requirements of humanity and the safety of the population on the use of armed force are restated and defined in the following rules.

In cases not specifically provided for, the civilian population shall continue to enjoy the protection of the general rule set forth in Article 1, and of the principles of international law.

CHAPTER I. OBJECT AND FIELD OF APPLICATION

Article 1

Since the right of Parties to the conflict to adopt means of injuring the enemy is not unlimited, they shall confine their operations to the destruction of his military resources, and leave the civilian population outside the sphere of armed attacks.

This general rule is given detailed expression in the following provisions:

Article 2

The present rules shall apply:
  (a) In the event of declared war or of any other armed conflict, even if the state of war is not recognized by one of the Parties to the conflict.
  (b) In the event of an armed conflict not of an international character.

Article 3

The present rules shall apply to acts of violence committed against the adverse Party by force of arms, whether in defence or offence. Such acts shall be referred to hereafter as "attacks."

Article 4

For the purpose of the present rules, the civilian population consists of all persons not belonging to one or other of the following categories:
  (a) Members of the armed forces, or of their auxiliary or complementary organizations.
  (b) Persons who do not belong to the forces referred to above, but nevertheless take part in the fighting.

Article 5

The obligations imposed upon the Parties to the conflict in regard to the civilian population, under the present rules, are complementary to those which already devolve expressly upon the Parties by virtue of other rules in international law, deriving in particular from the instruments of Geneva and The Hague.

Chapter II. Objectives Barred from Attack

Article 6

Attacks directed against the civilian population, as such, whether with the object of terrorizing it or for any other reason, are prohibited. This prohibition applies both to attacks on individuals and to those directed against groups.

In consequence, it is also forbidden to attack dwellings, installations or means of transport, which are for the exclusive use of, and occupied by, the civilian population.

Nevertheless, should members of the civilian population, Article 11 notwithstanding, be within or in close proximity to a military objective they must accept the risks resulting from an attack directed against that objective.

Article 7

In order to limit the dangers incurred by the civilian population, attacks may only be directed against military objectives.

Only objectives belonging to the categories of objectives which, in view of their essential characteristics, are generally acknowledged to be of military importance, may be considered as military objectives. Those categories are listed in an annex to the present rules.

However, even if they belong to one of those categories, they cannot be considered as a military objective where their total or partial destruction, in the circumstances ruling at the time, offers no military advantage.

CHAPTER III. PRECAUTIONS IN ATTACKS ON
MILITARY OBJECTIVES

Article 8

The person responsible for ordering or launching an attack shall, first of all:

(a) Make sure that the objective, or objectives, to be attacked are military objectives within the meaning of the present rules, and are duly identified.

When the military advantage to be gained leaves the choice open between several objectives, he is required to select the one, an attack on which involves least danger for the civilian population:

(b) Take into account the loss and destruction which the attack, even if carried out with the precautions prescribed under Article 9, is liable to inflict upon the civilian population.

He is required to refrain from the attack if, after due consideration, it is apparent that the loss and destruction would be disproportionate to the military advantage anticipated:

(c) Whenever the circumstances allow, warn the civilian population in jeopardy, to enable it to take shelter.

Article 9

All possible precautions shall be taken, both in the choice of the weapons and methods to be used, and in the carrying out of an attack, to ensure that no losses or damage are caused to the civilian population in the vicinity of the objective; or to its dwellings, or that such losses or damage are at least reduced to a minimum.

In particular, in towns and other places with a large civilian population, which are not in the vicinity of military or naval operations, the attack shall be conducted with the greatest degree of precision. It must not cause losses or destruction beyond the immediate surroundings of the objective attacked.

The person responsible for carrying out the attack must abandon or break off the operation if he perceives that the conditions set forth above cannot be respected.

Article 10

It is forbidden to attack without distinction, as a single objective, an area including several military objectives at a distance from one another where elements of the civilian population, or dwellings, are situated in between the said military objectives.

Article 11

The Parties to the conflict shall, so far as possible, take all necessary steps to protect the civilian population subject to their authority from the dangers to which they would be exposed in an attack—in particular by removing them from the vicinity of military objectives and from threatened areas. However, the rights conferred upon the population in the event of transfer or evacuation under Article 49 of the Fourth Geneva Convention of 12 Aug. 1949 are expressly reserved.

Similarly, the Parties to the conflict shall, so far as possible, avoid the permanent presence of armed forces, military matériel, mobile military establishments or installations, in towns or other places with a large civilian population.

Article 12

The Parties to the conflict shall facilitate the work of the civilian bodies exclusively engaged in protecting and assisting the civilian population in case of attack.

They can agree to confer special immunity upon the personnel of those bodies, their equipment and installations, by means of a special emblem.

Article 13

Parties to the conflict are prohibited from placing or keeping members of the civilian population subject to their authority in or near military objectives, with the idea of inducing the enemy to refrain from attacking those objectives.

CHAPTER IV. WEAPONS WITH UNCONTROLLABLE EFFECTS

Article 14

Without prejudice to the present or future prohibition of certain specific weapons, the use is prohibited of weapons whose harmful effects—resulting in particular from the dissemination of incendiary, chemical, bacteriological, radioactive or other agents—could spread to an unforeseen degree or escape, either in space or in time, from the control of those who employ them, thus endangering the civilian population.

This prohibition also applies to delayed-action weapons, the dangerous effects of which are liable to be felt by the civilian population.

Article 15

If the Parties to the conflict make use of mines, they are bound, without prejudice to the stipulations of the

VIIIth Hague Convention of 1907, to chart the mine-fields. The charts shall be handed over, at the close of active hostilities, to the adverse Party, and also to all other authorities responsible for the safety of the population.

Without prejudice to the precautions specified under Article 9, weapons capable of causing serious damage to the civilian population shall, so far as possible, be equipped with a safety device which renders them harmless when they escape from the control of those who employ them.

CHAPTER V. SPECIAL CASES

Article 16

When, on the outbreak or in the course of hostilities, a locality is declared to be an "open town," the adverse Party shall be duly notified. The latter is bound to reply, and if it agrees to recognize the locality in question as an open town, shall cease from all attacks on the said town, and refrain from any military operation the sole object of which is its occupation.

In the absence of any special conditions which may, in any particular case, be agreed upon with the adverse Party, a locality, in order to be declared an "open town," must satisfy the following conditions:

(a) It must not be defended or contain any armed force;

(b) It must discontinue all relations with any national or allied armed forces;

(c) It must stop all activities of a military nature or for a military purpose in those of its installations or industries which might be regarded as military objectives;

(d) It must stop all military transit through the town.

The adverse Party may make the recognition of the status of "open town" conditional upon verification of the fulfilment of the conditions stipulated above. All attacks shall be suspended during the institution and operation of the investigatory measures.

The presence in the locality of civil defence services, or of the services responsible for maintaining public order, shall not be considered as contrary to the conditions laid down in Paragraph 2. If the locality is situated in occupied territory, this provision applies also to the military occupation forces essential for the maintenance of public law and order.

When an "open town" passes into other hands, the new authorities are bound, if they cannot maintain its status, to inform the civilian population accordingly.

None of the above provisions shall be interpreted in such a manner as to diminish the protection which the civilian population should enjoy by virtue of the other provisions of the present rules, even when not living in localities recognized as "open towns."

Article 17

In order to safeguard the civilian population from the dangers that might result from the destruction of engineering works or installations—such as hydroelectric dams, nuclear power stations or dikes—through the releasing of natural or artificial forces, the States or Parties concerned are invited:

    (a) To agree, in time of peace, on a special procedure to ensure in all circumstances the general immunity of such works where intended essentially for peaceful purposes:

(b) To agree, in time of war, to confer special immunity, possible on the basis of the stipulations of Article 16, on works and installations which have not, or no longer have, any connexion with the conduct of military operations.

The preceding stipulations shall not, in any way, release the Parties to the conflict from the obligation to take the precautions required by the general provisions of the present rules, under Articles 8 to 11 in particular.

CHAPTER VI. APPLICATION OF THE RULES

Article 18

States not involved in the conflict, and also all appropriate organisations, are invited to co-operate, by lending their good offices, in ensuring the observance of the present rules and preventing either of the Parties to the conflict from resorting to measures contrary to those rules.

Article 19

All States or Parties concerned are under the obligation to search for and bring to trial any person having committed, or ordered to be committed, an infringement of the present rules, unless they prefer to hand the person over for trial to another State or Party concerned with the case.

The accused persons shall be tried only by regular civil or military courts; they shall, in all circumstances, benefit by safeguards of proper trial and defence at least equal to those provided under Articles 105 and those following of the Geneva Convention relative to the Treatment of Prisoners of War of August 12, 1949.

Article 20

All States or Parties concerned shall make the terms of the provisions of the present rules known to their armed forces and provide for their application in accordance with the general principles of these rules, not only in the instances specifically envisaged in the rules, but also in unforeseen cases.

Draft Additional Protocol to Article 3 Common to the Four Geneva Conventions of August 12, 1949

The High Contracting Parties,

Recalling that the human person remains at all times under the protection of the principles of humanity and the dictates of the public conscience,

Emphasizing that the humanitarian principles enshrined in Article 3 common to the four Geneva Conventions of August 12, 1949, constitute the foundation of respect for the human person in cases of armed conflict not of an international character,

Conscious of the need to develop the rules implicit in Article 3 common to the four Geneva Conventions of August 12, 1949, and applicable in armed conflicts not of an international character with a view to ensuring the basic humanitarian protection of all persons, whether combatants or non-combatants,

Agree on the following:

CHAPTER I

Scope of the Protocol

Article 1. Material field of application

The present Protocol, which elaborates and supplements Article 3 common to the four Geneva Conventions of August 12, 1949 (hereinafter referred to as common Article 3), shall apply to all conflicts not of an international character referred to in common Article 3 and, in particular, in all situations where, in the territory of one of the High Contracting Parties, hostilities of a collective nature are in action between organized armed forces under the command of a responsible authority.

Article 2. *Personal field of application*

The present Protocol shall apply to all persons, whether military or civilian, combatant or non-combatant, who are in the territory of one of the High Contracting Parties where an armed conflict within the meaning of Article 1 of the present Protocol is occurring.

Article 3. *Beginning and end of application*

The present Protocol shall apply from the time when the armed conflict begins until the end of hostilities. However, after the end of hostilities, persons who are interned or detained after sentence has been passed in respect of an act committed in relation to the armed conflict, and who have not been released, as well as persons arrested on charges relating to the armed conflict, shall enjoy the protection of Article 26 of the present Protocol for as long as their liberty shall be restricted.

CHAPTER II

General Protection of the Population

Article 4. *Torture and ill-treatment*

In order that the prohibition stipulated in common Article 3(1)(a) should obtain its fullest effect, the

Parties to the conflict shall take all necessary measures to ensure that their military or civilian agents should not commit, nor issue orders to commit, nor condone acts of torture or brutality.

Article 5. Terrorism, reprisals, pillage

1. Acts of terrorism, as well as reprisals against persons and objects indispensable to their survival, are prohibited.
2. Pillage is prohibited.
3. Women and children shall be protected, in particular against rape and any form of indecent assault.

Article 6. Measures in favour of children

1. Children shall be the object of special protection. The Parties to the conflict shall provide them with the care and aid which their age and situation require.
2. To this end the Parties to the conflict undertake, at least:

(a) to ensure the identification of children, particularly by making them wear identity discs;

(b) to take care that children who are orphaned or separated from their families as a result of armed conflict are not left abandoned;

(c) to endeavour to conclude local agreements for the removal of children from combat zones; such children shall be accompanied by persons responsible for ensuring their safety; all necessary steps shall be taken to permit the reunion of members of families temporarily separated;

(d) to take care that children under fifteen years of age do not take any direct part in hostilities.

3. The death penalty shall not be pronounced on ci-

vilians below eighteen years of age at the time when the
offence was committed, nor on mothers of infants or on
women responsible for their care. Pregnant women shall
not be executed.

Chapter III

Protection of the Wounded, Sick and Shipwrecked

Article 7. Protection and care

1. All wounded, sick and shipwrecked persons, military and civilians, as well as infirm persons, expectant
mothers and maternity cases, shall be the object of special
protection and respect.

2. Such persons shall, in all circumstances, be treated
humanely and shall receive, with the least possible delay,
the medical care that their condition requires, without
any discrimination.

3. All unjustified acts, whether of commission or omission, that endanger their person or their physical and
mental health are prohibited.

Article 8. Search

At all times, particularly after an engagement, Parties
to the conflict shall, without delay, take all possible measures to search for and collect the wounded, sick and shipwrecked and to ensure their adequate care.

Article 9. Role of the population

1. The civilian population shall respect the wounded,
sick and shipwrecked and refrain from committing acts
of violence against them.

2. No one shall be molested or convicted for having
tended the wounded, sick and shipwrecked.

Article 10. Medical and religious personnel

Military and civilian medical personnel as well as chaplains and other persons carrying out similar functions shall, in all circumstances, be respected and protected throughout their mission. Should they fall into the hands of the adverse Party, they shall be likewise respected and protected; they shall be granted all facilities necessary for the discharge of their functions and shall not be compelled to carry out tasks unrelated to their mission.

Article 11. Medical establishments and transports

1. Fixed establishments and mobile medical units, both military and civilian, which are solely intended for the care of the wounded, sick and shipwrecked, shall in no circumstances be attacked, but shall, together with their equipment, at all times be respected and protected by the Parties to the conflict.

2. Transports of wounded, sick and shipwrecked persons, or of medical personnel or equipment, shall be respected and protected in the same way as mobile medical units.

Article 12. Evacuation

The Parties to the conflict shall endeavour to conclude local agreements for the removal from areas where hostilities occur of the wounded, sick and shipwrecked, the infirm, expectant mothers and maternity cases.

Article 13. The distinctive emblem

1. The emblem of the red cross (red crescent, red lion and sun) on a white background is the distinctive emblem of the medical services of the Parties to the conflict

and of Red Cross organizations. It shall not be used for any other purpose and shall be respected in all circumstances.

2. From the outbreak of hostilities the Parties to the conflict shall adopt special measures for supervising the use of the distinctive emblem and for the prevention and repression of any misuse of the emblem.

CHAPTER IV

Civilian Population

Article 14. Definition of the civilian population

1. Any person who is not a member of the armed forces and who, moreover, does not take a direct part in hostilities is considered to be a civilian.

2. The civilian population is composed of all civilians fulfilling the conditions in paragraph 1.

3. Proposal I: The presence, within the civilian population, of individuals who do not conform to the definition given in paragraph 1, does not prevent the civilian population from being considered as such.

Proposal II: The presence, within the civilian population, of individual combatants, does not prevent the civilian population from being considered as such.

Article 15. Respect for and safeguarding of the civilian population

1. The civilian population as such, as well as individual civilians, shall never be made the object of attack.

2. In particular, terrorization attacks shall be prohibited.

3. Attacks which, by their nature, are launched against civilians and military objectives indiscriminately, shall be prohibited. Nevertheless, civilians who are within a military objective run the risks consequent upon any attack launched against this objective.

4. The civilian population or individual civilians shall never be used in an attempt to shield, by their presence, military objectives from attack.

Article 16. Respect for and safeguarding of objects indispensable to the survival of the civilian population.

Proposal I: 1. Objects indispensable to the survival of the civilian population shall not be the object of attack.

2. The Parties to the conflict under whose control objects indispensable to the survival of the civilian population are placed, shall refrain from:

(a) using them in an attempt to shield military objectives from attack;

(b) destroying them, except in cases of unavoidable military necessity and only for such time as that necessity remains.

Proposal II: 1. Objects indispensable to the survival of the civilian population shall not be the object of attack.

2. The Parties to the conflict under whose control objects indispensable to the survival of the civilian population are placed shall refrain from destroying them or using them in an attempt to shield military objectives from attack.

Article 17. Precautions when attacking

So that the civilian population, as well as objects indispensable to its survival, who might be in proximity to a military objective be spared, those who order or launch an attack shall, when planning and carrying out the attack, take the following precautions:

(a) they shall ensure that the objectives to be attacked are not civilians, nor objects of a civilian character, but are identified as military objectives; if this precaution cannot be taken, they shall refrain from launching the attack;

(b) they shall warn, whenever circumstances permit, and sufficiently in advance, the civilians threatened, so that the latter may take shelter.

CHAPTER V

Combatants

Article 18. Means of combat

1. Combatants' choice of means of combat is not unlimited.

2. It is forbidden to use weapons, projectiles or substances calculated to cause unnecessary suffering, or particularly cruel methods and means.

3. In cases for which no provision is made in the present Protocol, the principle of humanity and the dictates of the public conscience shall continue to safeguard populations and combatants pending the adoption of fuller regulations.

Article 19. Prohibition of perfidy

1. It is forbidden to kill or injure by resort to perfidy.

Unlawful acts betraying an enemy's confidence are deemed to constitute perfidy.

2. Ruses of war are not considered as perfidy.

Article 20. Recognized signs

It is forbidden to make improper use of the flag of truce, the protective sign of the red cross (red crescent, red lion and sun), the protective sign for cultural property and other protective signs specified in international conventions.

Article 21. Emblems of nationality

It is forbidden to make improper use of enemy insignia and uniforms. In combat their use is forbidden at all times.

Article 22. Safeguard of an enemy hors de combat

1. It is forbidden to kill or wound an enemy who, having laid down his arms, or having no longer means of defence, has surrendered at discretion.

2. It is forbidden to decide to leave no survivors and take no prisoners, to so threaten an enemy and to conduct the fight in accordance with such a decision.

3. A captor shall provide for persons falling in his power even if he decides to release them.

Article 23. Conditions of capture and surrender

1. A combatant is captured when he falls into the power of an enemy.

2. The following *inter alia* shall be considered to have fallen into the power of an enemy:

(a) any disarmed combatant unable to defend himself or express himself in territory taken, even temporarily, by an enemy;

(b) any combatant expressing by the usual means or by his attitude his intention to surrender, and abstaining from any violence.

Article 24. *Aircraft occupants*

The occupants of aircraft in distress who parachute to save their lives, or who are compelled to make a forced landing, shall not be attacked during their descent or landing unless their attitude is hostile.

CHAPTER VI

Persons Whose Liberty Has Been Restricted

Article 25. *Treatment of combatants who have fallen into the power of the adversary*

Members of regular armed forces and members of those armed forces which have fulfilled the conditions stipulated in Article 4A(2) of the Geneva Convention relative to the Treatment of Prisoners of War of August 12, 1949, shall receive, after having fallen into the power of the adversary, a treatment similar to that provided for prisoners of war in the said Convention.

Article 26. *Treatment of persons whose liberty has been restricted*

1. Subject to Article 25 of the present Protocol, all other persons whose liberty has been restricted, whether interned or detained after sentence has been passed, in respect of an act committed in relation to the armed conflict, shall in all circumstances be respected and treated humanely, without any adverse distinction.

2. All unjustified acts, whether of commission or omission, that endanger their person or their physical and mental health are prohibited.

3. The Parties to the conflict shall respect, as a minimum, the following provisions:

(a) they shall provide for the maintenance of the persons referred to in paragraph 1 above and for the medical attention which their state of health requires;

(b) places of internment and detention shall not be set up in areas close to combat zones. The persons referred to in paragraph 1 above shall be evacuated when the places where they are interned or detained become particularly exposed to dangers arising out of the conflict, if their evacuation can be carried out in adequate conditions of safety;

(c) the persons referred to in paragraph 1 above shall be allowed to practise their religion and receive spiritual assistance from chaplains and other persons performing similar functions;

(d) the persons referred to in paragraph 1 above shall be allowed to send and receive letters and cards. The Parties to the conflict may limit the number of letters and cards sent by each person if they deem it necessary;

(e) the persons referred to in paragraph 1 above shall be allowed to receive individual or collective relief.

4. Subject to temporary and exceptional measures, the Parties to the conflict shall agree to and facilitate visits to the persons referred to in paragraph 1 above, carried out by an impartial humanitarian body such as the International Committee of the Red Cross.

CHAPTER VII

Penal Prosecutions

Article 27. Individual responsibility

No person may be punished for an offence he or she has not personally committed. Collective penalties are prohibited.

Article 28. Penal prosecutions against combatants

After having fallen into the power of the adversary, combatants who will have fulfilled the conditions stipulated in Article 25 of the present Protocol, as well as those combatants who, without having fulfilled the conditions stipulated in Article 4A(2) of the Geneva Convention relative to the Treatment of Prisoners of War of August 12, 1949, will have at least, in the course of their operations, distinguished themselves from the civilian population by some distinctive sign or by any other means and who had complied with the provisions of the present Protocol, shall not be punishable by death if they become the object of penal prosecutions only by reason of having taken part in hostilities or having been members of armed forces.

CHAPTER VIII

Relief

Article 29. Relief for the population

The Parties to the conflict shall ensure, to the fullest extent of the means available to them and without any adverse distinction, the provision of foodstuffs, clothing, medical and hospital stores and shelter facilities necessary for the population in the territory under their control.

Article 30. Humanitarian assistance

1. If the population is inadequately supplied in foodstuffs, clothing, medical and hospital stores and shelter facilities, or if the wounded, sick and shipwrecked, military and civilian, need medical assistance, the Parties to the conflict shall, to the fullest possible extent, agree to and facilitate impartial relief activities undertaken by

humanitarian bodies, such as the International Committee of the Red Cross and National Red Cross Societies.

2. The Parties to the conflict shall have the right to prescribe the technical arrangements under which the passage of relief supplies shall be allowed. They shall in no way whatsoever divert relief consignments from the purpose for which they are intended or delay the forwarding of such consignments.

3. In no circumstances shall this assistance be considered as interference in the conflict.

Article 31. Consignment of essential supplies for the civilian population

1. In cases of blockade or siege, the Parties to the conflict or any High Contracting Party concerned shall allow the free passage of all consignments of essential foodstuffs, clothing, medical and hospital stores and shelter facilities, intended only for civilians.

2. The Parties to the conflict or any High Contracting Party concerned shall have the right to prescribe the technical arrangements under which the passage of relief supplies shall be allowed. They shall in no way whatsoever divert relief consignments from the purpose for which they are intended or delay the forwarding of such consignments.

3. The Parties to the conflict or any High Contracting Party concerned may make such permission conditional on the distribution only to the persons benefited thereby being made under the supervision of an impartial humanitarian body.

Article 32. Recording and information

1. The International Committee of the Red Cross shall, if it deems necessary, propose to the Parties to the conflict the organization of information bureaux to which

they shall communicate all relevant information on victims of the events who may be in their power. The dead shall also be recorded.

2. Each information bureau shall transmit to the other bureaux, if necessary through the Central Tracing Agency, the information thus obtained and shall transmit them to the next of kin concerned; the information bureaux shall also be responsible for replying to all enquiries concerning victims of the events and shall take the necessary steps to search for them; this is subject to reservations concerning cases where the transmission of information or the search might be detrimental to the victims of the events or to their relatives.

Article 33. National Red Cross and other relief societies

1. Subject to temporary and exceptional measures taken by the Parties to the conflict to guarantee their security, the National Red Cross (Red Crescent, Red Lion and Sun) Society and its branches shall be able to pursue their activities in accordance with the rules of the Red Cross as stated by International Red Cross Conferences. Other relief societies shall be permitted to continue their humanitarian activities under similar conditions.

2. Other humanitarian relief organizations created during the hostilities shall be permitted to carry out their activities in accordance with the principles of humanity, impartiality and neutrality.

3. In no circumstances shall the fact of having taken part in the humanitarian activities of the organizations referred to in paragraphs 1 and 2 above be considered to be punishable.

Article 34. Civil Defence Organizations

1. Subject to temporary and exceptional measures taken by the Parties to the conflict to guarantee their security, civil defence organizations shall be allowed to carry out their humanitarian tasks; they shall at all times be protected.

2. In no circumstances shall the fact of having taken part in the humanitarian activities of such organizations be considered to be punishable.

CHAPTER IX

Executory Provisions

Article 35. Regulations

The Regulations concerning special cases of armed conflicts not of an international character (hereinafter called the Regulations) shall constitute an integral part of the present Protocol; the procedure by which the present Protocol is to be applied is also valid for the Regulations.

Article 36. Special agreements

The Parties to the conflict shall endeavour to bring into force, either by means of special agreements, or by declarations addressed to the International Committee of the Red Cross, all or part of the other provisions of the four Geneva Conventions of August 12, 1949, and of the Additional Protocol to the said Conventions.

Article 37. Co-operation in the observance of the present Protocol

Each Party to the conflict, to the fullest possible extent, shall call upon a body which offers all guarantees of impartiality and efficacy to co-operate in the observance of the provisions of the present Protocol and its Regulations and of the other provisions of the four Geneva Conventions of August 12, 1949, and of the Additional Protocol to the said Conventions brought into force in accordance with Article 36 of the present Protocol.

Article 38. Legal status of the Parties to the conflict

The legal status of the Parties to the conflict shall not be affected by the application of the provisions of the present Protocol and its Regulations and of all or part of the other provisions of the four Geneva Conventions of August 12, 1949, and the Additional Protocol to the said Conventions brought into force in accordance with Article 36 of the present Protocol, and by the conclusion of any other agreement.

Article 39. Dissemination of the present Protocol

1. The High Contracting Parties undertake, in time of peace, to disseminate the text of the present Protocol as widely as possible to the whole population; they shall include the study thereof in their programmes of military and civil instruction.

2. In time of armed conflict, the responsible authorities of the Parties to the conflict shall take appropriate measures to bring the provisions of the present Protocol and its Regulations to the knowledge of all, combatants and non-combatants alike.

Article 40. Rules of application

The High Contracting Parties shall communicate to one another, through the Depositary State, the laws and regulations which they adopt to ensure the application of the present Protocol and its Regulations.

CHAPTER X

Final Provisions

Article 41. Signature

The present Protocol shall be open until ... ... 197... at ..., for signature by the Parties to the four Geneva Conventions of August 12, 1949.

Article 42. Ratification

The present Protocol is subject to ratification. The instruments of ratification shall be deposited with the Depositary State.

Article 43. Accession

1. The present Protocol shall remain open for accession by any Party to the four Geneva Conventions of August 12, 1949, which has not signed the present Protocol.

2. The instruments of accession shall be deposited with the Depositary State.

Article 44. Entry into force

1. The present Protocol shall enter into force when ... instruments of ratification or accession have been deposited.

2. Thereafter, it shall enter into force, for each High Contracting Party, as soon as its instrument of ratification or of accession has been deposited.

Article 45. Treaty relations upon entry into force of the present Protocol

When the Parties to the four Geneva Conventions of August 12, 1949, are also Parties to the present Protocol, common Article 3 shall apply as elaborated and supplemented by the present Protocol.

Article 46. Notifications

The Depositary State shall inform all the Parties to the present Protocol of the following particulars:

(a) signatures affixed to the present Protocol, ratifications and accessions under Articles 43 and 44 of the present Protocol;

(b) the date of entry into force of the present Protocol under its Article 45.

Article 47. Registration and publication

After its entry into force, the present Protocol shall be transmitted by the Depositary State to the Secretariat of the United Nations Organization for registration and publication, in accordance with Article 102 of the United Nations Charter.

Article 48. Authentic texts and official translations

1. The original of the present Protocol, of which the French and English texts are equally authentic, shall be deposited with the Depositary State.

2. The Depositary State shall arrange for official translations of the present Protocol to be made into Arabic, Chinese, Russian and Spanish.

IN WITNESS WHEREOF the undersigned, being duly authorized thereto, have signed the present Protocol.

DONE AT ..., this ... day of ..., 197... .

ANNEX

Regulations Concerning Special Cases of Armed
Conflicts Not of an International Character

*Article 1. Effective organization of the Party oppos-
ing the authorities in power*

When, in case of armed conflict not of an international
character in the territory of one of the High Contracting
Parties, the Party opposing the authorities in power has
a government which exercises effective power, by means
of its administration and adequately organized armed
forces, over a part of the territory, the Parties to the conflict shall apply all the provisions of the four Geneva
Conventions of August 12, 1949, and the Additional
Protocol to the said Conventions.

*Article 2. Outside aid in armed conflict not of an
international character*

When, in case of armed conflicts not of an international character in the territory of one of the High Contracting Parties, the armed forces of other States take a
direct part in the hostilities, the relations between the
Parties to the conflict shall be governed as follows:

(a) the relations as between the authorities in power
and the States that aid the Party opposing the authorities
in power shall be governed by the four Geneva Conventions of August 12, 1949, and the Additional Protocol
to the said Conventions; the same shall apply to the relations between States aiding the authorities in power
and States aiding the Party opposing the authorities in
power;

(b) the relations between the authorities in power and

the Party opposing those authorities shall be governed by at least the provisions in common Article 3 and in the present Protocol. Moreover, the Parties to the conflict shall grant to all captured combatants prisoner-of-war treatment as laid down in the Geneva Convention relative to the Treatment of Prisoners of War of August 12, 1949, and shall apply to civilians the provisions of Part IV relative to the civilian population of the Additional Protocol to the Geneva Conventions:

(1) when only the authorities in power benefit from other States' assistance;

(2) when both authorities in power and the Party opposing them benefit from other States' assistance.

(c) all the relations between the Parties to the conflict shall be governed by the four Geneva Conventions of August 12, 1949, and the Additional Protocol to the said Conventions, when the Party opposing the authorities in power fulfils the conditions stipulated in Article 1 of these Regulations, whether or not it is aided by other States.

III

DRAFT RESOLUTION CONCERNING DISARMAMENT AND PEACE TO BE ANNEXED TO THE FINAL ACT OF THE DIPLOMATIC CONFERENCE

The Conference,

noting that the Geneva Conventions and their Additional Protocols do not contain any express provision concerning weapons of mass destruction, blind, poisonous and particularly cruel weapons, and weapons with indiscriminate effects, *believing* nevertheless that these weapons are contrary to the dictates of humanity and that, in armed conflicts, the members of the international community must absolutely renounce their use,

expresses the hope that the prohibition of the production, stockpiling and use of such weapons will be confirmed or proclaimed and that these measures will lead to general and complete disarmament,

urges, moreover, the Parties to the Conventions to spare no effort for the preservation of peace.

Geneva Convention Relative to the Protection of Human Rights in Internal Armed Conflicts

Article 1.

1. The High Contracting Parties undertake to respect and to ensure respect for the present Convention in all circumstances.

2. Each party to an armed conflict to which this Convention applies is responsible for ensuring compliance with this Convention by members of its armed forces and other persons in its service or subject to its control.

Article 2.

1. In addition to the provisions which shall be implemented in peace time, the present Convention shall apply to any case of armed conflict not of an international character which is carried on in the territory of a High Contracting Party and in which organized armed forces carry on hostile activities in arms against the authorities in power and the authorities in power employ their armed forces against such persons.

or

[1. In addition to the provisions which shall be implemented in peace time, the present Convention shall apply to any case of armed conflict *not of an international character* which is carried on in the territory of a High Contracting Party and in which

(1) organized armed forces, subject to a system of internal discipline and exercising effective authority over some part of the territory of the

state, carry on hostile activities in arms against the authorities in power, and

(2) the authorities in power employ their armed forces against such persons.]

2. The present Convention has no application to situations of internal disturbance or tension.

3. The operation of the present Convention is without prejudice to the application of Article 3 of the Geneva Conventions for the Protection of War Victims of August 12, 1949 by the High Contracting Parties to those Conventions.

4. The application of this Convention shall not affect the legal status of the parties to an armed conflict. [In particular, the application of the present Convention by any party to an armed conflict shall not be taken to imply the recognition, legitimacy, or international standing of that or any other party to the armed conflict.]

Article 3.

1. The provisions of this Convention cover the whole of the population of the High Contracting Party in the territory of which a non-international conflict is taking place.

2. In the treatment of the population, no adverse distinction shall be made based on race, colour, caste, nationality, religion, sex, birth, wealth or any other similar criterion.

Article 4.

An impartial humanitarian body, such as the International Committee of the Red Cross, may offer its services to the parties to the conflict. The acceptance of such services by a party to the conflict is not dependent on the authorization of any other party to the conflict.

PROTECTION OF THE WOUNDED AND SICK

Article 5.

1. The wounded and sick, whether non-combatants or combatants rendered hors de combat, as well as the infirm, expectant mothers, and maternity cases, shall be the object of particular protection and respect.

2. In all circumstances these persons shall be treated humanely and shall receive with the least possible delay the medical care and attention necessitated by their condition, without any adverse distinction or discrimination based on political opinion or any of the criteria referred to in Article 3.

3. Any unjustified act or omission which seriously endangers the health or physical or mental well-being of any person referred to in paragraph 1 is prohibited.

Article 6.

1. At all times, and particularly after an engagement, the parties to the conflict shall, without delay, take all possible measures to search for and collect the wounded and sick, to protect them against pillage and ill-treatment, to ensure their adequate care, and to search for the dead and to prevent their being despoiled.

2. The parties to the conflict shall communicate to each other or, when this is not possible, publish all details of wounded and sick and dead of the adverse party in their hands.

Article 7.

1. The civilian population shall respect the wounded and sick, and in particular abstain from offering them violence.

2. No one may ever be molested or convicted for having nursed or cared for the wounded or sick.

Article 8.

Military and civilian medical personnel as well as chaplains and others performing similar functions shall be respected and protected in all circumstances during the period of the performance of their medical, religious, or humanitarian duties. If they should fall into the hands of the adverse party, they shall continue to be respected and protected. They shall receive all available facilities for the discharge of their functions and shall not be compelled to perform any work outside their professional duties.

Article 9.

1. Fixed establishments and mobile medical units, both military and civilian, which are solely intended for the care of the wounded and sick shall under no circumstances be the object of attack; they and their equipment shall at all times be respected and protected by the parties to the conflict.

2. The protection to which fixed establishments and mobile medical units are entitled shall cease if they are used to commit, outside their humanitarian duties, acts harmful to the adverse party. Protection may, however, cease only after a due warning has been given, naming, in all appropriate cases, a reasonable time limit, and after such warning has remained unheeded.

3. Transports of wounded and sick or of medical personnel or equipment shall be respected and protected in the same way as mobile medical units.

Article 10.

The parties to the conflict shall endeavour to conclude local arrangements for the removal from areas where hostilities are taking place of the wounded and sick, infirm persons, expectant mothers, and maternity cases.

Article 11.

1. An offer of medical assistance by another State or by an impartial humanitarian organization to aid in the relief of persons suffering as a consequence of the conflict shall not be considered as an unfriendly act and neither such an offer nor its acceptance shall have any effect on the legal status of the parties to the conflict.

2. An offer by another State to receive wounded, sick, or infirm persons, expectant mothers, and maternity cases on its territory shall not be considered as an unfriendly act and neither such an offer nor its acceptance shall have any effect on the legal status of the parties to the conflict.

Article 12.

The emblem of the red cross (red crescent, red lion and sun) on a white background is retained as the distinctive emblem of the medical services of the parties to a conflict. It shall not be used for any other purposes and shall be respected in all circumstances.

TREATMENT OF THE POPULATION

Article 13.

Non-combatants and combatants rendered hors de combat in the territory of a High Contracting Party within which a non-international conflict is taking place are entitled, in all circumstances, to respect for their persons, their honour, their family rights, their religious convictions and practices, and their manners and customs. They shall at all times be humanely treated, and shall be protected especially against all acts of torture and unlawful violence, against threats thereof, and against insults and public curiosity.

Article 14.

1. The parties to the conflict are forbidden
   a. to employ poison or poisoned weapons;
   b. to kill or wound individuals treacherously;
   c. to employ arms, projectiles, or material calculated to cause unnecessary suffering;
   d. to destroy property, unless such destruction be imperatively demanded by considerations of security;
   e. to pillage;
   f. to impose collective penalties or to take measures of intimidation, terrorism or assassination;
   g. to take reprisals against non-combatants and combatants rendered hors de combat; and
   h. to take hostages.
2. The parties to the conflict are not precluded from the use of herbicides and of lachriminatory gases and other riot control agents.

Article 15.

1. Persons taking no active part in the hostilities shall not intentionally be made the object of attack. The presence of such persons may not be used to render certain points or areas immune from military operations.
2. Except when urgent military necessities prevent, a bombardment of a place in which there are persons who

take no active part in the hostilities shall be preceded by
a warning adequate to permit such persons to remove
themselves to a safe place.

Article 16.

The parties to an armed conflict shall endeavour to
establish by agreement hospital and safety zones and
localities to protect from the effects of the conflict,
wounded, sick and aged persons, children, expectant
mothers, and mothers of small children.

Article 17.

1. The parties to the conflict shall not force the displacement of any portion of the population except if the
security of the population or imperative military reasons
so demand.
2. The parties to the conflict shall not under any circumstances force any portion of the population to leave
the territory of the state within which the armed conflict
is taking place.

Article 18.

The parties to the conflict shall, to the extent possible,
take or permit measures to facilitate the renewing of
contact by members of families dispersed by or during
the conflict. A party to the conflict shall encourage in
particular the work of organizations engaged on this task,
provided they are acceptable to it and conform to its
security regulations.

RELIEF ACTIVITIES

Article 19.

1. The parties to the conflict shall allow and facilitate
the free passage of consignments of medical and hospital

stores, essential foodstuffs, clothing, and tonics intended for the relief of those taking no active part in the hostilities. They shall give particular regard to the needs of children under fifteen, expectant mothers and maternity cases.

2. The party which allows the passage of the consignments referred to in paragraph 1 may make such permission conditional on the distribution to the persons to be benefited thereby being made under the effective supervision of an organ of the United Nations, the International Committee of the Red Cross, or other humanitarian organization.

3. Such consignments shall be forwarded as rapidly as possible, and the party which permits their free passage shall have the right to prescribe the technical arrangements under which such passage is allowed.

4. The party to the conflict to which a consignment is made may not refuse it unless the consignment is not needed to meet the needs of those persons for whose benefit it was intended.

5. An offer of supplies of the nature described in paragraph 1 shall not be considered as an unfriendly act and shall not affect the legal status of the parties to the conflict.

Penal Proceedings

Article 20.

No person may be punished for an offence which he or she has not committed.

Article 21.

No sentence shall be passed or execution carried out without previous judgment pronounced by a regularly

constituted court affording all the judicial guarantees
which are recognized as indispensable by the principal
legal systems of the world.

Article 22.

A person convicted of an offence shall be entitled, in
accordance with the laws in force, to avail himself of
the right of appeal or petition from any sentence pronounced upon him. He shall be fully informed of his
right to appeal or petition.

Article 23.

At the conclusion of the hostilities; the parties to the
conflict should endeavour to grant amnesty to as many
as possible of those who have participated in the conflict
or have been convicted of offences or deprived of liberty
in connection with the conflict.

INTERNMENT AND DEPRIVATION OF LIBERTY

Article 24.

Persons who have been confined, detained, interned, or
otherwise deprived of their liberty shall be released when
the reason for their confinement, detention, internment or
other deprivation of liberty ceases to exist.

Article 25.

Persons who have been confined, detained, interned,
or otherwise deprived of their liberty shall be humanely
treated. They shall in particular:

> (a) be accommodated in buildings or quarters
> which afford reasonable safeguards as re-
> gards hygiene and health and provide effi-
> cient protection against the rigours of the
> climate and the effects of the war;

(b) be provided with adequate supplies of water and with food rations sufficient to keep them in a good state of health;

(c) be permitted to secure adequate clothing or be provided with such clothing;

(d) be permitted to practice their religion and to receive spiritual assistance from ministers of their faith; and

(e) be enabled to receive individual or collective relief sent to them.

Article 26.

1. The parties to the conflict should endeavour to avoid setting up places of internment, confinement, or detention in areas exposed to the dangers of war.

2. Whenever military considerations permit, internment camps shall be indicated by the letters IC, placed so as to be clearly visible in the daytime from the air, or by such other system of marking as may be agreed upon by the parties to the conflict.

Article 27.

Except as provided in Article 28, women who are confined, detained, interned, or otherwise deprived of their liberty shall be placed in separate accommodation and shall, in so far as possible, be placed under the direct supervision of women.

Article 28.

Throughout the duration of any internment members of the same family, and in particular parents and children, shall be lodged together in the same place of internment, except when separation of a temporary nature is necessitated for reasons of employment or health or for

the service of a term of imprisonment under sentence of
a court. Internees may request that their children who
are left at liberty without parental care shall be interned
with them.

FINAL PROVISIONS

[The Convention would contain the normal final
clauses, including the same provision contained in the
Geneva Conventions of 1949 that it would be open to
accession by "any Power"—whether or not a party to one
or more of the Geneva Conventions of 1949. It would be
stipulated that in relations between Powers that are
bound by the Geneva Conventions of 1949, this Convention would be supplementary to Article 3 of those Conventions. All of this implies, as is intended, that even a
non-party to the Geneva Conventions of 1949 may become a party to this agreement.]

Canadian Draft Protocol to the Geneva Conventions of 1949 Relative to Conflicts Not International in Character

Prepared and Presented by the Canadian Expert

CHAPTER 1. APPLICATION

Article 1. Purpose and Application of the Protocol

1) The present provisions, which reaffirm and supplement existing provisions of the Geneva Conventions of August 12, 1949 (hereinafter referred to as "the Conventions"), apply to all cases of armed conflict occurring in the territory of one of the High Contracting Parties, involving government military forces on one side and military forces whether regular or irregular on the other side, and to which common Article 2 of the Conventions is not applicable.

2) The present provisions shall apply as a minimum with respect to all persons, whether military or civilian, combatant or non-combatant, present in the territory where a conflict such as is described in 1) of this article is occurring.

3) The Parties to the conflict should endeavour to bring into force all or part of the provisions of the Conventions not included in this Protocol.

4) Each Party to the conflict should arrange for, or agree to, the presence in territory under its control of impartial observers who shall report to the party who has so arranged for or agreed to their presence, on the

observance by persons in the territory under the control of that party of the provisions of this protocol. Where such action has not been taken by a Party to a conflict other states may request and encourage that Party to consider having recourse to such impartial observers.

CHAPTER 2. SPECIAL PROTECTION

Article 2. Protection and Care

1) All persons who are wounded or sick as well as the infirm, expectant mothers, maternity cases and children under fifteen, shall be given particular protection and respect.

2) They shall in all circumstances be treated humanely and, with the least possible delay, shall receive the care necessitated by their condition, without any adverse distinction.

Article 3. Search and Recording

1) At all times and particularly after an engagement, Parties to the conflict shall without delay take all possible measures to search for and collect the wounded and the sick, to protect them against pillage and ill treatment and to ensure their adequate care.

2) Parties to the conflict shall endeavour to communicate to each other all details on persons who are wounded, sick or who have died while in their hands.

Article 4. Role of the Population

1) All persons shall respect the wounded and the sick and in particular shall abstain from offering them violence.

2) No one may ever be molested or convicted for having nursed the wounded or sick.

Article 5. Medical Personnel

1) Military and civilian medical personnel and chaplains shall be, in all circumstances, respected and protected during the period they are engaged. If they should fall into the hands of an adverse party they shall be respected and protected. They shall receive all facilities to discharge their functions and shall not be compelled to perform any work outside their mission.

2) Medical personnel may be authorized by a party to the conflict to wear the distinctive emblem of the Red Cross (Red Crescent, Red Lion and Sun) on a white background.

3) Personnel so authorized shall wear the emblem on the armlet affixed to the left arm and shall carry an appropriate identity card indicating in what capacity he is so entitled to wear the emblem.

Article 6. Medical Establishments and Transports

1) Fixed establishments, including blood transfusion centres and mobile medical units, both military and civilian, which are solely intended to care for the wounded and the sick, the infirm and maternity cases, shall under no circumstances be attacked; they and their equipment shall at all time be respected and protected by the Parties to the conflict.

2) Transports of wounded and sick, or of medical personnel or equipment shall be respected and protected in the same way as mobile medical units. Such transports may be marked by the emblem of the Red Cross (Red Crescent, Red Lion and Sun) when being used solely for such purpose.

3) With authorization from a Party to the conflict, fixed and mobile medical establishments and units shall be marked by means of the emblem of the Red Cross

(Red Crescent, Red Lion and Sun) on a white background.

Article 7. Evacuation

The Parties to the conflict shall endeavour to conclude local arrangements for the removal from areas where hostilities are taking place of wounded or sick, infirm, expectant mothers, maternity cases, and children under fifteen.

Article 8. Medical Assistance by Other States

1) An offer of medical assistance by another state to aid in the relief of any persons suffering as a consequence of the conflict shall not be considered as an unfriendly act or have any effect on the status of the Parties to the conflict.

2) An offer by another state to receive wounded, sick or infirm persons, children under fifteen, expectant mothers and maternity cases on its territory shall not be considered as an unfriendly act or have any effect on the status of the Parties to the conflict.

Article 9. The Distinctive Emblem

The emblem of the Red Cross (Red Crescent or Red Lion and Sun) on a white background is the distinctive emblem of the medical services of the Parties to a conflict. It shall not be used for any other purposes and shall be respected in all circumstances.

CHAPTER 3. RELIEF

Article 10. Consignment of Medical Supplies, Food and Clothing

1) Each Party to the conflict shall allow the free passage of all consignments of medical and hospital stores,

essential foodstuffs, clothing and tonics intended only for non-combatants belonging to or under the control of another Party to the conflict.

2) The obligation of a Party to the conflict to allow the free passage of the consignments is subject to the condition that that Party is satisfied that there are no serious reasons for fearing that the consignments may be diverted from their destination or intended use.

3) The Party to the conflict which allows the passage of the consignments may make such permission conditional on the distribution to the intended beneficiaries being made under the local supervision of the ICRC or other appropriate agency.

4) Consignments shall be forwarded as rapidly as possible and the Party to the conflict which permits their free passage shall have the right to prescribe under what reasonable technical arrangements the passage is to be allowed.

5) The Party to the conflict to whom a consignment has been made may not refuse it unless the consignment is not needed to meet the needs of those persons for whose benefit it was intended.

6) An offer of supplies as described in paragraph 1) of this article shall not be considered as an unfriendly act or have any effect on the status of the Parties to the conflict.

Article 11. Applications to Relief Organizations

1) All parties belonging to or under the control of a Party to the conflict shall have the right to make application to the ICRC, the National Red Cross (Red Crescent, Red Lion and Sun) Society or other organization in the country in which the conflict is occurring which might assist them.

2) The several organizations referred to in this article shall be granted all facilities for carrying out their purposes by the authorities within the bounds set by military or security considerations.

Chapter 4. Hostages, Pillage, Reprisals and Torture

Article 12. Hostages, Pillage and Reprisals

1) The taking of hostages is prohibited.
2) Pillage is prohibited.
3) Reprisals against persons and property are prohibited.

Article 13. Prohibition of Torture, etc.

All persons shall be treated humanely and in particular no party to the conflict shall, with respect to persons belonging to it or under its control, take any measure of such a character as to cause them physical suffering or extermination. This prohibition applies not only to murder, torture, mutilation and medical or scientific experiments not necessitated by the medical treatment of such persons, but also to any other measures of brutality whether applied by civilian or military agents.

Chapter 5. Penal Procedures

Article 14. Individual Responsibility, Collective Penalties

No person may be punished for an offence he or she has not personally committed. Collective penalties and likewise all measures of intimidation or of terrorism are prohibited.

Article 15. Passing and Execution of Sentences

With respect to any accused person, the passing of sentences and the carrying out of executions without previous judgment pronounced by a regularly constituted court affording all the judicial guarantees, including the right to be represented by counsel, which are recognized as indispensable by civilized peoples, are prohibited.

Article 16. Appeals

A convicted person shall be advised of his rights of appeal or petition and such rights shall not be denied except in accordance with laws normally applicable thereto.

Article 17. Presence of Red Cross Representatives

1) Representatives of the National Red Cross (Red Crescent or Red Lion and Sun) Society and of the International Committee of the Red Cross, shall have the right to attend the trial of any accused person, unless the hearing is, as an exceptional measure, to be held *in camera* in the interests of security.

2) Where an accused is to be tried for an offence arising out of his participation in the conflict the punishment for which may be death, the National Red Cross (Red Crescent or Red Lion and Sun) Society and the ICRC shall be notified as to the date and place such trial is to take place.

Article 18. Death Penalty

1) Death sentences imposed upon persons whose guilt arises only by reason of having participated as combatants in the conflict shall not be carried out until after hostilities have ceased.

2) Death sentences imposed on any person shall not, in any event, be carried out until the convicted person has exhausted all means of appeal and petition for pardon or reprieve.

CHAPTER 6. PERSONS IN RESTRICTED LIBERTY

Article 19. Persons Whose Liberty Has Been Restricted

All persons who for any reason are confined, detained, interned or whose liberty has otherwise been restricted shall be humanely treated, and in particular shall:

a) receive necessary medical attention including periodical medical examinations and hospital treatment;

b) be allowed to practise their religion and to receive spiritual assistance from ministers of their faith;

c) be adequately fed, clothed and sheltered, having particular regard to their health, age, condition and employment;

d) be enabled to receive individual or collective relief sent to them;

e) be removed if the area in which they are confined, detained, interned or restricted, becomes particularly exposed to dangers arising out of the conflict;

f) if female, be confined in separate quarters under the direct supervision of women; and

g) shall be allowed to send and receive letters and cards, except that where it is considered necessary to limit the number of letters and cards sent by a person the said number shall not be less than two letters and four cards monthly.

Article 20. Interned Families

Wherever possible, interned members of the same family shall be housed in the same premises and given separate accommodation from other internees, together with facilities for leading a proper family life. Internees may request that their children who are left at liberty without parental care shall be interned with them and, except where compliance with the request would be contrary to the interests of the children concerned, it shall be granted.

Article 21. Placing and Marking of Internment Camps

1) Places of internment shall not be set up in areas particularly exposed to dangers arising out of the conflict.

2) Whenever military considerations permit, internment camps shall be indicated by the letters IC placed so as to be clearly visible in the daytime from the air. The Parties to the conflict may, however, agree upon any other system of marking. No place other than an internment camp shall be marked as such.

3) The Parties to the conflict shall give each other information concerning the location of internment camps.

CHAPTER 7. GENERAL

Article 22. Dispersed Families

A Party to the conflict shall, to the extent possible, take or permit such measures or enquiries as shall facilitate the renewing of contact by members of families dispersed by or during the conflict. Parties to the conflict in particular shall encourage the work of organizations engaged on this task provided they conform to security regulations.

Article 23. National Red Cross and Other Relief Societies

Subject to temporary and exceptional measures imposed for reasons of security by the Parties to the conflict, the National Red Cross (Red Crescent, Red Lion and Sun) Society shall be able to pursue its activities in accordance with Red Cross principles as defined by International Red Cross Conferences. Other relief societies shall be permitted to continue their humanitarian activities under similar conditions.

Article 24. Responsibilities

Each Party to the conflict is responsible for the treatment accorded by its agents to all persons belonging to it or under its control irrespective of any individual responsibility which may be incurred.

Minimum Rules for the Protection of Non-Delinquent Detainees

Considering that, in application of universally recognized principles of human rights for all sorts and conditions of men, a body of minimum rules for the treatment of detained delinquents has been drawn up on the basis of resolutions and recommendations adopted by the Congress of the United Nations, which met for that purpose in Geneva from August 22 to September 3, 1955;

Considering also that social conscience would not be satisfied if, whilst penitentiary science is increasingly adapting the treatment of delinquents deprived of their liberty to the requirements of justice and humanity, minimum guarantees were not granted to persons deprived of their liberty without having been prosecuted for penal offences and accused or convicted of an infringement of national or international law;

Considering, further, the absence of such guarantees for administrative, political and military internees and persons arrested for security reasons in the event of danger or internal and external strife;

There should be drawn up for the protection of these people a general statute prescribing minimum standards derived from the principle contained in article 94 of the Standard Minimum Rules for persons detained after legal conviction, even for civil offences, the letter and the spirit of which are to be found in the fundamental rules of the Universal Declaration of Human Rights of December 10, 1948, which stipulates that no one shall be subjected to torture or to cruel, inhuman or degrading treatment or punishment (Article 5).

I. General principles

1. Nothing in these Rules shall justify or encourage measures of detention dictated by exceptional circumstances. Their sole object is to attenuate the hardships of detention.

2. The minimum Rules set forth in the following articles shall, in accordance with the requirements of Article 2 of the Universal Declaration of Human Rights, be applied impartially and without distinction of any kind based on race, colour, national or social origin, sex, language, religious, political or other opinion, property or other considerations of a similar personal order.

3. Specific rules suitable for particular categories of non-delinquent detainees, taking their condition and need for special treatment or work into account, are not precluded, provided they are consistent with these general Rules, notably in so far as they extend the guarantees or benefits herein provided.

II. Registration—Identification and control of detainees

4. In any place, institution or camp in which persons are detained, there shall be maintained complete and up-to-date lists or registers with numbered pages showing:

a) The identity of each detainee, his citizenship or nationality and the conditions of his detention;

b) the date of his arrival, details of any transfers from place to place, the date of release or departure.

5. Personal effects which cannot be left in his possession shall be recorded and maintained in proper condition to be returned to him upon his release.

III. Separation of detainees

6. Men and women detainees shall be accommodated in separate institutions or parts of institutions. In the event of collective detention, family or communal accommodation shall be provided wherever possible.

7. In the event of collective civilian detention, children shall remain with the family or family circle whenever detention conditions and organization make this possible. Notwithstanding, exceptions justified by educational or professional training requirements shall be permitted.

Children less then six years of age shall in no case be separated from their mothers.

8. Civilian or military detainees or internees belonging to countries which are hostile to one another shall be separated. They may be accommodated together in other cases, taking into account national, linguistic or other affinities.

9. Non-delinquent detainees shall in all cases and without exception be distinguishable and separated from penal law detainees and convicted prisoners.

IV. Premises, fixtures and fittings

10. All institutions or places of detention shall satisfy the necessary requirements of safety, health and hygiene, taking the number of detainees and climatic and seasonal conditions into account. They shall be sufficiently large to avoid overcrowding and demoralizing promiscuity. They shall be properly maintained and cleaned.

11. There shall be adequate space, ventilation, lighting and heating for each detainee, in a manner consistent with scientifically acknowledged standards of hygiene to provide normally healthy living conditions and to avoid any risk of impairing the health of persons detained. (As a general rule, 8 cubic metres of space of each detainee is an acceptable standard.)

12. Premises shall be appropriate to the demands of any work performed, particularly as regards space, lighting, ventilation and any other essential condition to enable work to be carried out normally and to maintain the health of the workers.

13. When detainees need not be kept in individual cells, but are in rooms and dormitories (when detainees are not in individual cells but in rooms and dormitories) they shall be grouped by selection according to their suitability for such accommodation, in accordance with disciplinary and moral requirements. Night supervision should be appropriate.

14. Each detainee shall, in keeping with local or national standards, have an individual bunk or bedding; the latter shall be properly maintained and changed often enough to ensure its cleanliness. Detainees shall be responsible for keeping rooms, premises and beds neat and tidy in accordance with standing regulations.

15. Amenities for baths, showers and cleanliness shall be adequate and maintained in proper operating condition at temperatures suited to the climate so that each detainee shall be enabled and required to use them as frequently as hygiene demands. Sanitary facilities shall be such as to enable detainees to comply with the needs of nature at any time in a manner proper and decent.

V. Hygiene, personal cleanliness, clothing, exercise

16. The authorities shall demand personal cleanliness of the detainees and provide them with the facilities therefor (water toilet requisites, necessities for care of the hair and the beard), to enable detainees to maintain a decent appearance, dignity and self-respect. The authorities' demands shall not be of a vexatious nature under the pretext of hygiene (e.g. head shaving or forbidding beards).

17. If detainees are not permitted to wear and change their own clothing, that which is issued shall be appropriate to the climate and shall afford adequate protection. It shall not be degrading or humiliating nor give rise to confusion with the garb issued to convicted penal law offenders.

All clothing shall be clean and well maintained. When detainees are permitted to wear their own clothing arrangements shall be made to ensure that it is clean, decent and fit for use at the beginning of the detention period. Provision shall be made for the cleaning and changing of underclothing as frequently as is consistent with the demands of hygiene.

18. Every detainee shall be entitled to daily physical exercise (in the open air) for at least one hour; this may take the form of sport, gardening or supervised walks within the detention institution and to the extent permitted by climatic conditions. Grounds, equipment and other necessities appropriate to the number of detainees shall be provided as far as possible. (Detainees in single cells shall be permitted to leave them during the day to associate with other detainees. They shall be confined to their cells only during the night.)

VI. Work and diet

19. Work which detainees are compelled to perform shall not be harmful or degrading. It shall as far as possible be appropriate to their physical and intellectual ability. It shall not last for an excessive length of time and there shall be the necessary breaks to avoid impairing the health of those obliged to perform it.

Means of compulsion to enforce the performance of work or the standard output are subject to general rules in this respect (Art. 30 and 31).

20. (1) Every detainee shall at normal hours be decently served a wholesome meal of nutritious value sufficient to maintain health and strength. Drinking water shall be available as detainees require.

The daily diet shall be issued free and its calorific value and vitamin content shall be consistent with acknowledged standards appropriate to age and work performed.

(2) Permission for non-delinquent detainees to obtain extra food at their own expense or at the expense of their family, friends or of a relief society, shall be provided for in the internal regulations on condition that such facilities are not abused.

If circumstances permit, detainees may themselves prepare the food with which they are provided.

VII. Medical care

21. (1) Every place of detention shall have the services of at least one doctor. The medical service shall be organized in close co-operation with the public health administration.

Provision shall be made for the services of a psychiatrist for diagnosis and treatment of mental disorders.

Any place of detention where treatment is given shall,

as far as possible, have experienced personnel, equipment, means for treatment and the pharmaceutical products required for nursing and for suitable and appropriate medical and dental treatment.

(2) When places of detention do not have the necessary doctors, personnel, equipment and means, provision shall be made for transfer of detainees to suitable civilian or military hospitals, subject to the essential security measures.

22. In every institution where women are detained there shall be suitable provisions for pre- and post-natal treatment of maternity cases, and for child-birth. In the absence of such facilities provision shall as far as possible be made for transfer to hospital subject to the necessary security measures.

Nurseries shall be provided, with experienced personnel, where nursing infants may be cared for whenever they cannot be left with their mothers.

23. The doctor shall watch over detainees' health in accordance with the generally acknowledged principles of medical ethics. He shall carry out the necessary regular inspections and examinations.

In particular he shall:

a) examine detainees on arrival and whenever necessary thereafter, in order to isolate detainees who have or are suspected of having infectious or contagious diseases and those liable to be dangerous to their fellow detainees; to prescribe, order or take precautionary measures and give necessary treatment; to decide every detainee's capacity for work;

b) visit regularly and as the need arises, special cases, sick detainees, those who display or complain of symptoms of illness and those to whom his or the staff's attention has been drawn;

c) advise the director of the institution on matters of hygiene and cleanliness of premises, dormitories, work rooms and quarters, on the need for and operation of occupational equipment and sanitary installations (lighting, ventilation, heating, etc.), on diet, suitable clothing, regulations for physical exercise, rest periods, and any other requirements for the health of the detainees.

24. The doctor shall report to the director regularly and whenever any circumstance involving a detainee or detainees makes this necessary.

The director shall take into consideration the advice and reports of the doctor responsible for hygiene and the detainees' health. If the director agrees with the doctor he shall immediately take any necessary measures. If he disagrees he shall submit the matter without delay to higher authority.

VIII. Discipline and outside contacts

25. (1) Order and discipline shall be firmly maintained but shall not involve restrictions unnecessary to good order, security and organization of community life.

(2) No detainee shall be empowered to exercise disciplinary measures. According to circumstances, systems of good order and discipline, the operation of which is to some extent confided in the detainees themselves, with responsibility for organizing certain social, educational, sporting or recreational activities subject to supervision, may be justified.

(3) Detention conditions, the rights and obligations of detainees, working hours, leisure time, and the nature and duration of disciplinary punishment, shall be determined by legislation or administrative regulations.

26. (1) To an extent compatible with the mainte-

nance of good order, administrative needs and security requirements, detainees shall be permitted to correspond with their families and relatives as well as with the legal representatives, agents or advisers whose services they require for the defence of their interests.

(Detainees shall be permitted to correspond with their families and relatives as well as with the legal representatives, agents and advisers whose services they require for the defence of their interests. They shall be permitted to receive visits from these persons. There shall be a strict time limit to any restrictions in this connection.)

Death, illness, serious accidents, transfer to an institution for mental cases or to another place of detention shall be communicated to the detainee's family or relatives either by the administration or by the detainee himself when he is able to do so or by a relative or friend at his dictation. Likewise detainees shall be kept informed of events concerning their families.

(2) Unless serious and exceptional circumstances demand otherwise, foreign detainees shall be granted reasonable facilities to communicate with their country's diplomatic or consular representatives or with those of the State entrusted with their interests, and with any authorities or national or international humanitarian institutions whose task it is to assist or protect detainees.

27. Detainees shall be kept regularly informed of major current events either through newspapers, periodicals, other publications, radio broadcasts, lectures or any similar media authorized or controlled by the administration.

IX. Culture, recreation and moral comfort

28. Subject to the same conditions of authority and control, reasonable recreational and educational amenities appropriate to the circumstances and place of deten-

tion shall be provided in the form of lectures, slide or film projections, musical, theatrical, sport and other programmes, reading material and various games.

29. Detainees shall as far as possible be provided with spiritual or religious comfort. If there is a sufficient number of detainees of the same religion a minister thereof should be authorized to organize religious services and visit the detainees at specific times.

A detainee shall never be refused the right to contact a qualified representative of any religion. If a detainee refuses to receive a minister of religion or to take part in religious service his attitude shall be respected; no compulsion shall be used or punishment inflicted for that reason.

X. Instruments of restraint and punishment

30. (1) No means of restraint such as handcuffs, chains, irons or strait-jackets shall be used except in the following cases:

a) As a precaution against escape, during transfer or in conditions and circumstances involving a risk thereof; such implements shall be removed when the detainee appears before a judicial or administrative authority and when the risk of which there was reasonable apprehension no longer obtains;

b) On orders of the director, if need be after urgent consultation with the doctor, when normal means of controlling a detainee have failed or proved inadequate to prevent him from injuring himself and others and from damaging property;

(2) The nature and use of restrictive measures shall be prescribed by the general administration, to which the director of the institution shall report imme-

diately on serious or urgent cases. They shall not be applied for longer than is strictly necessary.

31. (1) No detainee shall be punished otherwise than in conformity with legal provisions and regulations, and never twice for the same offence.

Punishment shall not be inflicted, except in very minor cases, without the detainee's being informed of the accusation against him and his being given the possibility of presenting his defence, if necessary through an interpreter, and without a full and impartial enquiry by the director.

(2) Corporal punishment, confinement to cells which are dark or too small to permit normal posture, blows, and all cruel or degrading treatment shall be prohibited.

Solitary confinement, reduction of diet or any other punishment likely to impair physical or mental health shall be inflicted only to an extent which is reasonable or certified in writing by a doctor to be bearable and without great danger.

The doctor shall visit detainees undergoing such disciplinary punishment and report to the director immediately if he considers the punishment should be changed or ceased for physical or mental health reasons.

XI. Transfers

32. In the event of transfer from one place of detention to another, detainees shall be protected as much as possible from the public gaze, unwelcome or hostile curiosity, humiliation, insult or violence.

33. The cost of transferring detainees shall be borne by the administration and transfers shall be carried out in the same conditions for all, subject to special consid-

eration for age, sex or sickness and even rank where appropriate.

Transfer of detainees, prisoners or internees under conditions which are inhuman or dangerous for their health due to overcrowding, lack of air, light, or food or for any other circumstances affecting their physical wellbeing, shall be prohibited.

34. On arrival, each detainee shall be given, through posters or otherwise, precise, written, and clearly understandable information on conditions and rules applicable to detainees of his category, regulations for discipline, authorized methods of obtaining information and lodging requests or complaints, and any other details necessary for him to know his rights and obligations and to adapt to life in the penitentiary institution.

If a detainee is illiterate such information should be given to him orally.

35. Every detainee shall have the opportunity of making requests or complaints to the director of the place of detention or to an official authorized to represent him, either through the ordinary channels adopted in the institution or by addressing himself to the inspector or panel of inspectors in the course of their inspection.

He shall be permitted to talk with the inspector or any officer appointed to carry out inspection, without the presence of the director, other members of the detention institution's staff or any other person.

Unless a request or complaint is obviously groundless it shall be investigated quickly and impartially by the director and a reply shall be given as soon as possible. If rejected, the grounds therefor must be stated.

Detainees shall not be punished for making complaints even if they are rejected.

XIII. Staff professional qualifications and character

36. (1) The administration responsible for places of detention and for their proper organization and conduct shall exercise care in the recruitment of its officials and staff of all ranks in places of detention of all types (including detention camps and internment camps), by enquiring into their character, qualifications and sense of duty and responsibility.

(2) Any official or staff member committing a breach of legal and professional obligations or duties shall be punished by disciplinary or penal measures.

XIV. Inspections and supervision

37. Qualified and experienced inspectors appointed by the authorities shall regularly and frequently inspect places of detention and the conditions therein.

Inspectors shall, in particular, check that:

a) places of detention are run in conformity with the law, regulations, agreements or prevailing provisions, including the present Minimum Rules, with a view to ensuring observance of the conditions and aims thereof;

b) detainees and internees are treated in accordance with principles of humanity, justice and dignity consistent with the present Rules and those postulated by the Universal Declaration of Human Rights.

38. Inspection and control shall be authorized, particularly by qualified representatives of the International Committee of the Red Cross or other international or regional institutions of which the objectives are humanitarian and the action and impartiality acknowledged and known to be reliable.

The necessary arrangements for such inspections shall

be made with the relevant administration and directors of institutions, camps and other places of detention or internment.

Visits and inspections shall be permitted without let or hindrance by conditions or obstacles which would vitiate them and impede the achievement of their humanitarian purpose. (Persons carrying out such inspections shall be given facilities to talk in private with detainees of their own choosing.)

Bibliography

BOOKS, TREATISES AND PAMPHLETS

THE AIR WAR IN INDO-CHINA (R. Littauer and N. Uphoff ed. 1972).

B. Ayala, DE JURE ET OFFICIIS BELLICIS ET MILITARIS LIBRI (J. Wisttake ed. 1912).

G. Baker, I. HALLECK'S INTERNATIONAL LAW (1908).

G. Baker, II. HALLECK'S INTERNATIONAL LAW (1908).

R. Baxter, THE LAWS OF WAR (1957).

D. Bindschedler-Robert, THE LAW OF ARMED CONFLICT (1970).

J. Blaustein, HUMAN RIGHTS (1964).

J. Brierly, THE LAW OF NATIONS (6th ed. 1963).

I. Brownlie, BASIC DOCUMENTS ON HUMAN RIGHTS (1971).

J. Carey, U.N. PROTECTION OF CIVIL AND POLITICAL RIGHTS (1971).

I. CHALLENGE AND RESPONSE IN INTERNAL CONFLICT (1967).

II. CHALLENGE AND RESPONSE IN INTERNAL CONFLICT (1967).

Che Guevara, GUERRILLA WARFARE (1961).

CHEMICAL AND BIOLOGICAL WARFARE (S. Rose ed. 1968).

M. Cranston, WHAT ARE HUMAN RIGHTS (1962).

G. Draper, THE RED CROSS CONVENTIONS (1958).

T. Farer, THE LAWS OF WAR 25 YEARS AFTER NUREMBERG (1971).

A. Gentilis, DE JURE BELLI LIBRI TRES (J. Scott ed. 1931).

M. Greenspan, THE MODERN LAW OF LAND WARFARE (1959).

THE GUERRILLA AND HOW TO FIGHT HIM (T. Green ed. 1962).

S. Hersh, CHEMICAL AND BIOLOGICAL WARFARE: AMERI-
CA'S HIDDEN ARSENAL 151 (1968).

A. Higgins, THE HAGUE PEACE CONFERENCES (1909).

Institute of World Polity, THE LAW OF LIMITED INTER-
NATIONAL CONFLICT (1965).

INTERNAL WAR (H. Eckstein ed. 1963).

International Commissions of Jurists, THE RULE OF LAW
AND HUMAN RIGHTS (1966).

THE INTERNATIONAL LAW OF CIVIL WAR (R. Falk ed.
1971).

Jabhat al-Tahrir al-Quami, WHITE PAPER ON THE APPLI-
CATION OF THE GENEVA CONVENTIONS OF 1949 TO
THE FRENCH-ALGERIAN CONFLICT 7 (1960).

M. Keen, THE LAWS OF WAR IN THE LATE MIDDLE AGES
(1965).

H. Lauterpacht, II. OPPENHEIM'S INTERNATIONAL LAW
(7th ed. 1952).

M. McDougal and F. Feliciano, LAW AND MINIMUM
WORLD PUBLIC ORDER (1961).

MODERN GUERRILLA WARFARE (I. Osanka ed. 1962).

L. Montross, WAR THROUGH THE AGES (3rd ed. 1960).

C. Phillipson, I. INTERNATIONAL LAW AND CUSTOMS OF
ANCIENT GREECE AND ROME (1911).

C. Phillipson, II. INTERNATIONAL LAW AND CUSTOMS OF
ANCIENT GREECE AND ROME (1911).

J. Pictet, THE PRINCIPLES OF INTERNATIONAL HUMANI-
TARIAN LAW (1970).

M. Royse, AERIAL BOMBARDMENT (1928).

G. Schwarzenberger, II. INTERNATIONAL LAW (1968).

G. Schwarzenberger, THE LAW OF ARMED CONFLICT
(1968).

G. Schwarzenberger, THE LEGALITY OF NUCLEAR WEAP-
ONS (1958).

J. Scott, REPORTS TO THE HAGUE CONFERENCE OF 1899 AND 1907 (1916).

N. Singh, NUCLEAR WEAPONS AND INTERNATIONAL LAW (1959).

J. Siotis, LE DROIT DE LA GUERRE ET LES CONFLICTS ARMIES D'UN CARACTERE NON-INTERNATIONAL (1958).

J. Spraight, AIR POWER AND WAR RIGHTS (3rd ed. 1947).

J. Stone, LEGAL CONTROLS OF INTERNATIONAL CONFLICT (1959).

Tenurick, INTERNATIONAL LAW (3rd ed. 1948).

R. Trinquier, MODERN WARFARE (1961).

United Nations Office of Public Information, THE DANGERS OF CHEMICAL AND BACTERIOLOGICAL (BIOLOGICAL) WEAPONS (1969).

E. Vattel, LE DROIT DES GENS OU PRINCIPES DE LOI NATURELLE (J. Scott ed. 1916).

I. THE VIETNAM WAR AND INTERNATIONAL LAW (R. Falk ed. 1968).

II. THE VIETNAM WAR AND INTERNATIONAL LAW (R. Falk ed. 1969).

III. THE VIETNAM WAR AND INTERNATIONAL LAW (R. Falk ed. 1969).

Von Bynkershoek, A TREATISE ON THE LAW OF WAR (Du Sonceau ed. 1810).

Von Clausewitz, ON WAR (Jolles trans. 1943).

H. Wheaton, LAW OF NATIONS (1845).

W. Wintrop, MILITARY LAW AND PRECEDENTS (2nd ed. 1920).

World Health Organization, HEALTH ASPECTS OF CHEMICAL AND BIOLOGICAL WEAPONS (1970).

Q. Wright, A STUDY OF WAR (Abridged ed. 1964).

JOURNAL ARTICLES

Baldwin, *New Look at the Law of War: Limited War and FM 27-10*, 4 MIL. L. REV. 1(1959).

Baxter, *The Geneva Conventions of 1949*, 9 NAVAL WAR COLLEGE REV. 59 (1956).

Baxter, *So-called "Unprivileged Belligerency": Spies, Guerrillas, and Saboteurs* 28 BRIT. YB. INT'L. L. 323 (1951).

Baxter and Burgenthal, *Legal Aspects of the Geneva Protocol of 1925*, 64 AM. J. INT'L. L. 853 (1970).

Blum, *The Beirut Raid and the International Double Standard*, 64 AM. J. INT'L. L. 73 (1970).

Brownlie, *International Law and Activities of Armed Bands*, 7 INT'L. AND COMP. L. Q.712 (1958).

Coursier, *The Prohibition of Torture*, 11 INT'L. REV. OF THE RED CROSS 475 (1971).

Delaney, *Reflections on Political Communication and Insurgency*, 22 NAVAL WAR COLLEGE REV. (1969).

DeSaussure, *The Laws of Air Warfare: Are There Any?*, 23 NAVAL WAR COLLEGE REV. 35 (1971).

Downey, *The Law of War and Military Necessity*, 47 AM. J. INT'L. L. 251 (1953).

Draper, *The Ethical and Juridical Status of Constraints in War*, 55 MIL. L. REV. 169 (1972).

Falk, *The Beirut Raid and the International Law of Retaliation*, 63 AM. J. INT'L. L. 415 (1969).

Farer, *Humanitarian Law and Armed Conflicts: Toward The Definition of "International Armed Conflict,"* 71 COLUM. L. REV. 37 (1971).

Ford, *Resistance Movements and International Law*, 7-8 INT'L REV. OF THE RED CROSS 515, 579, 627, 7 (1967-8).

Friedmann, *Intervention, Civil War and the Role of International Law*, 1965 PROC. AM. SOC. INT'L. L. L. 67.

Glod and Smith, *Interrogation Under the 1949 Prisoners of War Convention*, 21 MIL. L. REV. (1963).

Gozybowski, *The Polish Doctrine of the Law of War in the Fifteenth Century: A Note on the Genealogy of International Law*, 8 JURIST 386 (1958).

Greenspan, *International Law and Its Protection for Participants in Unconventional Warfare*, 341 ANNALS OF THE AMERICAN ACADEMY OF POLITICAL AND SOCIAL SCIENCES 30 (1962).

Help to War Victims in Nigeria, 9 INT'L. REV. OF THE RED CROSS 353 (1969).

Johnson, *Civilian Loyalties and Guerrilla Conflict*, 14 WORLD POLITICS 646 (1962).

Kalshoven, *Human Rights, the Law of Armed Conflicts, and Reprisals*, 11 INT'L. REV. OF THE RED CROSS 183 (1971).

Kelly, *Assassination in War Time*, 30 MIL. L. REV. 101 (1965).

Kelly, *Gas Warfare in International Law*, 9 MIL. L. REV. 3 (1960).

Kelly, *Legal Aspects of Military Operations in Counterinsurgency*, 21 MIL. L. REV. 95 (1963).

Levie, *Some Major Inadequacies in the Existing Law Relating to the Protection of Individuals During Armed Conflict*, 14 HAMMARSKJÖLD FORUM (1970).

Lillich, *Forcible Self-help under International Law*, 22 NAVAL WAR COLLEGE REV. 56 (1970).

McDougal and Reisman, *Rhodesia and the United Nations: the Lawfulness of International Concern*, 62 AM. J. INT'L. L. (1968).

Mirimanoff, *The Red Cross and Biological and Chemical Weapons*, 10 INT'L. REV. OF THE RED CROSS 301 (1970).

Moore, *The Control of Foreign Intervention in Internal Conflict*, 9 VA. J. INT'L. L. 205 (1969).

Neuman, *The International Civil War*, 1 WORLD POLITICS 333 (1949).

Ney, *Guerrilla War and Modern Strategy*, 2 ORBIS 66 (1958).

Note, *The Geneva Conventions and Treatment of Prisoners of War in Vietnam*, 80 HARV. L. REV. 851 (1967).

O'Brien, *The Meaning of Military Necessity in International Law*, 1 YEARBOOK OF WORLD POLITY 109 (1957).

Pictet, *International Humanitarian Law*, 6 INT'L. REV. OF THE RED CROSS 456, 466 (1966).

Protection of Civilian Populations Against the Dangers of Indiscriminate Warfare, 7 INT'L. REV. OF THE RED CROSS 300 (1967).

Pye, *The Roots of Insurgency and the Commencement of Rebellions*, 9 NAVAL WAR COLLEGE REV. 157 (1956).

Scholgel, *Civil War*, 10 INT'L. REV. OF THE RED CROSS 123 (1970).

Schwarzenberger, *Law of Air Warfare and the Trend Toward Total War*, 8 AM. U. L. REV. 1 (1959).

Trainin, *Questions of Guerrilla Warfare in the Law of War*, AM. J. INT'L. L. 534 (1946).

Trathcer, *The New Law of Land Warfare*, 22 MO. L. REV. 143 (1957).

Treymond, *Aid to Victims of the Civil War in Nigeria*, 10 INT'L. REV. OF THE RED CROSS 65 (1970).

Veuthey, *The Red Cross and Non-International Conflicts*, 10 INT'L. REV. OF THE RED CROSS 411 (1970).

Wales, *Algerian Terrorism*, 22 NAVAL WAR COLLEGE REV. 26 (1969).

Wosepka, *Repatriation and the Chieu Hoi Amnesty Approach in Vietnam: Consequences and Prospects*, 5 INT'L. LAWYER 637 (1971).

Wright, *Legal Aspects of the Vietnam Situation*, 60 AM. J. INT'L. L. 750 (1966).

PUBLIC PUBLICATIONS

COUNTERGUERRILLA OPERATIONS (Dept. of the Army FIELD MANUAL 31-16).

D. deHuan and J. Tinker, REFUGEE AND CIVIL WAR CASUALTY PROBLEMS IN INDOCHINA (Staff Report of the United States Senate Subcommittee on Refugee Problems 1971).

FIELD MANUAL 27-10 THE LAW OF LAND WARFARE (Dept. of the Army Pamphlet 1956).

FINAL RECORD OF THE DIPLOMATIC CONFERENCE OF GENEVA, 1949.

HANDBOOK OF EXISTING RULES PERTAINING TO HUMAN RIGHTS (OEA/Ser. L/V/II.23, Doc. 21 17 Dec. 1970).

I. INTERNATIONAL LAW (Dept. of the Army Pamphlet 27-161-1).

II. INTERNATIONAL LAW (Dept. of the Army Pamphlet 27-161-2).

J. Kelley and G. Pellatier, LEGAL CONTROL OF THE POPULACE IN SUBVERSIVE WARFARE (Judge Advocate General's School text 1966).

Note, INTERNATIONAL LAW DOCUMENTS 1950-51 (Navy
  Pamphlet 1952).

RED CROSS PUBLICATIONS

I. COMMENTARY ON THE GENEVA CONVENTIONS OF 1949
  (J. Pictet ed. 1952).
II. COMMENTARY ON THE GENEVA CONVENTIONS OF 1949
  (J. Pictet ed. 1960).
III. COMMENTARY ON THE GENEVA CONVENTIONS OF
  1949 (J. Pictet ed. 1960).
IV. COMMENTARY ON THE GENEVA CONVENTIONS OF
  1949 (J. Pictet ed. 1958).
PRELIMINARY REPORT ON THE CONSULTATION OF EX-
  PERTS CONCERNING CONFLICT AND GUERRILLA
  WARFARE (1970).
PROTECTION OF THE CIVILIAN POPULATION AGAINST
  DANGERS OF HOSTILITIES (1971).
REPORT AID TO VICTIMS OF INTERNAL DISTURBANCES
  (1962).
REPORT APPLICABILITY OF HUMANITARIAN PRINCIPLES
  IN CASES OF INTERNAL DISTURBANCES (1955).
THE ICRC AND THE ALGERIAN CONFLICT (1962).
THE ICRC AND THE YEMEN CONFLICT (1964).

125; detention criteria, 164; detention facilities, 167; food, 125; housing, 124; medical care, 124; parallel provisions in civilian convention, 107. (See also prisoners of war.)

Civilian Convention (IV): Article 23, 134, 172, 177, 180; Article 30, 180; Article 33, 149; Article 49, 105; Article 51, 106; Article 53, 68; Article 63a, 178; Article 74, 174; Article 78, 107; Draft Preamble, 69. (See also Article 3, Geneva diplomatic conference.)

1949 Geneva diplomatic conference, 38, 54, 137, 178, 192

Geneva Gas Protocol, 24, 36, 70, 93, 101

Grotius: on ancient practices, 10, 11; impact upon the modern law of war, 15-16; influence on Gustavus Adolphus, 12; reaction to the Thirty Years' War, 14; as synthesizer, 8; on treaties as a source of the law of war, 18

1899 Hague Convention with respect to the laws and customs of war on land, 21

1899 Hague Peace Conference, 21

1907 Hague Convention, 26

1954 Hague Convention on cultural property, 70, 81, 100

Hague regulations, 22, 67: Article 22, 143; Article 23, 68, 92, 111, 143; Article 25, 69, 82; Article 27, 82-83, 146; relief, 132

high command case, 68, 112, 131

Ho Chi Minh, 32

hostages, 100, 148

hostages case, 111

human rights, 42, 61: Act of Athens, 95; Bangkok conference (1965), 75; Covenant of Civil and Political Rights, 138; derogation, 72, 73-74; European Human Rights Convention, 120; human rights legislation in general, 61-63; influence upon law of war, 42-43; Inter-American Convention on Human Rights, 62-63, 120; Lagos conference (1961), 64; Teheran conference (1968), 41, 140-141; theoretical rationale, 64-79; U.N. covenants, 72, 138; Universal Declaration of Human Rights, 61, 71, 124, 138

internal conflict, incidence of, 32: applicability of the laws of war thereto, 31, 33-34, 49-50; destruction of property and loss of life therein, 45-49; as distinguished from international conflict, 31-32; prevalence of guerrilla tactics, 32-33; suggested criteria

internal conflict (*cont.*)
  for applicability of laws of
  war, 182-185
ICEHRAC, 189
ICRC: appeal to Greek government during Greek civil
  war, 59; authorized to determine when laws of war
  apply, 190; contribution to
  development of law of war,
  24-25, 39-40; inspection of
  detention facilities, 60, 61,
  114, 123; on the lawfulness
  of chemical and biological
  weapons, 94-95; in Yemenese civil war, 48, 60
interrogation practices, 37, 126
intervention, 3, 28, 50, 133,
  182, 193

Johnson, Samuel, 129
just war, 12-13

Kellogg-Briand Pact, 26, 27
Kriegsraison theory, 65

"law of arms," 13
law of spoils division, 15
law of war: ancient anteced-
  ents, 8-12; "classical" theory,
  15-19; codification, 19-26;
  demand for reform, 39-43;
  developments during the
  Middle Ages, 12-15; normative ambiguity, 65-71; recent
  changes, 28-33; relationship
  to human rights, 42-43;
  restraints on use of force,
  26-29
lawless case, 62, 124

League of Nations Covenant,
  26
London Declaration (1909),
  133

Mao, 86
military manuals, 17, 186-187
military necessity, 17-18, 65,
  111

Napoleon, 17, 66
Napoleonic wars, 30
neutrality, 75
Nigerian civil war: amnesty,
  121; applicability of self-
  determination principles, 72;
  Biafra as a belligerent, 34;
  genocide, 87; loss of life, 45,
  48; relief programs, 129-
  130, 134; respect for Article
  3, 59; summary execution,
  117; treatment of rebels at
  end of conflict, 114; use of
  air power, 95
non-international conflict:
  criteria for determination of,
  184; definition, 51. (See also
  internal conflict.)
Nuremberg War Crimes Tri-
  bunal, 27

Pakistani civil war, 45-46, 48
Pax Romana, 7
pillage, 148, 183
Plato, 7, 10
population safety zones (open
  towns), 74, 147, 149
protecting power, 187-188
prisoners of war, 24: "detained
  combatant," 158, 165; guer-

Library of Congress Cataloging in Publication Data

Bond, James Edward, 1943-
     The rules of riot.

     Bibliography: p.
     1. Civil war. 2. War (International law)
3. Guerrillas   (International law)   I. Title.
JX4541.B65   341.6'8   73-12196